Teaching STEM in the Early Years

Other Redleaf Press Books by Sally Moomaw

More Than Singing: Discovering Music in Preschool and Kindergarten

By Sally Moomaw and Brenda Hieronymus

More Than Counting: Standards-Based Math Activities for Young Thinkers in Preschool and Kindergarten, Standards Edition

More Than Counting: Math Activities for Young Thinkers in Preschool and Kindergarten

Much More Than Counting: More Math Activities for Young Thinkers in Preschool and Kindergarten

More Than Letters: Literacy Activities for Preschool, Kindergarten, and First Grade

More Than Magnets: Science Activities for Young Thinkers in Preschool and Kindergarten

More Than Painting: Exploring the Wonders of Art in Preschool and Kindergarten

By Guy W. Jones and Sally Moomaw

Lessons from Turtle Island: Native Curriculum in Early Childhood Classrooms

Teaching
STEM
in the Early Years

Activities for Integrating

Science

Technology

Engineering

and Mathematics

SALLY MOOMAW, EdD

Redleaf Press®
www.redleafpress.org
800-423-8309

Published by Redleaf Press
10 Yorkton Court
St. Paul, MN 55117
www.redleafpress.org

First edition 2013
Cover design by Jim Handrigan
Cover photograph © Ocean Photography/Veer
Interior design by Percolator
Typeset in Mrs. Eaves XL and Mr. Eaves XL
Interior photographs by Sally Moomaw
Printed in the United States of America

Table 3.25 on page 113 was originally published in "STEM Comes to Preschool," *Young Children* 65,
no. 5 (2010): 12–18. Reprinted with permission from the National Association for the Education of
Young Children.

Oil paintings in Activity 7.10 (*New Playmate*, © 2004; *Painted Pony*, © 2007; *Firewood*, © 2009) are by
Carol Kelley. Included with permission from the artist.

Library of Congress Cataloging-in-Publication Data
Moomaw, Sally, 1948- author.
  Teaching STEM in the early years : activities for integrating science, technology, engineering,
and mathematics / Sally Moomaw, EdD.
    pages cm
  Summary: "The foundation for science, technology, engineering, and mathematics education
begins in the early years. Teaching STEM in the Early Years provides activities and learning center
ideas that seamlessly integrate STEM throughout your early childhood classroom"—Provided by
publisher.
  Includes bibliographical references.
  ISBN 978-1-60554-121-1 (pbk.)
  ISBN 978-1-60554-253-9 (e-book)
  1. Science—Study and teaching (Early childhood)—United States. 2. Technology—Study and
teaching (Early childhood)—United States. 3. Engineering—Study and teaching (Early childhood)—
United States. 4. Mathematics—Study and teaching (Early childhood)—United States.   I. Title.
LB1139.5.S35M66 2013
372.35'044—dc23
                    2012037237

Printed on acid-free paper

U15-07

For Charlie, without whose help there would be no book,
and for Sonya, a true STEM explorer

Contents

Acknowledgments

I would like to thank my editor, David Heath, for his astute guidance in the preparation of this book, and Charles Moomaw for his extensive technical assistance. I am grateful to Dr. Peter Moomaw for lending his scientific expertise and to artist Carol Kelley for graciously allowing her artwork to be included in this book. I greatly appreciate the participation of Andrew, Ashley, Caroline, Charlie, Emily, Max, Nancy, Peter, Sonya, Tamara, and Vivian, who appear in the photographs.

STEM Education

Sonya decided to build an arena for her toy horses. Her parents made blocks for her by covering half-pint-, pint-, and quart-size dairy containers with contact paper. Sonya carefully stacked four half-pint containers to make a column. Next to this stack of blocks, she built another column by matching new blocks to the four blocks in her original tower. Sonya slid her second stack of blocks about a foot away from the first stack. By repeating this process, Sonya soon had four corner towers for her arena.

Next, Sonya placed a quart-size block on the floor between two of the towers to make a fence. She noticed a gap between the towers and her fence, so she carefully pushed the towers closer together until they touched the fence block. Sonya repeated this process for two additional sides of her arena but used a pint-size block on the fourth side to allow space for an entrance. Delightedly, she moved her horses through this opening into the arena.

Sonya now prepared to add a roof. Running into her father's office, she found a clipboard and brought it back to her building area. Sonya attempted to lay the clipboard across the columns, but it fell into the arena. Frustrated, she looked around her room and noticed a doll blanket, which she draped over the columns of her building. The blanket was large enough to make a roof, but it sagged in the middle. Dissatisfied with the result, Sonya continued to look around her room. In the closet, she found a square box lid from a game. Much to her delight, the box lid fit almost perfectly across her columns. "Daddy," Sonya called. "Come see what I made."

Sonya and her father discussed the arena. "I want to e-mail a picture to Grandma," Sonya exclaimed. "She'll like my arena." Sonya's father handed her his smartphone, and she took a picture of her building. He helped her text a message, and together they sent it, along with the photo, to Grandma.

• • •

This vignette about Sonya encompasses the four disciplines of STEM education: science, technology, engineering, and mathematics. It also illustrates how children's play can provide fertile ground for learning in each of the STEM disciplines. Through her block building, Sonya experimented with balance, **symmetry**, and the properties and effects of materials. These are all important concepts in science. In mathematics, she used **one-to-one correspondence** to produce towers of the same height, and she explored measurement through her fence and roofing dilemmas. The entire play experience related to engineering, where concepts of science and mathematics must be applied to real-world problems. Finally, Sonya used technology to quickly preserve and communicate the results of her efforts. Teachers, parents, and caregivers can support and extend children's knowledge in these critical areas by recognizing the four disciplines of STEM education in the play experiences of children.

INTRODUCTION TO STEM EDUCATION

The acronym STEM originated with the National Science Foundation (NSF). STEM refers to NSF's education-related programs in the disciplines of science, technology, engineering, and mathematics. Some educators regard STEM as any of the individual STEM disciplines. On the other hand, many others require that some, if not all, of the disciplines be integrated in order to receive STEM designation (Carnegie Mellon University 2008). In this book, STEM education indicates integration of at least two of the STEM disciplines within a curricular activity.

In recent years, STEM education has become a focus of attention in the United States for several reasons. First, U.S. students continue to trail their peers in many developed countries in science and mathematics, as reported by the Trends in International Mathematics and Science Study (National Center for Education Statistics 2009). Second, there is concern that the United States is not adequately developing students in the areas of technology, engineering, science, and mathematics. In a recent report to Congress, the United States ranked twentieth internationally in the number of students who received degrees in science and engineering (Kuenzi 2008). Third, application of content knowledge from STEM disciplines is increasingly required in jobs at all levels. Individuals must process information from STEM areas to make informed societal decisions, such as evaluating conflicting political statements on global warming. Finally, STEM education has been linked to scientific leadership in the world and to economic growth (National Research Council 2011).

The foundations of STEM education begin in a child's early years. Recently, there has been a surge of interest in early childhood mathematics (Clements and Sarama 2007). A substantial body of research attests to the importance of number sense for achievement in school mathematics (Duncan et al. 2007; National Research Council 2009; Starkey, Klein, and Wakeley 2004). In fact, Gersten and Chard (1999) believe that the concepts embedded in number sense are as important to early mathematics learning as concepts of phonemic awareness are to early reading. Understanding of geometry and measurement is also viewed as important and relevant for children in the primary years (Clements and Sarama 2007; National Council of Teachers of Mathematics 2006). Young children are also capable of considerable learning in science during the preschool and kindergarten years (Moomaw and Davis 2010; Moomaw and Hieronymus 1997). Nevertheless, research on science education in preschool and kindergarten is notably lacking. Neither the *Handbook of Research on Science Education* (Abell and Lederman 2007) nor the *Handbook of Research on the Education of Young Children* (Saracho and Spodek 2006) contains any research on science education with young children. This is a critical lack; during early childhood, children can develop a love for science and a feeling of efficacy for their own abilities that can support their learning in the years ahead.

The concept of an integrated curriculum is familiar to many early childhood teachers (see the More Than . . . curriculum series from Redleaf Press, www.redleafpress.org). Teachers may develop math games to coordinate with a favorite children's book, plan the dramatic play and block areas in preparation for an upcoming field trip, or introduce natural materials into the art area to coordinate with the seasons. Such integration of curricular materials is supported by professional teaching organizations. For example, a National Association for the Education of Young Children (NAEYC) position statement on developmentally appropriate practice advises that "teachers plan curriculum experiences that integrate children's learning *within* and *across* . . . the disciplines" (Copple and Bredekamp 2009, 21).

Teachers are accustomed to planning integrated curriculum activities that relate to literature or literacy. They may be less accustomed, however, to planning activities that integrate mathematics and science. Yet this coordination of curricula is important to young children's learning and lies at the heart of STEM education. Professional organizations in mathematics and science echo this need. For example, the National Council of Teachers of Mathematics (2000) encourages teachers to help children connect mathematics to other contexts, and the National Science Education Standards urge teachers to coordinate science and mathematics programs (National Research Council 1996).

COMPONENTS OF STEM

Although four disciplines are included in the acronym STEM, science and mathematics are the most familiar to teachers of young children. Even so, many early childhood teachers fail to capitalize on the science opportunities that are embedded throughout the classroom. Adult support is critical if young children are to maximize their foundational learning. As an example, most preschool classrooms incorporate water wheels in the sensory table, and children delight in watching these wheels spin as they pour water through them. Yet most children won't consider the relationship between the amount of water they pour over the wheel and how fast the wheel spins unless an adult is there to stimulate this thinking. A simple question such as, "How can you make the wheel go slowly?" can focus children's attention on the *force* of moving water and factors that affect it. Children who are stimulated in their early years by insightful questions like this become immersed in scientific inquiry. They develop the desire to experiment and learn more. So it is essential that early childhood teachers begin to think of themselves as science teachers who can stimulate children's thinking throughout the day.

Many early childhood teachers also do not think of themselves as math teachers, even though mathematics is a critical component of the curriculum in preschool and kindergarten. Teachers may feel uncomfortable with mathematics, their math anxiety often dating to their own elementary school experiences (Philipp 2007). While teachers may count objects with children or read counting books, they often do not engage in math discussions and problem-solving activities that expand children's thinking. Here is an example. Wendy and Jason begin to argue during snack because Jason thinks Wendy has more grapes than he does. The teacher responds, "I gave you each five. You have the same." This type of response shuts down conversation and mathematical thinking. Instead, the teacher might ask Jason why he thinks Wendy has more grapes. Perhaps Jason's grapes are clumped together and Wendy's are spread apart, making it appear that Wendy has more. If the teacher asks Wendy and Jason how *they* can figure out if one of them has more grapes, then the children become the problem solvers. They may decide to match their grapes in a **one-to-one correspondence** fashion, or they may actually count them. Either way, the children will have gained confidence in their ability to solve their own problems. Sometimes teachers may be unwilling to accede power to children because they are afraid the children will come up with the wrong answer. What if they decide Wendy really does have more grapes? At this point, the teacher can provide further scaffolding. She might say, "Wait a minute. When you paired up the grapes on your plate, this grape on Jason's plate got left out." This type of intervention can help children recognize and correct their own mistakes.

Because engineering is a profession that is pursued in college, it seldom occurs to teachers to connect children's activities to real-life engineering jobs. When children design and build block structures, they need to know that this is also what architects and engineers do. A walk around the neighborhood might stimulate children to incorporate unique features into their own block designs, especially if photographs (technology) are used to preserve the images of the neighborhood buildings. Similarly, when children have difficulty creating a bridge to span two block structures, the teacher should let them know that engineers also must solve problems when they design bridges and roads. A children's book about bridges may provide ideas about how engineers have solved problems similar to their own. As another example, a child tries to create a building in the sand table, but it keeps falling down. This is an opportunity to talk about the different characteristics of building materials. Allowing the child to create the same building with clay may yield a more effective result. The properties and characteristics of building materials is something that engineers and architects must also consider when designing and building structures. Engineering is connected to many of the concepts children explore in the early childhood classroom. For this reason, background information for teachers is included in many of the activities in this book. Teachers can use this information to help children connect their school activities to engineering professions in the adult world.

This is the age of technology, when each year brings more amazing inventions—smartphones, smaller and more powerful computers, enhanced interactive games, global positioning systems, and so on. Some elementary school classrooms now have Smart Boards that allow teachers and students to instantly access information from around the world. Nevertheless, while there are some computer applications that are effective learning tools for young children, and while teacher-guided use of the Internet can help children answer questions they may have, it is important to remember that technology did not begin in the digital age. People have been inventing and using tools for millennia, and we continue to use these simple devices in our everyday life. For example, tools that are used in the kitchen, such as apple slicers and peelers, hand-held juicers, and mortars and pestles, are applications of **simple machines** and technology that children can understand and therefore apply. In fact, experimentation with simple machines, such as **pulleys**, **inclines**, and **wedges**, can greatly expand chil-

dren's understanding of physics. For this reason, tools that can be used throughout the classroom are a focus of curriculum applications of technology in this book.

Recently, some educators have suggested that the acronym STEM be changed to STEAM, with the letter *A* designating *art*. Science and mathematics are indeed deeply embedded in both art and music. The incorporation of science and mathematics concepts into art and music activities is emphasized throughout this book. With that in mind, it seems unnecessary to alter the spelling of STEM, which is rapidly becoming familiar to educators.

EFFECTIVE TEACHING PRACTICES

Four teaching practices are critical to early learning in science and mathematics:

1. Intentional teaching

2. Teaching for understanding

3. Encouraging inquiry

4. Providing real-world contexts

Intentional teaching within the STEM disciplines means that teachers thoughtfully plan learning experiences with science and math goals in mind. They utilize technology as a learning tool and make connections to engineering when appropriate. Learning goals should focus on *understanding* so that children can apply their knowledge in science and mathematics to new situations. Both mathematics and science are creative disciplines in which individuals ask questions, establish relationships, and communicate ideas. For this reason, a focus on inquiry should be at the heart of education in both areas. Young children learn best when they can interact with concrete materials and make connections to experiences from their own lives. Therefore, learning in both science and mathematics should focus on materials, situations, and experiences that are important, interesting, and meaningful to young children.

Intentional Teaching

As with all areas of the curriculum, children learn more effectively when teachers incorporate developmentally appropriate practices when implementing activities in the STEM disciplines. The third edition of *Developmentally Appropriate Practice in Early Childhood Programs Serving Children from Birth through Age 8* (Copple and Bredekamp 2009) emphasizes the importance of *intentional teaching*. This means that effective teachers are purposeful in all aspects of teaching. They plan the curriculum and environment with specific outcomes and children in mind. They remain alert for teachable moments as they occur throughout the classroom. Effective teachers understand the developmental learning trajectories for children in each area of the curriculum. They also know what individual children understand based on the child's development. This knowledge allows teachers to plan a multilevel curriculum that meets the learning needs of a range of children. The teacher can intervene as children interact with the materials to structure the learning for each child.

The following example illustrates how intentional teaching guides learning for a range of children.

> *Ms. Ortega has introduced a collection of various sizes and types of pinecones into the science area. She expects that children will explore the similarities and differences among the pinecones and also begin to measure them. When Anna interacts with the pinecones, Ms. Ortega notices that Anna groups the large pinecones together and moves the smaller pinecones into a different pile. Building on Anna's interest in size comparison, the teacher helps her use direct comparison to put six of the pinecones in order based on their length. Later Eric and Wei visit the pinecone collection. They are older than Anna and have had more experience with measurement. For these boys, Ms. Ortega introduces a set of interlocking cubes and suggests that they use the cubes to measure the length of several pinecones. She even gives them a recording sheet (prepared ahead of time) so that they can notate their results.*

In the above example, the teacher was effective in working with all three children for several reasons:

1. She had identified measurement as one of her goals for the activity.

2. She knew the developmental trajectory for measurement concepts and where individual children in her class were likely to fall along this continuum.

3. She had considered how to implement the activity with various children as part of her planning.

Teaching for Understanding

In its *Principles and Standards for School Mathematics*, the National Council of Teachers of Mathematics (2000) addresses effective teaching practices through its Teaching and Learning Principles. The Teaching Principle emphasizes that mathematics teachers must understand what students know, what students need to know, and how to support students in their learning. This principle applies equally to teachers of preschool through high school.

Teaching for understanding is a focus of all of the activities in this book. The Learning Principle, which also relates to development, focuses on the importance of learning mathematics with understanding. Regardless of age, students use their prior knowledge and experience to construct new knowledge. Conceptual understanding of mathematics is critical because students can then use their mathematical knowledge to solve new problems. Learning at the conceptual level, rather than simply memorizing facts, is equally important in science education.

In both mathematics and science, teachers should encourage children to solve problems through their own thinking rather than supplying them with answers. This allows children to build upon their previous knowledge and deepen their conceptual understanding. The following example, from a preschool classroom, would be considered a STEM activity because it incorporates both science and math.

> In helping cut up an apple for snack, the children discover that there are seeds inside. One of the children wonders how many seeds there are, and he counts them to find out. Following his revelation that there are nine seeds from the apple, the children speculate that all apples must have the same number of seeds. The next time the children cut up an apple, the teacher reminds them of their prediction that all apples will have nine seeds. Several children quickly count the seeds in the new apple and discover that there are eight. "This apple doesn't have as many seeds as the last one," they say. Isaac, however, is not convinced, so the teacher hands him the seeds from the original apple. "What's another way to find out if the new apple has as many seeds as the first apple had?" she asks. Carefully, Isaac puts the seeds from the original apple in a row. Then he places one of the seeds from the new apple next to each seed from the original apple. There is one seed left over. Isaac smiles and says, "Yep. The first apple had more seeds."

In this example, Isaac was allowed to solve the problem in a way that made sense to him. Had the teacher simply agreed with the other children, she would have deprived Isaac of the opportunity to build upon his own level of thinking to solve the problem.

Encouraging Inquiry

The National Science Education Standards, as developed by the National Research Council (1996), emphasize that inquiry into questions generated by students should be the focus of science teaching. This does not mean that the teacher never introduces a topic for study. Nevertheless, the teacher should determine what questions children have about the topic and provide support as they experiment and determine answers to their questions. Again, this emphasis on inquiry extends to the youngest learners: "Lifelong scientific literacy begins with attitudes and values established in the earliest years" (National Research Council 1996, 114).

Likewise, inquiry should be a guiding force in learning mathematics. As children interact with materials, they form relationships, such as grouping objects into various categories. This indicates that they have developed a general rule to govern placement of the items, an important algebra concept. As an example, children may decide that all the large animals should go into one field, and all the smaller animals into another field. Once this is accomplished, children may want to make comparisons. Are there more large or small animals? Is there a small animal to go with each large animal? Can the animals be arranged from largest to smallest for a parade? All of these questions involve important mathematical concepts, and children's inquiry drives their formation of these mathematical relationships. While inquiry often stems from the child, teachers can stimulate investigation through carefully posed questions related to the child's play. The teacher might ask, "Will all of the animals fit into this truck? How many trucks do you think we will need to carry all of the animals?" This intentional teaching through inquiry presents more interesting questions for children to answer and moves their learning forward. The teacher has modeled questions that children may ask themselves in the future.

Providing Real-World Contexts

All of the examples used previously in this chapter involve children engaged in everyday experiences, such as playing and eating. Young children learn best when activities are relevant to their lives. In science, it is particularly important that young children have real materials to explore, because preschoolers and kindergartners are still determining the difference between reality and fantasy. By observing a classroom goldfish, children may notice that this real-life example does not behave at all like the fish in some popular storybooks. Similarly, the rabbits at the petting zoo don't wear coats with gold buttons and drink tea. Experiences with living plants and animals can spur discussions about the difference between real and pretend.

Likewise, in physical science children need to interact with materials, experiment, and observe the results. This helps dispel notions that scientific processes are magical. While a car viewed in a video game or on a cartoon show may jump vertically or fly through the air, the cars that children use on ramps that they have constructed in the classroom behave in consistent, predictable ways.

CONTENT STANDARDS IN STEM EDUCATION

STEM education in children's early years, which centers around science and mathematics, strongly supports learning in the content standards for these disciplines. In science, there are three general areas:

1. physical science
2. life science
3. earth and space science

Physical science includes the physical properties of materials, the movement of objects, and the *forces* that affect materials, such as magnetism and gravity. State preschool and kindergarten indicators that address physical science typically focus on the characteristics of objects—weight, shape, size, texture, color, form, and temperature. In addition, movement-related concepts and actions are often addressed. These might include lifting, pushing, blowing, floating, and so forth. Indicators often suggest that young children engage in sensory experiences and sort objects by various properties. Since inquiry is considered a main focus in science, children should engage in many experiments that involve the physical attributes of materials and reveal how forces may affect them.

Life science is concerned with living things—both plants and animals. It includes growth cycles, the environmental needs of plants and animals, habitats, and the observation of particular characteristics of various plants and animals. For young children, life science standards generally focus on the plants and animals in the children's immediate environment. Indicators often include

- developing an awareness of the changes that occur as plants and animals grow,
- demonstrating appreciation and respect for plants and animals,
- differentiating between living and nonliving (or real and pretend) things, and
- developing an understanding of the needs of various plants and animals.

Earth science encompasses the study of the earth's components, including patterns of change over time. For this reason, earth science standards generally incorporate the examination of materials such as *rocks*, shells, and soil, as well as changes in the environment, including weather, seasons, and erosion. Space science is combined with this standard. It involves patterns of day and night and phenomena created by light, such as shadows and *reflections* (also part of physical science). Space science also involves observations of objects in space, such as the sun, moon, and stars. Preschool indicators under this standard might include

- awareness of the properties of earth materials,
- use of terminology to indicate day and night,
- exploration of how an individual's actions may cause changes in materials, and
- observations about the weather.

There are five content standard domains in mathematics:

1. number and operations
2. algebra
3. geometry
4. measurement
5. data analysis and probability

Although the focus in early childhood education is on number and operations, geometry, and measurement (National Council of Teachers of Mathematics 2006), all five content standards are interconnected and important for STEM education.

For young children, **number and operations** includes

- quantifying small amounts,
- comparing sets of objects as more, less, or equal,
- counting,
- ordering numbers (first, second, last, and so on),
- combining sets (early addition)
- taking away from sets (early subtraction), and
- dividing materials among friends (early division).

It involves understanding underlying relationships, such as **one-to-one correspondence** (one number word for each object counted) and **cardinality** (the last number counted equals the total). Much of the mathematical learning that occurs through children's play involves number and operations.

Algebra includes understanding patterns and relationships, as well as analyzing, representing, and modeling mathematical situations. In preschool and kindergarten, children construct algebraic relationships by sorting and classifying materials and eventually arranging them in patterns. The language of math that permeates math-rich classrooms helps children analyze problem situations. An example of this might be whether three friends can go to the gross-motor room together when only two spaces are open on the waiting list. The concrete materials that are a mainstay in quality programs enable children to represent mathematical problems in ways that they can understand.

Geometry in the early years involves much more than naming shapes. It also includes understanding spatial relationships, positional statements, and the properties of two- and three-dimensional objects. Through concrete experiences with blocks and other materials, children form the foundation for later, analytic processes in geometry.

Measurement for young children includes

- understanding the measurable attributes of objects,
- constructing the concept of an appropriate unit of measure,
- the application of number to measurement, and
- measurement comparisons.

Seriating, or ordering objects by size, is an aspect of measurement frequently explored by young children.

Data analysis encompasses

- gathering information,
- organizing the information in a useful way, and
- asking and answering questions related to it.

For young children, data come from their life experiences. They may sort their toys into groups, compare how many buttons are in two groups, or vote for their favorite fruit. Preschool and kindergarten teachers often help children organize this information on a bar graph. The probability component of this standard centers around likelihood, including whether or not something is possible. For example, children may wonder if it is likely to rain on the day of a field trip. If it is sunny, they may conclude that it is not likely, but it is possible for it to rain if the sky starts to get cloudy.

INTEGRATING STEM DISCIPLINES

Science and mathematics pair naturally within the curriculum. When children are conducting investigations in science, they often make measurement comparisons, such as which plant has grown the tallest or which *incline* allows cars to roll the fastest. Measurement is a component of both the science and math disciplines. Also, as children closely examine items in nature, they often notice mathematical elements, such as patterns, *symmetry*, and geometric configurations. Stripes on angelfish and zebras create an alternating color pattern. Ladybugs (a type of beetle) and maple leaves are symmetrical, with shape patterns that are a mirror image on either side of their midlines. The shells of box turtles are composed of interlocking pentagonal shapes.

Quantification is also an important aspect of science. Children can differentiate insects from *arachnids*, such as spiders, by counting their legs—insects have six legs and spiders have eight. With help, children can count the rings on a tree stump to determine the age of the tree. Children may also want to quantify and compare the number of legs on various animals, the number of grooves on a pumpkin, and the amount of pebbles needed to sink a toy boat. When planning science activities for the classroom, teachers should simultaneously identify the mathematical components involved and include them as a focus of the curriculum. In this way, learning in both science and mathematics is increased, and children begin to understand the natural connection between the two disciplines.

If mathematics augments the science curriculum, science can also enhance the mathematics curriculum. Many teachers plan quantification games for their classrooms because these materials strongly support children's construction of number concepts (Ramani and Siegler 2008; Whyte and Bull 2008; Young-Loveridge 2004). When science materials are used as part of the game, such as shells or *fossils* for counters, or toy representations of fish or insects for movers, they spark children's interest in learning about science. This can lead to more in-depth explorations in the science area of the classroom. Manipulative materials that incorporate geometric shapes are standard components of many preschool and kindergarten classrooms, yet children may quickly tire of these familiar materials. It is much more exciting and educational to examine shapes within the context of science. Animal habitats, such as nests and holes, are typically round. Many shells have a spiral shape, a special type of pattern. Starfish, many flowers, eucalyptus pods, and the configuration of seeds in apples are examples of pentagons in nature. Bee combs, snowflakes, and many types of coral have hexagonal shapes. By observing the geometry in nature, children gain a much more comprehensive understanding of geometric shapes.

Technology integrates with science and mathematics primarily through the tools that children employ for observation, experimentation, and measurement. In science, children often use magnifying glasses to enlarge images and expose detail. Several types of microscopes are available. A simple, handheld magnifier incorporates a mirror so that children can see the top and the bottom of objects. They can carry this magnifier outside and explore insects or items that they find from both perspectives. A more elaborate microscope for children connects to a computer and greatly expands the image of the object under investigation. This type of microscope allows a group of children to share their observations with one another. Other technology tools that children often use in science explorations include tongs, eyedroppers, pumps, plastic knives, sifters, and funnels. These tools frequently incorporate *simple machines* that can themselves become the focus of experimentation. Technology, therefore, serves two purposes in the early childhood curriculum. First, it can enhance scientific learning by expanding opportunities to observe and experiment. Second, children can study the technology itself to enhance their understanding of science.

Children may also use technology as part of the mathematics curriculum, particularly in the area of measurement. Balance scales, thermometers, wind wheels, weather vanes, measuring cups and spoons, and timers (particularly the hourglass styles in which falling sand marks elapsed time) are examples of appropriate technology for early childhood mathematics investigations. In addition, items such as kaleidoscopes and mirrors can help children create symmetrical images.

Connections to engineering were presented previously in this chapter. Children learn about engineering through their exploration of materials, such as building with blocks, experimenting with solid and liquid materials, and adhering materials with glue, tape, staples, twine, and even nails. In addition, the objects that children use in these explorations (from various shapes of blocks to boxes and paper rolls) strongly support geometry. Shape and position are critical components of building stability.

Although science and mathematics have natural connections in the curriculum, children's learning mechanisms in these two disciplines are somewhat different. Piaget's (1971) framework of three types of knowledge can help teachers understand how learning occurs in science and mathematics. The first type of knowledge, *physical knowledge*, encompasses the physical properties of objects, such as color, texture, temperature, weight, and shape. Children discover these properties by interacting with objects, manipulating them, and observing the results. Conceptual understanding of the physical properties of materials comes from this direct interaction, not from reading or being told about them. For example, children learn that coldness is a property of ice by touching it. They observe that ice begins to melt and turn to water as they hold it in their warm hands. This type of experience is the essence of physical knowledge. Much of science involves understanding the physical properties of objects, as well as manipulating materials and observing the results. Most scientific learning, particularly for young children, involves physical knowledge.

The second type of knowledge is *logical-mathematical knowledge,* which is constructed internally by the child. Children form all kinds of relationships based on their experiences—numeric, similar/different/same/opposite, more/less/same, symmetrical/asymmetrical, difficult/easy, and so forth. All of this knowledge resides inside the child rather than within the properties of objects or experiences. For example, there is nothing about a truck and a car that makes them similar until an individual decides they are closely related, perhaps because both have wheels and are used for transportation. Another person might determine that the same two objects are different because the truck is larger and is used to carry cargo. Since virtually all of mathematics involves the formation of relationships, learning in mathematics centers around logical-mathematical knowledge.

Although physical knowledge and logical-mathematical knowledge are different, they often occur almost simultaneously as children learn. It is through their experiences with objects that children discover characteristics that they use to form relationships. By lifting a ball and a balloon, children discover that one is heavier than the other, a logical-mathematical relationship that is constructed after children discover a physical property of the two objects. By grouping shells and pebbles into two categories based on their physical characteristics, children may discover that there are more shells than pebbles. In this case, the physical properties of the shells and pebbles provide a context for making a numeric comparison.

The third type of knowledge in Piaget's framework is *social knowledge,* information agreed upon by cultural groups. Manners, rules, vocabulary, and customs are examples of this type of knowledge. The only way children can learn this information is through reading about it or being told. Constructivist educators have long voiced concern that science and mathematics are frequently taught as if children can understand the underlying concepts by simply reading or being told the information. Reading about *simple machines* rather than actually experimenting with them is an example from science. In mathematics, telling children specifically how to solve a problem exemplifies this concern. Social knowledge related to science and mathematics is largely confined to scientific or mathematical vocabulary. While it is important for children to learn this vocabulary, it should be introduced within the context of direct interactions with scientific and mathematical situations. In this way, social knowledge supports conceptual development rather than leading to only a surface level of understanding.

DESIGNING A STEM CURRICULUM

An integrated STEM curriculum often revolves around scientific inquiry. This encourages children to ask questions, conduct explorations, and form inferences in much the same manner as scientists. Teachers support scientific inquiry by providing interesting curricular materials that challenge children to explore and learn while building on their previous knowledge and understanding. For example, a class that discovered and collected *fossils* on a recent field trip might be very interested in comparing them to seashells and sea creatures of today. The questions that teachers pose and the conversations they have with children as they interact with materials can expand children's use of scientific inquiry, increase their thinking skills, and provoke deeper investigations. The following are some of the components of scientific inquiry:

- predicting: forming an idea or expectation based on previous experiences that guides scientific investigation
- observing: carefully examining the

characteristics of an object, either in its natural environment or in an experimental setting

- experimenting: creating a situation to investigate a prediction or manipulate an object to gain knowledge
- comparing: forming relationships through observation or experimentation with objects
- measuring: formulating or using a method to compare or quantify particular attributes of objects, such as length, weight, distance, and speed
- inferring: forming an assumption based on repeated observations or experimentation
- communicating: sharing knowledge gained through inquiry by talking, writing, drawing, or reenacting a situation

Children can engage in scientific inquiry through exploring materials in STEM learning centers and investigating materials throughout the curriculum, including the outdoors. In addition, STEM learning can be a major component of class projects and a focus of field trips. Simple adjustments to regular classroom activities can also lead to STEM learning outcomes.

Creating STEM Learning Centers

Science learning centers are a component of many preschool and kindergarten classrooms. Effective teachers redesign and change these centers regularly to build on the interests of the children, to coordinate with other aspects of the curriculum, or to introduce materials related to a particular content standard. Science centers can be strengthened by turning them into STEM learning centers. The introduction of mathematics, such as the inclusion of measurement tools or graphs for data analysis, adds to the information children can construct. Technology also supports learning by providing children with a range of tools to use in their explorations. Digital and video cameras can preserve children's scientific interactions and allow them to revisit and analyze their experiences. Finally, the inclusion of nonfiction books written for young children can help them understand the connection between their explorations in the STEM center and the professions of adults, including various types of engineering. Chapter 2 provides a variety of ideas for creating STEM learning centers.

Exploring STEM throughout the Classroom

Science and mathematics are embedded in all areas of the classroom, and teachers should take advantage of these learning opportunities throughout the day. Cooking experiences introduce children to **simple machines** through a variety of tools and gadgets. Children also discover changes in materials caused by heat, cold, or combination with other materials. Children use measurement and quantification as they add ingredients.

In the block area, children can explore simple machines, such as **inclines** and **pulleys**, while they engage in engineering-related projects. They can also investigate natural building materials and compare a variety of rigid, soft, and semirigid materials. The application of geometry and measurement concepts is strongly related to play in the block area.

At the sensory table, children can compare the characteristics of liquid and dry materials and experiment with air and water pressure. Through art activities, children can investigate the behavior of materials, create patterns, and engage in explorations that involve earth science, physics, and life science.

Finally, through music, children can create patterns and explore the physical properties of instruments. STEM activities in all of these areas are presented in chapter 3.

STEM in Outdoor Areas

Outdoor areas provide opportunities for STEM explorations that are not available in the class-room. Children can investigate shadows, wind, and bubbles and observe insects, birds, and neighborhood animals. The outdoor area allows children to explore simple machines on a larger scale. Pulleys can be used to move materials to areas that are too far to reach. Inclines can be explored through activities that use the whole body. Outdoor planting activities can often be longer in duration than those conducted in the classroom, and they can be connected to natural light and weather cycles. Designing STEM activities for outdoor areas is the subject of chapter 4.

Integrating STEM into Class Projects

Many preschool and kindergarten teachers have become interested in fostering learning through class projects, particularly following widespread interest in the Reggio Emilia schools in Italy. Whether introduced by the teacher based on the perceived interests of the children or initiated by a group of children who share a particular interest, projects focus on inquiry. Often there is a central question that children hope to answer through their investigations. Teachers provide support and guidance by mediating discussions, providing needed materials, introducing new but related experiences, and documenting learning.

Regardless of the nature of a class project, science is almost always involved, and mathematics often adds an important dimension. Sometimes a project may center around an area of science, as when a class wants to build a life-size dinosaur or discover seasonal changes in the environment. At other times, the project may seem unrelated to science, such as a class that wants to produce a play. However, even when science is not the focus of a project, it is often an important component. In the play project, backdrops and props may be desired. As children select materials and use them to construct props, they will encounter science and engineering situations related to balance and the properties of materials. They may also need to measure as they develop costumes and stage sets. For this reason, teachers can use class projects to integrate mathematical and scientific learning. Examples of a variety of class projects and the related STEM learning are included in chapter 5.

Quick STEM Activities

Early childhood teachers have many required standards and curricular components to integrate into each day's schedule. Even in preschool and kindergarten, many teachers feel pressured to fit so many requirements into the day. However, many opportunities for learning in the STEM disciplines go unaddressed each day. Many of these involve daily activities that are already part of the schedule but can be "tweaked" through a slight change, addition, or focus. These can provide rich experiences in science and mathematics. Chapter 6 investigates numerous simple changes to regular classroom activities that create opportunities for learning in the STEM disciplines.

STEM Field Trips

Field trips provide preschool and kindergarten children with the opportunity to visit settings they may not typically experience, or to more fully explore their own community. Chapter 7 discusses ways to create richer learning opportunities on field trips by planning for STEM learning outcomes and documenting the experiences. Some field trips already have a science component, such as trips to the zoo, a farm, or the park. Still, children's learning can be enriched by adding mathematics, technology, and engineering to the experience. Other field trips, such as a walk around the neighborhood, may not initially appear to be STEM oriented, but with proper planning they can be. Teachers can encourage closer scientific investigation, such as observing and recording the plants and animals that are part of the community. Or children can focus on the design and structure of various buildings, connecting children to the science, mathematics, and engineering that are all around them.

SUMMARY

After a decade of intense focus on literacy development in early childhood programs, attention is now shifting to the importance of early learning in mathematics and science. STEM education integrates learning in both of these disciplines and includes connections to technology and engineering. By focusing on the connections between science and mathematics, teachers can accommodate curriculum goals and learning standards in both disciplines while helping children understand the ways in which mathematics and science are woven into their daily experiences. Learning in each area reinforces the other.

A Note about Terminology
Glossary terms appear throughout the text in **bold and italic type**.

STEM Learning Centers

Mina attached a small plastic ramp, backed with Velcro, to a felt board that was mounted to the wall in the class's STEM learning center. She placed a plastic ball on the ramp and watched as it rolled down the incline and dropped into a tub below. Next, Mina added a second ramp, placed directly beneath the first ramp, to the felt board. This time, as she again rolled the ball down the top ramp, Mina noticed that the ball completely missed the ramp below it. Carefully, Mina adjusted the lower ramp so that it extended beyond the top ramp. When she rolled the ball for a third time, it dropped off the top ramp, landed in the middle of the lower ramp, and rolled down it before dropping into the tub.

"That's neat," said Mina's friend Zach, who had approached the STEM area and was watching. "I know a way to make the ball go the other way, like in this picture." Zach pointed to a photograph of a street that zigzagged down a hill.

"How?" asked Mina.

Zach removed Mina's bottom ramp and repositioned it so that the downward slope slanted in the opposite direction. When Zach rolled the ball down the top ramp, it dropped onto the bottom ramp and rolled the opposite direction before falling into the tub. Mina and Zach continued experimenting with the ramps until they could make the ball change directions several times on its downward course.

• • •

The STEM center in this vignette is described in Activity 2.2 of this chapter. At first glance, it looks like an interesting science center that allows children to experiment with the properties of **inclines**. But in this case, the teacher has also planned the center so that children can experiment with the geometric concepts of positioning, directionality, and angle. The photograph of Lombard Street in San Francisco, often called the "Crookedest Street in the World" because of its hairpin turns, was deliberately added to the center to encourage children to model its pattern of directional change in their own experiments.

After the children have had a week to freely explore the effects of directional change and positioning, the teacher plans to introduce a different concept. She will encourage children to construct two kinds of inclines, those that are almost parallel to the ground, and therefore have a very gradual slope, and others that are steep. The children can then compare the speed of cars rolling down them. To more accurately measure the speed of the cars, the teacher plans to help the children count the clicks on a **metronome** as the cars roll down the slopes. (A metronome is a device used in music to help musicians maintain a steady beat or tempo.) The use of a timing device integrates technology into the center. It also focuses on quantification as a component of measurement. The teacher also plans to create short video clips of each child experimenting in the center and e-mail them to the children's homes. That way, the children can discuss their scientific experiments at home with their families. Finally, the teacher hopes to introduce children's books related to road construction (civil engineering) and draw connections to the children's experiments with inclines. The intentional planning of the teacher transforms a nice science center into an integrated STEM center that stimulates children's thinking in all four STEM disciplines.

PLANNING STEM LEARNING CENTERS

Throughout this book, STEM education is defined as the integration of at least two of the STEM disciplines, typically mathematics and science. Establishing connections across curriculum areas is regarded as important by professional educational organizations in early childhood (Copple and Bredekamp 2009), mathematics (National Council of Teachers of Mathematics 2000), and science (National Research Council 1996). By establishing a STEM learning center as a regular component in the classroom, teachers can ensure that children have many opportunities to investigate concepts in science and mathematics and to connect learning in the two disciplines.

When planning STEM learning centers, teachers can start with a science or mathematics topic and then integrate goals and materials from one or more of the other STEM disciplines. Although educators often think first of science when planning a STEM curriculum, either science or mathematics provides a good starting point. For example, in a class that has been exploring **pendulums**, the teacher might decide to use a magnet as the weight (bob) on the pendulum and provide paper clips for the children to try to pick up as they swing the pendulum (Activity 2.5). The experience quickly takes on a mathematical

element when the teacher encourages the children to quantify and compare how many paper clips they collect with the magnet. This activity is an example of a science topic that is extended to include mathematics, thereby making it a STEM experience. Or perhaps the children have been exploring geometric shapes at the math center in their classroom. The teacher, who wants to extend their understanding of geometry to include discussions about how geometric shapes appear in nature, brings in an assortment of natural items that illustrate this concept. The children sort the natural objects into categories based on their shapes. In this example (Activity 2.16), the teacher extends a mathematics topic to include science. Both of these examples illustrate how learning can increase when teachers make connections across content domains.

Like traditional science centers, STEM learning centers should include a small table or bench to hold materials for exploration. It should offer enough space for several children to use the center at a time. Interaction with peers, as the story with Mina and Zach illustrates, allows children to exchange ideas, model learning strategies, and compare results. Communication is an important component of STEM learning.

In addition to science and math materials, STEM centers should include technology tools to facilitate learning. Magnifying glasses, balance scales, and interlocking cubes for measuring length are examples of simple technology. More sophisticated technological devices, such as computers, digital cameras, and overhead projectors, may be kept nearby to extend or record learning. Books and pictures that connect the STEM learning materials to examples in the real world should also be regular components of the center.

The location of STEM learning centers within the classroom is also important. Positioning the STEM center near a window may be advantageous since some activities require natural light. Also, auxiliary items such as bird feeders, thermometers, or window-box planters can be located outside the window to connect indoor and outdoor curricula. The STEM center should allow easy access for children and welcome their involvement. If the center is located in a dark corner of the classroom, children may be less likely to explore it.

This chapter describes twenty STEM learning centers to guide teachers in integrating science, mathematics, technology, and engineering. Each of the following subcategories are a focus of five centers: physics, life science, earth science, and mathematics (algebra, geometry, number and operations, measurement, and data analysis). Each center integrates learning objectives from at least one other STEM discipline, and often two or three. Learning through inquiry is the major goal of each center and is therefore highlighted in each description. Related background information for teachers in science and mathematics is also included.

LIGHT AND COLOR

PHYSICS

Materials

○ deep cardboard box

○ white piece of paper

○ 3 flashlights, modified to create red, blue, or green light (see description)

○ red, blue, green, yellow, cyan, and magenta color tiles

○ documentation sheets

Center Description

This STEM center allows children to observe the results of mixing red, blue, and green light, which are the primary colors of light used to produce the secondary colors of *magenta*, *cyan*, and yellow. Magenta is a deep purplish red, and cyan (pronounced *SIGH-an*) is a greenish blue. Both colors are used in photography and color printing. Mixing colored light does not produce the same outcome as mixing colored pigments. Children can compare the results of combining colored lights with what happens when they mix colored paints in the art area.

In this experiment, children use flashlights to produce colored light. The flashlights are modified in one of three ways: (1) the lighted end is covered with red, blue, or green cellophane; (2) the lighted end is covered with clear plastic that has been colored with red, blue, or green permanent marker; or (3) red, blue,

or green bulbs are substituted for the clear flashlight bulbs. A cardboard box creates the darkened area needed for children to observe the effects of mixing colored lights. A piece of white paper mounted in the back of the box provides a colorless surface for the experiment.

Red, blue, green, yellow, cyan, and magenta color tiles, made by clipping the appropriate colors from free paint-sample cards, mounting them to note cards, and printing the name of the color on the card, are also included in the center. Children can use the tiles to show the results of mixing the colored lights. Children can record their observations on documentation sheets.

 ## Science Content

When colors that are emitted directly from a light source are combined, new colors are produced by an additive process. This is different from the subtractive process that is involved when colored pigments, such as paint or colored water, are combined (see Activity 4.11). Red and green lights combine to produce yellow; green and blue lights produce cyan; and red and blue lights produce magenta. Red, green, and blue lights produce white when all three are combined.

 ## Mathematics Content

The mathematics content in this center involves comparing the results of mixing two primary colors of light, which produce a secondary color, with combining three colors of light, which produces white.

Comments and Questions to Support Inquiry

- What color of light do you see when you mix the red and green lights? Does that happen when you mix red and green paint? Let's write down that red and green light make yellow, and later we'll try mixing red and green paint.

- If you work together, you can combine three colors of light. Let's see what happens.

- How would you describe the color of light you made by combining green and blue? That color is called cyan.

❗ Misconception Alert

When mixing colored lights, the primary colors are red, blue, and green. This is different from the primary colors for mixing pigments, which earlier color theory identified as red, blue, and yellow and are now known to be magenta, cyan, and yellow.

CHILD-DESIGNED INCLINES

PHYSICS

Materials

- ○ flannel or magnetic board
- ○ 4 to 8 small ramps (see description)
- ○ several small balls
- ○ Velcro or magnetic tape

Center Description

This center allows children to experiment with the effects of changing the slope and direction of inclined planes. It integrates concepts from physics and geometry. The activity is similar to marble-track toys that children may have played with in the classroom. This activity, however, gives children more control in the investigative process; therefore, it allows for more scientific learning.

The center consists of either a flannel or magnetic board, mounted to the wall or propped vertically; four to eight small ramps, constructed by the teacher; and small balls to roll down the ramps. Depending on the type of backboard being used, the ramps have either Velcro or magnetic tape affixed to one of their sides. This allows children to position the ramps wherever they like on the backboard. Children can change the angle, position, and direction of each ramp segment and observe how the change affects the movement of the balls.

There are many inexpensive and simple ways to make the ramp segments for this center. Perhaps the easiest method is to cut the lips off of the short ends of jewelry gift boxes that are approximately 8 inches long and 2 inches wide. Affix the Velcro or magnetic tape to the long edges. Each jewelry box makes two ramp sections if the tops and bottoms of the boxes are used. Empty jewelry boxes can be purchased at craft or party supply stores.

Another quick way to make ramp segments is to cut plastic or wood corner molding approximately 1¼ inches wide into 8-inch lengths. Overlap two strips and glue them together so that there is a lip along

each side of the ramp to keep the balls from rolling off the edge. Easier still is to use a plastic ceiling wall bracket, also 1¼ inches wide and cut into 8-inch strips, since it already has lips along both edges (see photograph). (Ceiling wall brackets are the long, horizontal pieces used to hold suspended ceilings.) All of these materials are inexpensive and are available in hardware or building supply stores.

Science Content

An **inclined plane** is one of six types of **simple machines** that children encounter daily in their lives. It consists of a flat surface positioned at an angle (less than 90 degrees) in relation to a horizontal surface. In other words, one end is higher than the other. Children experience inclined planes at entrance ramps to buildings, sloped sidewalk intersections, and when they run, slide, or roll down a hill. From a scientific perspective, inclined planes allow individuals to slide or roll objects from one level to another.

This requires less *force* than lifting them because the force is distributed over a greater distance. The speed at which an object moves down an incline is related to the slope, or steepness, of the incline.

 ## Mathematics Content

Position, direction, and angle are important geometric concepts that children encounter in this activity. Teachers should model positioning terms (*top, middle, side, bottom, above, below,* and *next to*) as children experiment with the inclines. In this way, children learn to pair placement patterns with the appropriate vocabulary. Directional terms, which describe movement patterns, include *up, down, across, opposite, left to right,* and *right to left,* although children are not expected to master the latter two in preschool. Finally, teachers can use the inclines to illustrate angles by comparing the slanted line formed by the incline with the horizontal line formed by the bottom of the flannel board frame.

 ## Connections to Technology and Engineering

The inclined plane is itself an example of technology, since it is one of the six classical simple machines. Teachers may want to take digital photographs of children's experiments with the ramps. These photographs can be shared with the class in a slide show or PowerPoint display, and children can recollect and share the results of their experiments.

Inclined planes are an important component of engineering, particularly in designing and building roads. Photographs of roadways, including overpasses and exit ramps, can be added to the STEM center to help children notice and make connections to inclines they experience in their daily lives.

Comments and Questions to Support Inquiry

- Let's put some ramps on this flannel board and see if the balls roll down them.

- Oops! Your ball missed the bottom ramp. Where can you put the lower incline so that the ball hits it?

- Look, your incline doesn't go straight across like the bottom of the flannel board. It moves downward at an angle.

THE GREAT INCLINE RACE

PHYSICS

Materials

- ○ wooden board, 12 inches by 18 inches
- ○ narrow strip(s) of wood, to be cut into sections as described below (72 inches of wood are needed)
- ○ wood glue
- ○ 1 piece of self-adhesive felt, quilted fabric, and mesh shelf liner, each approximately 2 inches by 15 inches
- ○ ruler
- ○ 4 identical toy cars

Center Description

Young children love to race cars. This center incorporates four *inclines*, each with a different surface, and a simple starting gate to ensure that the cars all begin the race at the same time. Children can observe how fast the cars move along the four paths and measure the distance each car travels.

The base of the racetrack is a lightweight piece of wood, 12 inches wide and about 18 inches long. Lines are drawn to divide the wood into four lengthwise sections, each 2½ inches wide, to form the racing lanes. Narrow strips of wood are then glued along these lines in the following configuration: 2½-inch-long strips at the top of each line, followed by a gap wide enough to fit the edge of a ruler, and finally strips of wood that extend to the bottom of the base. Different surfaces are created for each racing lane by "paving" three lanes of the track with the following materials: self-adhesive felt, quilted fabric, and mesh shelf liner. The fourth track remains uncovered wood. A ruler is inserted horizontally through the gaps in the wood strips to create the starting gate, and that end of the board is raised about 4 inches by propping it with blocks or a box. Children can then race four identical cars down the track and compare how fast and how far cars on the various tracks travel.

At first, children can observe the relative posi-

tions of the cars to determine which has moved the farthest. After several days, grid lines can be taped at 5-inch intervals along the floor. Children can count how many lines each car crosses. For kindergarten children, teachers may wish to tape a yardstick or a tape measure to the floor to connect the activity to standard measuring tools.

Science Content

This activity encourages careful observation and inquiry as children try to determine which car reaches the bottom of the track first and why. Children will notice that the car on the wood track consistently reaches the bottom first, followed by the car on the felt. The wheels of the car on the soft, quilted track deform the fabric as they press into it, which absorbs some of the energy that would otherwise go into moving the car forward. Similarly, the bumps on the mesh shelf liner shake the car, which also diverts energy from moving the car forward. This is why the cars on these two tracks move more slowly.

 ### Mathematics Content

This activity encourages measurement of both speed and distance. While younger children will judge speed and acceleration based on visual perception, older children can clap at regular intervals to measure the time a car takes to reach the bottom of each track. (In this case, they will need to race the cars one at a time.) A *metronome*, which produces sounds and light flashes at regular intervals for musicians to follow, is even better to use. These devices are not expensive and can be used in a variety of activities. The gridlines along the floor help children begin to quantify measurements of distance. Children can also link together manipulative materials, such as snap blocks, to measure distance. This helps children realize that measurement involves use of a designated item as a unit, and the number of units used is the distance.

Children will likely want to discuss the order of finish of the cars, which leads to the learning and application of *ordinal numbers*—first, second, third, and fourth. They may even want to record the order of finish on a score sheet.

  ### Connections to Technology and Engineering

Use of a digital video camera to preserve some of the ramp experiments allows children to review the results and the teacher to lead discussions with groups of children. As children watch the cars move down the various tracks, they can together clap and count pulses to determine speed. Children can also communicate about the experiments and share their inferences regarding what affects the speed of the cars.

Understanding how the surface of roads affects speed is important to civil engineers. Sometimes curves on a steep road have ridges to help prevent vehicles from going too fast. Teachers can introduce these concepts through their discussions with children.

Comments and Questions to Support Inquiry

- Does the car on the wood ramp always get to the bottom first? Why do you think that happens?
- This time let's watch for the car that comes in third place.
- Can you predict which car will go the farthest?
- Does the fastest car always go the farthest?
- Does the slowest car always go the shortest distance?

WISHING WELL: USING A WHEEL AND AXLE

PHYSICS

Materials

- ○ 2 pieces of wood, 24 by 2½ by ½ inches
- ○ 1 piece of wood, 13 by 12 by ½ inches
- ○ 1 dowel, ¾ inch in diameter and 13 inches long
- ○ 2 circular pieces of wood, 5 and 2 inches in diameter, respectively
- ○ 2 large stick pins
- ○ twine or cord
- ○ small bucket
- ○ plastic shoe box
- ○ small plastic fish or toys

Center Description

The **wheel and axle** is another of the **simple machines**. It consists of a wheel attached to a rod, so that turning the wheel also turns the rod. In this activity, children can experiment with two sizes of wheels, either of which can be turned to lower a bucket into the well and fish for a surprise.

The wishing-well frame is made from two pieces of wood, 24 by 2½ by ½ inches, that are mounted with paneling nails to a baseboard that is 13 by 12 by ½ inches. A third piece of wood, 14 by 2½ by ½ inches, is nailed to the two side pieces to form the top. A ¾-inch hole is drilled 4 inches from the top of each side of the frame, and a 13-inch-long piece of ¾-inch dowel is threaded through both holes. The wheels are made from two circular pieces of wood, one approximately 5 inches and the other 2 inches in diameter. Holes ¾ inch in diameter are drilled part way through the centers of the wheels. The ends of the dowel are then glued into these holes. Large stick pins are inserted into the two circular wood pieces to form handles for the cranks. To complete the wishing well, a piece of 15-inch-long twine or cord is stapled to the middle of the dowel, and the twine is tied to a small bucket. A plastic shoe box, filled halfway with water, is placed on the base of the frame, and small plastic fish or toys are added.

Children can compare the effects of the two sizes of cranks as they lower the bucket to fish for trinkets. If desired, the wood can be painted or stained to preserve it.

Science Content

Like the *inclined plane*, the wheel and axle allows an individual to use less *force* to move an object because the force is spread out over a greater distance. In this activity, the smaller wheel requires more force to move the bucket than the larger wheel because the larger wheel spreads the force over a greater distance; however, turning the smaller wheel requires less force than turning the rod itself. Teachers can point out the distance the handle moves on the large circle compared with the distance the handle on the small wheel must travel. If children are interested, they can stretch cord around the edges (circumferences) of both circles and compare the lengths.

 ## Mathematics Content

An interesting mathematical component of this activity is for children to compare the number of turns of the large versus the small wheel needed for the bucket to reach the water. Although the large wheel itself moves much farther than the small wheel, it does not move the bucket any farther than the small wheel does because one rotation of the wheel, independent of its diameter, completes one rotation of the rod. Therefore, both wheels must rotate the same number of times before the bucket reaches the water.

  ## Connections to Technology and Engineering

The wheel and axle is itself an example of technology that has evolved over thousands of years yet is still a fixture of modern life. It is an important component of engineering designs in areas such as the automobile industry. Teachers can help children understand the importance of this technology by asking questions throughout the day when children encounter examples of the wheel and axle, as in the following:

- How would you move the wagon if it didn't have wheels?

- Is it easier to move this big block by pushing it along the ground or by pushing it on the wagon?

- How could we open the door without the doorknob?

Comments and Questions to Support Inquiry

- How many times do you need to turn the big wheel before the bucket reaches the water? How many times do you need to turn the little wheel?

- Does the bucket move farther when you move the big wheel one time around versus the little wheel? Let's put a stick in the well and mark the distance the bucket moves when we move each wheel one complete turn.

- What makes the bucket move?

> **⚠ Misconception Alert**
>
> Not every wheel mounted to a rod constitutes a wheel and axle. In a true wheel and axle, the rod and wheel are firmly attached so that when one rotates, so does the other.

PENDULUM PICK-UP

PHYSICS

Materials

- ○ 2 pieces of wood, 16 by 2 by ¾ inches
- ○ 1 piece of wood, 12 by 2 by ¾ inches
- ○ 1 piece of wood, 18 by 12 by ½ inches
- ○ magnetic wand
- ○ string
- ○ screw eye
- ○ assortment of paper clips, both metal and plastic

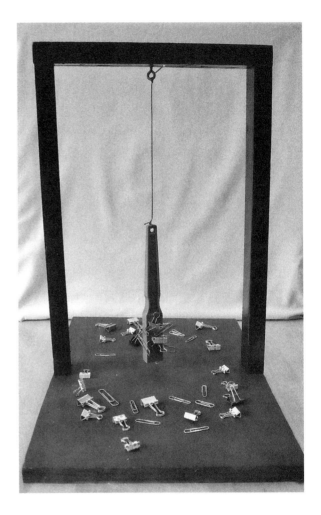

Center Description

A **pendulum** is a weight that is suspended from a fixed point so that it is free to move. In this STEM center, the weight suspended from the pendulum is a magnetic wand that children can use to pick up various types of paper clips scattered below. Two variables affect whether or not the paper clips are picked up by the magnet: (1) the material the paper clips are made from, and (2) the distance of the paper clips from the magnet. Some of the paper clips are plastic and are therefore not attracted to the magnet; others are made from a metal alloy containing iron and are easily picked up by the magnet; and the third type are covered with a plastic coating but have a metallic core that is attracted to the magnet. Children will need to investigate the differences between the paper clips that are attracted to the magnet and those that are not.

The second factor that affects whether or not the magnetic wand picks up a paper clip is how far away the paper clip is from the magnet. Children may notice that the magnet picks up more paper clips that are directly below it than paper clips that are along the edge of the pendulum frame and therefore farther away. As part of the investigative process, teachers can help children measure the distance between the magnet and the paper clips when the magnet is at various positions in its swing. Children can mark the distance on a stick or attach interlocking cubes to use as measurement units.

The pendulum frame used in the photograph consists of two sides made from pieces of ¾-inch wood, 16 by 2 inches; a top made from ¾-inch wood, 12 by 2 inches; and a baseboard made from ½-inch plywood, 18 by 12 inches. The frame is screwed together, as pictured, and the pendulum is suspended from a screw eye.

Science Content

The pendulum weight is called a *bob*, and the time that the pendulum takes to swing back and forth one time (for example, left to right, and back to the right again) is called a *period*. These are terms that children will quickly acquire if teachers model them while children explore the pendulum.

A magnet is an object that produces an invisible magnetic field, a **force** that pulls other ferromagnetic materials (chiefly iron) toward it. It is incorrect to tell children that magnets attract all metallic objects, because in most cases this is true only for materials that contain iron. Notice that magnets will not pick up an aluminum pop-top, a silver necklace, or current American coins, although these objects are made of metal. Kindergarten and older preschool children may be interested in the book *What Makes a Magnet?* by Franklyn M. Branley.

+ Mathematics Content

Two areas of mathematics are involved in the investigations in this STEM center: number concepts and measurement. To integrate number concepts, teachers can help children count the number of periods before the pendulum comes to rest. Also, if teachers clap a steady beat along with the children and count the number of claps per period, children will discover that even though the arc of the pendulum gets smaller and smaller, the number of claps per period remains the same. Teachers can also help children measure the distance between the pendulum bob (magnet) and the paper clips, as previously described.

  ### Connections to Technology and Engineering

During their life experiences, children may have noticed the wrecking ball on a crane that is used to knock down buildings. This is an application of the properties of a pendulum to achieve an engineering-related purpose. The wrecking ball is the bob of the pendulum. Children's books, such as *Bam, Bam, Bam* by Eve Merriam and *Machines at Work* by Byron Barton, document this process.

Comments and Questions to Support Inquiry

- Why does the pendulum pick up so many more paper clips from the middle of the tray?

- Here's another magnetic wand. See if it will pick up any paper clips from the edge of the tray. Does it? Then why doesn't the magnetic wand on the pendulum pick up the paper clips on the edge?

- Which paper clips don't get picked up by the magnet?

- I agree that the magnet doesn't attract the plastic paper clips, but this paper clip got picked up, and it looks like plastic.

- Can you figure out how close the magnet has to be to this paper clip before it will pick it up?

- Let's count how many claps it takes for the pendulum to go back and forth each time.

! Misconception Alert

Adults often tell children that magnets are attracted to objects made of metal. This is inaccurate. Magnets are mainly attracted to objects that contain iron.

WORM TUNNELS

LIFE SCIENCE

Materials

○ clear plastic container, tall and narrow, filled with soil

○ material to cover the top of the container, such as burlap, gauze, or nylon, wire, or plastic mesh

○ several earthworms

○ fresh leaves

○ magnifying glass

○ paper and pencil, for recording observations

Center Description

Worms are kept inside for several days in this STEM center so that children can watch them. The indoor habitat for the worms is a narrow clear plastic container filled with moist soil. When earthworms are added to the container, children can watch them tunnel through the soil. The soil should be kept moist but not soaking wet. Nylon, wire, or plastic mesh taped to the top of the container keeps the worms from escaping but allows them to get air. Each day, fresh leaves for the worms to eat should be added to the container. Children may notice parts of the leaves disappearing as the worms take them belowground.

A narrow container is used for this activity so that children can observe the worms. Worms prefer the dark, so they are likely to stay near the center of the container, which will be out of sight if the container is too wide. In this case, a smaller container can be put inside the larger one, with the soil and worms housed in between the two containers.

Let's find out about earthworms.

What do earthworms look like?

What do earthworms eat?

Where do earthworms live?

The worm bin should be kept out of the sunlight so that the worms do not become overheated or too dry. Teachers should plan this activity for a time when the ground is not frozen. Worms can be dug up from any soil rich in plant growth. Teachers can also purchase earthworms at a fishing or bait store.

Paper and pencils should be included at the center so that children can draw and write about their observations. A magnifying glass may make the worms easier for children to see. Children's books, such as *An Earthworm's Life* by John Himmelman and *Wonderful Worms* by Linda Glaser, can enhance children's knowledge and understanding of earthworms.

 ## Science Content

Earthworms have a segmented, tube-shaped body that feels moist and slimy. Earthworms burrow through the ground by contracting their bodies, and they enrich the soil by converting organic materials, such as leaves, into **humus**. Their burrowing activity aerates the soil, which makes it easier for plants to take in moisture and nutrients. For these reasons, earthworms are considered welcome inhabitants of gardens.

 ## Mathematics Content

Some children may be interested in counting the segments on an earthworm's body. The earthworms can be removed from the container for brief periods and placed on a moist cloth for viewing. Earthworms dehydrate easily, so they should be kept out of the sun. Teachers can model using directional terms, an important component of geometry, to describe the worm tunnels. For example, the teacher might comment, "It looks like this worm moved straight down and then veered off at an angle. Now it's moving straight across."

 ## Connections to Technology

Teachers can download photographs and information about earthworms from the Internet. Use of magnifying glasses to enlarge the images of the earthworms is another connection to technology.

Comments and Questions to Support Inquiry

- Can you draw a picture of what the earthworm's tunnel looks like? Tomorrow we can observe the worms again and see if the tunnel has changed.

- What happens to the earthworm's body when it is digging a tunnel?

- Make an estimate of how many segments the body of this earthworm has. We'll take it out of the bin later in the week and count them.

- Are all three leaves still at the top of the worm bin? What do you think happened to them?

INSECTS AND SPIDERS

LIFE SCIENCE

Materials

- ○ large plastic insect and spider (as scientifically accurate as possible)
- ○ collection of toy insects and spiders
- ○ divided tray or small containers for sorting
- ○ bug jars
- ○ children's binoculars
- ○ simple information sheet, as pictured
- ○ information books about insects and spiders

Center Description

This STEM center features a large replica of an insect and a spider for children to examine, compare, and contrast. There are also small toy replicas of insects and spiders for children to sort and classify. Quality children's science books, such as *Insects* by Robin Bernard and *Spiders! Get Caught in the Web of These Eight-Legged Creatures* by Time for Kids, add to the appeal of the center, provide more specimens for children to discuss, and supply background information (not to mention reinforce literacy). Children can draw, dictate, or write their observations on individual clipboards or in an observation notebook.

After children have had some time to examine the materials in the center, the search for insects and spiders can expand to outdoors. Children can use bug jars to collect samples of insects or use children's binoculars to observe spiders and webs. The bug jars are clear plastic with mesh over the top to allow ventilation.

Science Content

Insects and spiders are part of the *arthropod* phylum of living things. Insects have an external skeleton, a three-part body (head, thorax, and abdomen), six legs (three pairs), and two antennae. Spiders belong to the *arachnid* class of arthropods. They have eight segmented legs (four pairs) and a two-part body (head and abdomen). Like insects, spiders also have an external skeleton. Children can differentiate spiders from insects by comparing the number of legs (or pairs of legs).

 ## Mathematics Content

Children will need to use quantification strategies to differentiate between insects and spiders. They may compare the legs on the models in a *one-to-one correspondence*, that is, in matching fashion, or count the legs. Children can also count the body parts— three for insects, and two for spiders. An interesting concept for young children is the idea that one pair of legs is actually two legs.

 ## Connections to Technology

Bug-collection boxes that have a built-in magnifier are commercially available, as are binoculars for young children. Both of these tools use technology to make the details on objects easier to see. Spraying spider webs with water from a plant mister makes the webs much more visible without harming the webs. Children can then more easily observe and discuss the patterns of lines and shapes that are part of the webs.

Comments and Questions to Support Inquiry

- The sign says that insects have six legs and spiders have eight. Is this a model of an insect or a spider?

- I see one, two, three—three body parts on this insect. Does the spider have three body parts?

- Angela brought a bug in from the playground. When you have a chance, see if you can tell whether it's an insect or a spider.

SEED SORT AND GROW

LIFE SCIENCE

Materials

- ○ several types of seeds, such as corn, pumpkin, bean, or sunflower
- ○ sorting tray
- ○ clear plastic container partially filled with soil
- ○ name label for each child
- ○ seed labels for each side of the container
- ○ straws
- ○ markers

Center Description

The purpose of this STEM center is to help children make connections between seeds and the plants that grow from them. A variety of seeds are available in the center for children to examine and sort before they are planted. Corn, pumpkin, bean, and sunflower seeds are large enough for children to handle without becoming frustrated. As they sort the seeds into a divided tray, children can speculate about what types of plants they will grow.

During the second phase of this activity, children can help the teacher plant the seeds. An interesting question to pose before the seeds are planted is: Do seeds that look alike grow plants that look alike? The seeds should be planted along the sides of a clear container, with one type of seed per side, so that children can view the roots of the plants and keep the seeds organized. Tape an example of each type of seed to the side of the box where that variety of seed

was planted. After each child plants a seed, a label with the child's name can be placed on the outside of the box in front of the seed. When the plants begin to grow, a straw can be inserted into the soil behind each plant. Each child can visit his or her plant daily and add a mark to the straw to measure the plant's growth. Additional straws can be added as needed by pinching the bottom of a new straw and inserting it into the original straw marker, thereby extending the height of the straw measuring stick.

Science Content

This activity can be a mystery investigation if teachers do not reveal the names of the seeds before the plants have grown. Children will discover that seeds that look alike do indeed grow plants that look alike, and they can identify a future plant by looking at its seed.

Mathematics Content

Two mathematics content standards are heavily represented in this activity: algebra and measurement. Sorting and classifying is an important algebraic concept because children must apply a general rule to a set of objects in order to determine which should go together. In this case, seeds that have a similar appearance (color, size, and shape) will likely be grouped together.

The connection between measurement and scientific observation is a highlight of this activity. Children can use their marks on the straws as visual indicators of daily growth. Older children may want to quantify their measurements by using interlocking units, such as Unifix cubes, to make a column as high as their plant. By counting the cubes, they can determine how many units tall their plant is.

Connections to Technology

Some children may be ready to use standard measurement tools, such as yardsticks or measuring tapes, to measure their plants. Applying a standard measurement device is an application of technology.

Comments and Questions to Support Inquiry

- Do the plants in this row look similar or different?
- Are all of the plants in this row the same height?
- Do all of the plants have a stem? Leaves?
- How can we measure the plants that are growing over the side of the box?

WHAT GROWS ABOVE AND BELOW THE GROUND?

LIFE SCIENCE

Materials

○ green bean, carrot, lettuce, and onion seeds

○ clear plastic shoe box, partially filled with soil

○ magnifying glasses

○ observation notebook with a section for each child

○ rulers and interlocking toy inchworms (commercially available) for measuring

○ several small cups of water with eyedroppers for watering (but not overwatering) the plants

Center Description

This center helps children explore the parts of plants that grow above and below ground, as well as the parts of particular plants that we eat. Children begin by planting green beans, carrots, lettuce, and onions in a clear plastic container that is narrow but relatively deep. You can purchase the seeds at garden stores, hardware stores, and online. If the seeds are planted close to the edge of the box, children can see the parts of the plant that grow below the ground.

Science Content

Children know that plants grow upward because they can see the parts that are above the ground. Many children, however, do not realize that important parts of plants are also under the ground. This center helps children observe growth below, as well as above, the ground. If the seeds are planted two months before the end of school, the plants will be ready to harvest and eat before the school year ends. Because of the types of seeds planted, children will be able to eat the leaves (lettuce), fruit (green beans), and roots (carrots and onions) of the plants from their garden.

 ## Mathematics Content

This center encourages children to use both standard and nonstandard measurement tools to quantify plant growth and make comparisons. The interlocking inchworms help children begin to construct important measurement concepts, such as the need to use units that are the same size, the importance of having the units touch one another, and the use of counting to quantify the number of units.

  ## Connections to Technology and Engineering

The eyedropper used by children to water plants provides a technology connection for this center. Children may be able to feel the air moving out of the eyedropper when they squeeze it, and they can see the movement of water into the eyedropper. A connection to engineering can be made by pointing out to the children that agricultural engineers help farmers grow better food more easily. The books *Food from Farms* and *Farm Machines*, both by Nancy Dickmann, help children better understand the function of farms.

Comments and Questions to Support Inquiry

- Do all of the plants have roots?

- Do the tops of the plants look the same or different?

- Do the roots of the plants look the same or different?

- Which plant has the longest root?

FIVE SPECIAL ROCKS AND MINERALS

EARTH SCIENCE

Materials

○ samples of mica, sandstone, talc, pumice, and granite (available from geologic supply companies)

○ Internet photos of sedimentary rock

○ recording sheet, such as the one pictured

○ magnifying glasses

○ balance scale

Center Description

The five *rocks* and *minerals* highlighted in this activity are *mica*, *sandstone*, *talc*, *pumice*, and *granite*. These rocks and minerals were selected because they have special characteristics that make them interesting to children. Mica is composed of layers that can be peeled endlessly into thin, *transparent* sheets. Sandstone and talc are tactile materials. When children rub sandstone, sand actually comes off of the rock. Talc initially feels hard, but when children rub it, they feel the softness of powder and can see it on their hands. Pumice is rough to the touch but very light in weight. Children can see numerous holes that are part of the rock's formation. Granite, on the other hand, is heavy and dense. It contains grains from a variety of minerals that are fused together.

Children should be encouraged to interact with the rocks and minerals in this collection to discover the unique properties of each. Children should not worry that they are "breaking" the mica when they peel it, or "ruining" the sandstone and talc when they rub it. These are the natural characteristics of the

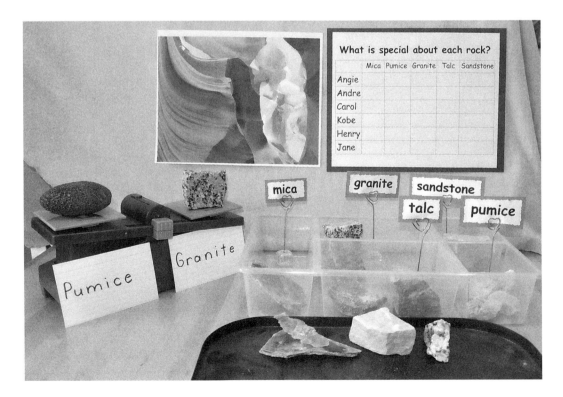

materials. Scientific tools should also be part of this center. Magnifying glasses help children see the holes in the pumice and the various minerals in the granite. A balance scale allows them to compare the weights of the rocks, which is particularly interesting with pumice.

All of these rocks are readily available at Internet sites. Often they come in packs of multiple specimens. Teachers may want to collaborate and each purchase one of the types of rocks. They can then share with one another and each have a complete collection.

 ## Science Content

A *mineral* is a naturally occurring substance that has a characteristic chemical composition and specific physical properties. *Rocks*, on the other hand, are combinations of minerals and therefore do not have a specific chemical composition. Mica is a mineral that forms in sheets. Due to the transparency of its layers, in the past mica has been used for windows. Sandstone is a *sedimentary rock*, meaning that it was formed by a layering of the earth's materials. Photographs of layers of sedimentary rock are available on the Internet. Talc is the softest known mineral and can be easily scratched by a fingernail. It is the most common ingredient in talcum powder. Both pumice and granite are volcanic rocks, formed from the molten lava of volcanoes that has cooled and solidified. In the case of pumice, rapid cooling and depressurization creates gas bubbles that leave noticeable holes in the rock.

 ## Mathematics Content

Geological and school supply companies often sell rocks and minerals in sets of five to ten pieces of the same type of material. Teachers can therefore put out a collection of samples of the five special rocks and minerals used in this activity for children to sort and classify. They may use color, feel, and weight as sorting categories. Sorting and classifying is a component of the algebra standard in mathematics.

  ## Connections to Technology and Engineering

This center incorporates technology through the use of magnifying glasses and a balance scale. Teachers with Internet access may wish to display photographs of the rocks and minerals used in the center or help children search for additional information. Minerals are often mined from deep beneath the earth's surface. The book *Life in a Mining Community* by Natalie Hyde has full-color photos and provides some information about mining. *Mining* by Ann Love, Jane Drake, and Pat Cupples contains more information but may need to be simplified by teachers.

An understanding of rocks and minerals is also important for construction engineers. Many older buildings and cathedrals are built of sandstone. Granite is used for building exteriors, floors, and kitchen countertops.

Comments and Questions to Support Inquiry

- Some of these rocks have sand or powder that comes off in your hand. Let's rub some rocks and try to find the sandstone and talc.

- Which of the rocks is the lightest? Let's use the scale to compare the weight of the rocks.

- Can you see through the thin sheet that you peeled from the mica?

⚠ Misconception Alert

Rocks and minerals are not the same thing. Each mineral has its own characteristic chemical composition. Rocks, on the other hand, are composed of various minerals and therefore do not have a specific chemical composition.

ONCE UPON A TIME: EXPLORING FOSSILS

EARTH SCIENCE

Materials

- ○ selection of several types of fossils
- ○ sorting tray
- ○ bowl of water, with several small brushes
- ○ labels for fossils (if desired)
- ○ information books on fossils
- ○ magnifying glasses
- ○ balance scale (optional)

Center Description

Fossils are the preserved remains or evidence of plants and animals that once lived on the earth. Young children are often fascinated with dinosaurs, so exploring fossils is a natural connection. This STEM center highlights several types of fossils, including individual specimens and fossils embedded in rock slabs. Photographs of similar fossils, downloaded from Internet sites, are available to help children identify the fossils in the center. Children's books, such as Aliki's *Fossils Tell of Long Ago* and *Digging Up Dinosaurs,* provide scientific information. The book *Bones, Bones, Dinosaur Bones* by Byron Barton includes clear illustrations and simple text for younger preschool children. Other materials at this center include magnifying glasses, a balance scale, a divided tray for sorting the fossils, and a bowl of water with brushes. When children spread water over the rock slabs, details of the fossils are more visible.

Fossils are readily available in many parts of the country. The website www.paleoportal.org displays a map of the type of fossils located in each state. Hilly

areas are a good place for teachers to look for fossils, particularly if there is a bare hillside with exposed rocks. Cuts in roads often reveal fossils, but safety is a concern when stopping along highways. Streambeds and beaches are also good places to look for fossils. Fossils can also be purchased inexpensively at many online sites.

 ## Science Content

Fossils may be the actual shells or bones of an animal that have hardened into stone, or impressions left by plants or animals, such as the indentation of a leaf or the footprints of an animal. The fossils used in this center are from the Ohio River valley, where they are so common they can literally be picked up off the ground almost anywhere one walks. Information about fossils is readily available on the Internet.

 ## Mathematics Content

Algebra is integrated into this activity when children sort and classify the fossils. Many of the fossils in the center shown in the photograph are **brachiopods**, which were sea animals with bivalve shells. They are good examples of **symmetry**, a special type of pattern in which one side is the mirror image of the other. Other fossils are **gastropods**, or ancient snails, which have a spiral shape—an interesting geometric design.

 ## Connections to Technology

The use of specific scientific tools, such as magnifying glasses and balance scales, connect this center to technology.

Comments and Questions to Support Inquiry

- Can you think of an animal today that looks like this fossil?

- Which of these fossils should go together in the sorting tray?

- There are so many fossils in this rock slab! Which kind of fossil appears the most often?

WHAT'S INSIDE A ROCK?

EARTH SCIENCE

Materials

○ geode, agate, amber, and petrified wood specimens

○ Internet images of geodes, agates, amber, and petrified wood

○ paper

○ colored pencils

Center Description

This center focuses children's attention on the inside of *rocks*, which in some cases is more interesting than what can be seen from the outside. Four specimens, all easily obtainable from websites, are featured: *geodes*, *agates*, *amber*, and *petrified wood*.

- Geodes, which often look like rock eggs from the outside, exhibit beautiful quartz crystals when cracked open. Children can put the parts together and take them apart like three-dimensional puzzles.

- Agates are rocks that, when sliced, reveal bands of color formed by quartz deposits. Agates are often polished to look like glass.

- Amber, which is the hardened resin of ancient trees, often contains the preserved remains of insects.

- Petrified wood is wood that has turned to stone. It often has beautiful bands of color created by *minerals*, which are deposited in the cells of the wood and harden into stone.

Agates
Can you describe or draw an agate?

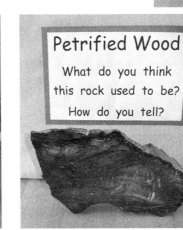

Amber
What can you find inside the amber? How do you think it got there?

Geodes
Can you find the geode that has not been opened?

Petrified Wood
What do you think this rock used to be? How do you tell?

When children have the opportunity to explore beautiful rocks such as these, they may develop an interest in science and geology that lasts a lifetime and points them toward a future career path. Most of the rocks mentioned above can be purchased rather inexpensively. The exception is amber. Real amber with plant or insect remains can be quite expensive, and the specimens are small—often 1 inch long or less. Man-made amber, however, looks like the natural substance and is relatively inexpensive even for larger specimens. For example, a manufactured piece of amber that is about 6 inches long and 4 inches wide can be purchased for less than ten dollars. The faux amber is actually a better choice for young children because it is easier to handle and the fossilized remains are readily observable.

A good addition to this center is colored pencils and paper. Children may wish to copy the beautiful designs they see in the rocks. This sharpens their observational skills.

 ## Science Content

Geodes form around cavities in rock formations when groundwater slowly deposits minerals inside the cavity, eventually producing crystals. Most agates form within cavities in *igneous* (volcanic) rock. As with geodes, water solutions deposit layers of minerals within the stone over time. When sliced, bands of colorful, parallel lines can be seen. Amber is itself a *fossil* (whether or not there are plant or animal remains encased in it) because it is plant resin that has been hardened under heat and pressure. Petrified wood is a special type of fossil that retains the original structure of the wood after all of the organic material has been replaced with minerals.

 ## Mathematics Content

The parallel bands of color formed in agates and petrified wood are wonderful geometric constructions. Teachers can help children observe and finger-trace these lines, which never cross. Children may then begin to notice other parallel lines in their environment, such as the balusters in stairway railings or fence rails.

  ## Connections to Technology and Engineering

Teachers who have Internet access can display beautiful images of the types of rocks included in this center on a classroom computer. Many minerals are mined from deep beneath the earth's surface. Mining engineering is a special type of engineering related to the extracting and processing of minerals. Picture books related to mining can help children make the connection between rocks and minerals and mining engineering. The book *Mining* by Ann Love, Jane Drake, and Pat Cupples provides illustrations and diagrams of a mine.

Comments and Questions to Support Inquiry

- Can you tell what this specimen (petrified wood) was before it became a rock?

- Look at the lines in this agate. Do they ever touch?

- Can you find the two halves of this geode and put it back together? From the outside, you'd never know it was full of beautiful crystals.

- What do you see inside this amber? You can use the magnifying glass to look more closely.

CAN A ROCK FLOAT?

EARTH SCIENCE

Materials

○ samples of mica, sandstone, talc, pumice, and granite (available from geologic supply companies)

○ container of water

○ recording sheet, such as the one pictured

○ balance scale

Can a rock float?

Geologist	Granite	Mica	Pumice	Sandstone	Talc
Mark					
Sonya					
Peter					
Jenna					
Jeff					
Claire					
Nancy					

Center Description

This center uses the five special *rocks* and *minerals* from Activity 2.10—*mica*, *sandstone*, *talc*, *pumice*, and *granite*—for further explorations. A common belief among both adults and children is that rocks cannot float. This center helps children disprove that notion. In the process, they discover some important principles related to *buoyancy*. The center includes a container of water deep enough to allow the largest rocks in the center to be submerged.

A bath towel spread across the science table can absorb any water that is displaced from the container. As children add small and large specimens of mica, sandstone, talc, pumice, and granite to the water, they will notice that some do not sink. Teachers should encourage children to examine the characteristics of the rocks that float to determine what makes this possible. Recording sheets can be added to the center so that children can preserve and compare the results of their experiments.

Science Content

A common misconception, and one regularly conveyed to children, is that heavy objects sink and lightweight objects float. Actually, objects float when the weight of the object is less than the weight of the water it displaces. Pumice is not a dense material (recall that it is full of holes), so the weight of the water it displaces is more than the weight of the pumice. For this reason, pumice usually floats. Granite, on the other hand, is dense, so even a small piece quickly sinks. Mica is twice as dense as water, so typically it will not float. However, a very thin sheet may float temporarily due to the *surface tension* of the water. Also, if the mica sheet is formed into a cup shape, it may float like a boat.

Mathematics Content

Mathematics content in this center relates to the relative weights of the rocks when compared to their volume. If two specimens of different rocks are close to the same size (volume), such as a piece of pumice and a piece of granite, then children can compare them on a balance scale. Be aware, though, that young children tend to believe that the side of the scale that goes up is the heaviest. Putting something that is very lightweight, such as a feather, on one side of the scale may help convince children that the heavier side goes down.

 ## Connections to Technology

Adding a balance scale to this center enables children to use technology to help increase their understanding.

Comments and Questions to Support Inquiry

- What do you think will happen when you put the rocks into the water?

- Did all of the rocks sink? Which one is floating? Let's put another piece of pumice into the water and see what it does.

- Which one of the rocks looks the most like a boat? Do you think its shape helps it float?

! Misconception Alert

The idea that lightweight objects float and heavyweight objects sink is incorrect. Objects float when the weight of the object is less than the weight of the water it displaces (moves aside).

WONDERS OF THE SEA

EARTH SCIENCE

Materials

○ assortment of seashells that vary by type, size, color, and shape

○ informational books that identify and illustrate seashells

○ sorting trays

○ sizing chart

○ magnifying glasses

Center Description

Many children are fascinated by the colors, shapes, designs, and textures of seashells. This center allows children to compare a wide variety of shells and sort them by their characteristics: size, shape, color, design, and texture. Several small sorting trays enable children to either sort shells by themselves or collaborate with a peer.

Magnifying glasses are available in the center so that children can more easily view the details of shells. A sizing chart, with lines drawn at 1-inch intervals, can be added to the STEM center for quick comparison of the length of the shells. Several inviting children's books help children identify the shells and find out more about the creatures that once lived in them. An example is *The Shell Book* by Barbara Hirsch Lember, which offers beautiful illustrations of seashells.

Seashells are easy to find and inexpensive to buy for teachers who do not live near the ocean. Craft stores often sell bags of assorted shells for a few dollars. Even larger specimens are often not costly. Although children enjoy sorting and handling small shells, it is instructive to have one or more large specimens for children to examine in greater detail. A large conch shell, for example, allows children to feel the spiral curvature of the inside of the shell. The beauty and intricacy of shells may inspire a lifelong interest in oceanography and geology for some children.

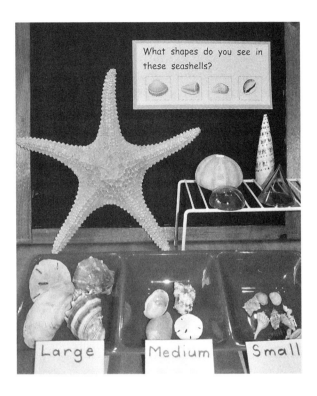

Science Content

Seashells are another of the earth's treasures that welcome children into the world of science. Teachers should learn the names of the seashells so that they can model this vocabulary for students. Children and teachers can learn together as they share the books included in the center. Teachers should not be afraid to use informational books that have more text than is appropriate for preschool and kindergarten children. If the illustrations are rich, teachers can select small bits of material from the text to share with the children.

✚ Mathematics Content

This center is rich in mathematics content. Seashells are excellent examples of the way in which geometry is woven throughout nature. Many shells have a spiral form, while others are round or elliptical in shape.

Conical forms are also common. To help children identify these shapes, teachers can add a set of geometric solids to the area for comparison. It is also interesting to note the shapes that are absent from the collection of shells, such as squares or rectangles.

The sorting component of this center incorporates the algebra content standard. Whether children choose to sort by type of shell, color, or size, they must create a general rule to apply to the placement of the shells. This application of an overarching rule is a key concept in algebra. Also related to both algebra and geometry is recognition of the symmetrical pattern of many of the shells.

After children have sorted the shells, they may want to compare the quantities of each type. This introduces concepts of quantification and data analysis into the learning. Some teachers may even decide to have children graph the various types of shells, perhaps by laying them on a board divided into sections. A group graph can be created by having children vote for their favorite shell. Finally, the sizing chart encourages measurement and allows children to quickly compare the lengths of various shells.

  ### *Connections to Technology and Engineering*

The main use of technology in this center is magnifying glasses, although teachers with Internet access can help children use the computer to find information about seashells and sea creatures. The study of sea creatures and their remains is part of the science of oceanography and, more specifically, marine biology and marine geology. A related area of engineering is marine engineering, which deals with the development of structures such as ships, harbors, and oil platforms that enable people to study and utilize the sea.

Comments and Questions to Support Inquiry

- Can you find a shell that looks like this cone? How many shells can you find that are this shape?

- I notice that you have a lot of cowrie shells and a lot of scallops. Which do you have the most of?

- This shell has rows of dots on it. Can you help me find it in the book? I don't know what it's called.

WHERE SHOULD THE DINOSAURS GO?

MATHEMATICS: ALGEBRA

Materials

○ 12 or more toy dinosaurs of various sizes and colors

○ sorting tray divided into boxes by tape

○ variety of children's nonfiction books on dinosaurs

Center Description

This center builds on the interest many young children have in dinosaurs by providing small replicas for them to examine. Although it is closely connected to science, the focus of this center is mathematics. The main objective is to find various ways to group a collection of small toy dinosaurs. Attributes that children can use to sort the dinosaurs include type of dinosaur, size, color, horns or no horns, and meat or plant eater (for budding *paleontologists*). Sorting trays help children keep the various groups separated.

Included in the center is a large tray divided into boxes by strips of tape. Once children have sorted the dinosaurs, they can use this tray to graph them. Teachers can model the idea of putting all the dinosaurs from a particular group in the same row on the

tray. Once the dinosaurs have been positioned on the tray, children can readily determine which group has the most, which has the fewest, and whether any groups have the same number of dinosaurs.

Various children's books about dinosaurs add to the science content of this center. Try to select more recent publications since information about dinosaurs is constantly being updated. For example, older books may identify the dinosaur now known as *apatosaurus* as *brontosaurus*.

 ## Mathematics Content

Sorting and classifying is an important component of algebra. To arrange the dinosaurs into groups, children must develop logical categories based on some general rule that they create. Children may decide that each type of dinosaur, regardless of size or color, should have its own section of the sorting tray. They must then apply this rule each time they position another dinosaur from the collection. Later in school, children will apply general rules to the manipulation of numbers, as in the application of the commutative principle in addition and multiplication or when they work with functions.

Data analysis is also a strong component of this center. In essence, the toy dinosaurs are the children's data, which they organize by grouping them into categories. The graph helps children make sense of the data. As children compare the number of dinosaurs in each row, they apply quantification concepts such as *one-to-one correspondence* or counting.

 ## Science Content

Although this center focuses on mathematical concepts, many children will be interested in learning more about the dinosaurs. Teachers should carefully select up-to-date informational books to include in the classroom. Based on the information and illustrations in these books, teachers can select toy dinosaurs that offer the most accurate depictions to include in the activity.

 ## Connections to Engineering

The science of *paleontology* employs engineering to help with excavations. Books such as *Digging Up Dinosaurs* by Aliki can help children make this connection.

Comments and Questions to Support Inquiry

- Where should I put this *tyrannosaurus*? I see tyrannosauruses in several compartments of your sorting tray.

- How many more *stegosauruses* do you need to have just as many as the number of *triceratopses*?

- I'm going to put the plant eaters over here, away from the meat eaters. Is this dinosaur a plant eater or a meat eater?

⚠ Misconception Alert

The dinosaur formerly known as brontosaurus is now called apatosaurus. Do not use books that depict people and dinosaurs as living during the same period. This is scientifically inaccurate.

NATURE'S SHAPES

MATHEMATICS: GEOMETRY

Materials

- ○ natural objects with geometric shapes (see center description)
- ○ plastic containers for sorting
- ○ photographs of geometric forms in nature
- ○ informational books that depict shapes in nature

Center Description

This center gives children the opportunity to identify geometric shapes found in nature and to group objects based on this attribute. Circular or spherical objects included in the center are a small bird's nest, a sand dollar, a buckeye, a sweet gum pod, and a sea urchin. Objects that are oval or ovoid include a cowrie seashell, a pumpkin seed, an avocado seed, a leaf from a jade plant, and a plastic bird's egg. Objects that are triangular or conical are a small replica of a spruce tree, a fern (preserved in self-laminating film), a pinecone, a naturally chipped *rock*, and a feather. Pentagons include a dried apple slice showing the core, a flower (preserved in self-laminating film), a locust pod, a sand dollar (the shape inside is a pentagon), and a starfish. Hexagons are represented by a wasp comb, a plastic snowflake replica, a large leaf, and a flower.

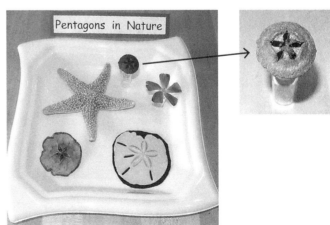

Included in the center are plastic containers with shape signs showing geometric shapes. There are also photographs of geometric shapes in nature to stimulate conversation. The wordless concept book *Shapes in Nature* by Judy Feldman and the children's book *Star in My Orange: Looking for Nature's Shapes* by Dana Meachen Rau can also contribute to discussions.

 ## Mathematics Content

This center focuses on geometry and helps children identify shapes in various representations. For example, the triangular feather is not the standard equilateral triangle that children typically see in manipulative toys. Instead, it is long and thin. Seeing shapes in a variety of configurations helps children focus on the attributes that designate each shape. Counting is reinforced as children quantify how many sides each shape has, particularly when they attempt to distinguish between pentagons and hexagons.

 ## Science Content

Squares and rectangles are not common in nature and are therefore not represented in the center. This is an interesting topic to discuss with children. Pentagonal shapes are extremely common in organic objects (matter from organisms that are living or were once living). While hexagonal shapes are prevalent at the molecular level in inorganic materials, they are less common in organic substances. Hexagons do appear, however, in flower petal arrangements and on the shells, or *carapaces*, of some turtle species.

Comments and Questions to Support Inquiry

- Can anyone find something with a triangular shape to go in this box?

- Can you explain why you put the sand dollar in the pentagon box? Gina says it's round.

- How can we tell whether this flower should go with the pentagons or the hexagons?

FEED THE ZOO ANIMALS GAME

MATHEMATICS: NUMBER AND OPERATIONS

Materials

- ○ math game board, as pictured
- ○ small toy truck for each player
- ○ 12 poker chips for each player (6 with a leaf sticker; 6 with a meat sticker)
- ○ 2 dice (1–6 dots)
- ○ teacher-made zookeeper book (see center description)

Center Description

This center is designed to build young children's number concepts through a board game that centers around zoo animals. The game board, which is made from poster board, has a road that passes the habitat of each type of animal. The animals are represented with stickers and are grouped in sets of one to twelve.

Each player has a truck to carry food for the animals. The "food" consists of poker chips (red for one player and blue for the other player); each player has six poker chips with a leaf sticker, for plant-eating animals, and six poker chips with a meat sticker, for meat-eating animals.

Although two standard 1–6 dot dice are available, children can choose to roll either one or two dice each time it is their turn. Based on the number rolled on the die/dice, children move their trucks to the habitat that has a corresponding number of animals. The goal is to visit each group of animals and distribute the appropriate food.

To help children determine whether to feed the animals a plant or a meat chip, the center contains a teacher-made zookeeper book with a photograph of each animal and both a written and pictorial designation of "meat eater" (**carnivore**) or "plant eater" (**herbivore**). The book also gives an example of the specific type of food that each animal usually eats.

Mathematics Content

This center focuses on the number and operations standard in mathematics. Each time children roll the dice, they have a new quantification problem to solve. While some children may match the dots on the dice to the animals in a given set, children who are experienced at using counting to determine how many are in a group will likely use that strategy. Rolling two dice encourages children to transition into addition by counting all of the dots together. Strategy, or logical thinking, is also a component of this game. For example, if the only habitat left on the board has one animal, it is necessary for the child to roll just one die.

Science Content

The science content in this center involves life science. The game helps children realize that not all animals eat the same type of food. It also builds vocabulary for children who have had little experience visiting or reading about zoo animals.

Comments and Questions to Support Inquiry

- Jenny counted seven dots on her dice. Can you help her find a group of seven animals?

- I have to feed the snakes. Help me find them in the book. I'm not sure what snakes eat.

- Look. You have the same number of dots on both dice. How many is that?

- If I want to get to the group with eight animals, should I roll one or two dice?

MEASURING PUMPKINS

MATHEMATICS: MEASUREMENT

Materials

○ 3 pumpkins—small, medium, and large

○ interconnecting plastic links, for measuring the pumpkins

○ paper, pencils, and scissors

○ balance scale

○ teeter-totter (if available) and blocks

○ large tub of water

Center Description

Three sizes of pumpkins are the subject of this center on measurement. Over several weeks, children can measure the pumpkins' height, circumference, bottom area, weight, and **buoyancy**. The measurement results can be recorded next to the children's names on a large sheet of paper on the wall.

The first focus is on height. While children will make initial height comparisons based on visual perception, they can obtain more exact measurements by using interconnecting plastic links, available in many early childhood educational catalogs. Children's measurements will likely vary, because many young children do not realize that the measuring tool must start at the bottom of the object and go to the top in as straight a line as possible. Also, children may have curves or bulges in the links that distort the measurement. An important part of the learning in this center is the conversations that children have about these discrepancies. These discussions help children construct important measurement concepts. Children can use the same interlocking links to measure the circumference of the pumpkins.

Obviously young children cannot compute the area of the bottom of the pumpkins. Nevertheless, they can begin to understand the concept of area by

tracing around the bottom of each pumpkin, cutting out the circular shapes, and laying them on top of one another. Some children may use the links to measure across the diameter of the area shapes. If children measure height and circumference during the first week the center is available, they may be ready to move on to area measurements during the second week.

The larger pumpkins are too big to measure on a typical school balance scale, but they can be measured on a teeter-totter, which is essentially a large balance. Children can place a pumpkin on one side of the teeter-totter and add blocks to the other side until balance is achieved. Blocks of the same size should be used so that the unit of measure remains the same. A bathroom scale can also be used, but the results will make little sense to most young children.

The final measurement activity is to observe the buoyancy of pumpkins. Before conducting the experiment, children should make predictions about whether the pumpkins will float near the top of the water, sink all the way to the bottom, or float somewhere in between. A tub of water deep enough to cover the largest pumpkin by several inches is needed. If desired, this part of the measurement cycle can be conducted outside.

 Mathematics Content

When children first begin to measure objects, they use direct comparison with another object to judge whether the item they are measuring is larger, smaller, taller, shorter, and so forth. There are three important concepts related to children's understanding of measurement: (1) a nonstandard unit can be used (not just standard units such as inches or pounds), (2) the units used to measure must all be the same (for example, the same size of block rather than some large and some small blocks), and (3) the units can be counted to get the total measurement. When young children are measuring length, they typically do not

understand that the units must touch each other but not overlap, must stretch from the beginning point to the end point of the distance or length being measured, and can have no curves or bulges in their line of measure.

 Science Content

Pumpkins are native to North America but are now grown all over the world, with the exception of Antarctica. Pumpkins can be orange, yellow, green, red, or white. There are many excellent children's books about pumpkins, including *Pumpkins* by Ken Robbins and *How Many Seeds in a Pumpkin?* by Margaret McNamara and G. Brian Karas.

Both adults and children may be surprised to discover that pumpkins float. The reason is that the weight of a pumpkin is less than the weight of the water it pushes aside (displaces). Each pumpkin has a large cavity inside filled with air, and the weight of this air is less than the weight of the water.

Comments and Questions to Support Inquiry

- I don't see any measuring links by this part of the pumpkin (*gesture*). Doesn't this part of the pumpkin get to be part of the measurement, too?

- How many times can you fit the circle from the little pumpkin across the circle from the big pumpkin? Wow! The big pumpkin is as far across as four of the little pumpkins.

- You two have different measurements for the big pumpkin. Why don't you both measure again and see if you can figure out why. I don't think the size of the pumpkin has changed!

- Does it take more links to measure the height of this pumpkin or the circumference—the distance around?

GRAPHING REPTILES AND AMPHIBIANS

MATHEMATICS: DATA ANALYSIS

Materials

- ○ toy replicas of reptiles and amphibians
- ○ tray, divided into columns and rows with plastic tape
- ○ sorting tray
- ○ chart depicting reptiles and amphibians
- ○ informational books about reptiles and amphibians

Center Description

Young children are often quite interested in **reptiles** and **amphibians**. While a main objective of this center is to encourage children to sort, classify, and analyze data, a co-objective is to familiarize them with common types of reptiles and amphibians.

The center includes a large container with plastic replicas of reptiles and amphibians; several sorting trays; a large tray divided into boxes with colored

tape; a chart, with photographs of reptiles and amphibians divided into the appropriate two categories; and several children's books about reptiles and amphibians. Children can use the sorting tray to classify the animals according to type, color, size, or whatever other criteria they may identify. They can work individually or with one or more partners. Once the animals have been sorted, children can align them in rows on the tray to create a graph.

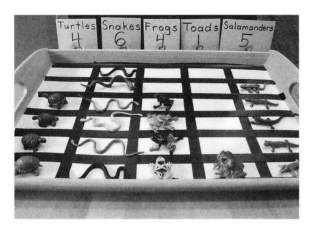

They can then answer questions, such as which row has the most or the fewest animals, and how many more are in one row than are in another. Teachers may choose to photograph the children's graphs for later discussion or for documentation of learning.

Mathematics Content

This center focuses on algebra and data analysis. Sorting and classifying objects and graphing them are methods children use to organize data (the animals) and answer questions, such as whether there are more amphibians or more reptiles in the collection. As children examine the animals and sort them into groups, they must develop specific rules for how they will classify the animals. Using a general rule that is applied broadly is a component of algebra.

Science Content

Reptiles are a class of animals that breathe air, lay eggs (although there are a few exceptions), and have scales. Crocodiles, snakes, and turtles are examples of reptiles used in this center. Although amphibians may seem similar to reptiles in appearance, most amphibians undergo a process of *metamorphosis*. They change from breathing water when they are young to breathing air as adults. Frogs, toads, and salamanders are examples of amphibians.

Connections to Technology

Kindergarten children may enjoy talking about the various ways they sorted the animals during group time. Teachers can facilitate these discussions by taking digital photographs of the children's work and projecting them for group discussion. Children will need to carefully analyze the work of their peers to determine what categories were used for sorting the animals in the various examples.

Comments and Questions to Support Inquiry

- Did you notice the chart that shows reptiles and amphibians? Let's see if we can sort these animals into those two categories.

- I didn't realize turtles and snakes could go together in a group, but they're both reptiles.

- Do you have more snakes or more frogs on your graph?

- How many more frogs do we need to find to have as many frogs as snakes?

CHOOSING A CLASS PET

LIFE SCIENCE

Materials

○ selected pet, in appropriate habitat and location

○ care chart, such as the one pictured

○ observation notebook, or pencils and paper

Center Description

Research on the effects of animals as classroom pets is sparse. Nevertheless, a growing number of studies indicate that experience with animals helps children develop empathy and caring attitudes toward animals. These attitudes extend to children's interactions with people (Gee 2011). A class pet allows children to learn about the specific needs of animals through observation and caretaking. Although many children may have a pet at home, others do not have this opportunity. Exposure to a class pet may encourage children to learn more about various types of animals and spark a lifelong interest in biology, animal care, and related subjects.

Some schools and licensing agencies have rules about animals. Teachers should check these regulations before planning for a class pet. Teachers should also be aware that not all animal agencies support the practice of incorporating animals as class pets. For example, the Humane Society of the United States (2012) recently changed its position from advocating

the use of class pets to not supporting this practice. Instead, they suggest periodically bringing animals to class as visitors or substituting stuffed animals for actual class pets. From a learning standpoint, however, neither alternative gives children the opportunity to develop observational skills over an extended period or to absorb the daily needs of the animal.

Bringing an animal to live in the classroom is a huge responsibility because the animal will need to be cared for over vacations. In addition, appropriate

Table 2.20: Choosing a Class Pet

SUGGESTED	SOME RESERVATIONS	NOT RECOMMENDED
Gerbils are easy to keep in the classroom and are interesting to children. Because they are desert animals, gerbils produce little urine or feces; hence, their environments do not smell and do not need to be cleaned frequently. Gerbils need the company of other gerbils, so at least two should be grouped together. Simply adding a toilet paper roll to their environment triggers a flurry of activity. While gerbils can be handled, care should be taken since they are small and hard to catch.	**Rabbits** usually do not make the best class pets because they are shy and easily frightened. This can cause them to scratch or bite. Their systems tend to be somewhat fragile, and bowel blockages are not uncommon. If allowed to hop around the classroom, rabbits will chew cords and carpet.	**Birds** are colorful and interesting to children, but they are also highly susceptible to breezes and are therefore difficult to keep in classrooms, where doors are often opening and closing. Birds are also messy and may bite.
Goldfish are inexpensive and easy to care for in a filtered aquarium. The aquarium does not need to be heated as long as the classroom stays above 50 degrees. It is helpful to keep an extra container of water handy that has been open to the air for twenty-four hours to dechlorinate it. Then, if an accident occurs (for example, a child tries to give the class fish a bubble bath) the fish can be quickly moved to the safe container.	**Ducklings** grow quickly. Some teachers like to incubate and hatch ducklings. These should be considered short-term pets because of their quick growth. A future home for the ducks should be secured before the eggs are brought into the classroom.	**Reptiles** are not recommended for classroom pets because of the danger of salmonella. This includes turtles, lizards, and snakes. An additional problem is feeding these animals. Snakes usually eat small rodents, so feeding them in an early childhood classroom is an issue. Lizards such as geckos eat crickets, which have to be kept alive until they can be fed to the gecko.
Guinea pigs are cute, furry, and generally docile. They can make excellent class pets that children quickly bond with. Guinea pigs are social creatures and need companionship. Two females is the best choice.	**Chicks** fall into the same category as ducklings. They are interesting to hatch but quickly outgrow the classroom space. Therefore, teachers must plan ahead for homes for the adolescent chickens.	**Wild or exotic animals** are best left in their natural habitat. They do not adapt well to the handling and commotion of a classroom. This includes animals such as ferrets, chinchillas, and chipmunks.

arrangements must be made for weather emergencies. Before a pet is selected, the teacher should research the needs of the animal. Ground rules should be firmly established in advance so that animals are treated respectfully by the children.

There are a variety of animals to choose among for class pets. Obviously teachers must be certain that the animal will not aggravate any child's health condition, such as an allergic reaction to pet dander. Teachers must also be sure that they can afford the expense of the animal, such as the cost of a secure cage and food. Information about caring for small animals, including the costs involved, can be found online at the ASPCA website (www.aspca.org/Pet-care /small-pet-care). Page 57 has additional information for teachers to consider about particular animals that are often considered for class pets. The information comes from the ASPCA website, books in the Animal Planet Pet Care Library—such as *Hamsters* by Sue Fox, *Rabbits* by Sue Fox, *Guinea Pigs* by Julie Mancini, and *Aquarium Care of Goldfish* by David E. Boruchowitz— and from personal experiences of classroom teachers.

 ### Science Content

A class pet provides children with the opportunity to observe another living creature carefully over a long period. Children learn about the animal's habitat and environmental needs, what it eats and drinks, and sometimes aspects of its life cycle, including birth and death. If the class has more than one pet, such as gerbils and fish, children can compare how the animals live and behave. Most importantly, children learn to care for and behave responsibly with animals.

 ### Mathematics Content

There are many ways to integrate mathematics into the observation and care of a class pet. Children can measure the size of the animal's habitat and how much it eats. They can count the animal's body parts and look for *symmetry*. Some pets, such as a guinea pig, can be weighed and measured.

Comments and Questions to Support Inquiry

Comments and questions should relate specifically to the type of pet the class acquires.

- What does the _____ have in its home? What do you have in your home?

- Where does the _____ sleep?

- Does the _____ like to play? How can you tell?

STEM throughout the Classroom

As soon as Khai and Aurelia arrived at school, they hurried to their favorite area—the blocks. Soon each child was busy building a tall block structure. "I'm making a lighthouse," said Aurelia. "We saw a lighthouse when we visited my aunt."

"I'm going to make a castle," said Khai, "with two towers and a moat."

After the children had been building for some time, Aurelia began to look for a toy person to put in her lighthouse. Instead, she found a basket filled with small wheels, each mounted in a metal frame. "What's this?" Aurelia asked, carrying the basket over to the teacher.

*"Those are **pulleys**," answered the teacher. "You can use them to move things up and down, like the flag outside, or across an area." The teacher showed Aurelia and Khai how to thread a string through two pulleys and attach a small bucket. "We could connect our buildings with the pulleys!" Khai exclaimed, becoming increasingly excited. "How can we hook the pulleys onto the buildings?"*

The teacher showed Khai some pipe cleaners. "Would these help?" she asked.

"I think so," replied Khai. He carefully threaded a pipe cleaner through the hole on one of the pulleys and then wrapped the ends of the pipe cleaner around one of the horizontal blocks on his castle. "Now you do it," Khai said to Aurelia. "Put a pulley on your building."

Aurelia looked at Khai's building to see where he had positioned his pulley, and then added a pulley to her lighthouse directly across from Khai's pulley. Next, Aurelia cut a long piece of string. "Put this through your pulley like Miss Amanda did," Aurelia ordered Khai. Meanwhile, Aurelia threaded the other end through her pulley.

"Can you tie this string together?" Aurelia asked Khai.

"I think so," Khai replied.

After several unsuccessful attempts, Khai finally managed to secure the ends of the string together. Aurelia ran to the art area and returned with a piece of tape, which she used to attach a small bucket to the string on the pulley. "Now we can send stuff between the two buildings," Aurelia announced.

The teacher had returned to the block area to check on the progress of Khai and Aurelia. "I knew two master builders would find a way to use the pulleys," she commented. "Well done. I'm going to put a sign on the block area that says you are the consulting engineers for any new pulley projects."

• • •

STEM IS EVERYWHERE IN THE CLASSROOM

Opportunities for learning in science and mathematics abound throughout the early childhood classroom. Some children find certain areas of the curriculum particularly interesting, so it is important for teachers to intentionally integrate science and mathematics into all parts of the classroom. As the preceding vignette illustrates, the addition of carefully selected materials can expand opportunities for learning in the STEM domains, stimulate higher-order thinking, and enable children to incorporate science, mathematics, engineering, and technology into their creative endeavors. In this case, the pulleys represent a historic technological invention that is still widely used today. Experimenting with simple machines such as pulleys allows children to construct important scientific relationships, including the ability of a pulley to reverse direction. As Khai and Aurelia adapt pulleys to meet their own engineering needs, they must employ the mathematical concepts of direction and measurement to solve a real-world problem—connecting two buildings so that materials can be interchanged between them. All four STEM domains are incorporated into their play. This chapter examines STEM learning in the cooking, block, sensory, art, and music areas of the curriculum.

STEM LEARNING IN COOKING ACTIVITIES

Cooking activities connect to two important content areas in science: life science and physics. The ingredients in recipes come from plants (grains, vegetables, and fruits) and animals (eggs, dairy products, and meat). Through the conversations that teachers have with children during cooking activities, children can begin to understand the connection between their own lives and the plants and animals that help meet their needs. These are important concepts in life science.

Teachers can also introduce related books and pictures to further enhance the learning.

As part of the cooking process, children engage in activities that include chopping, stirring, mixing, spreading, pouring, and measuring. The tools that assist in these endeavors are often applications of the six *simple machines*. For example,

- the crank on a hand-held eggbeater is a *wheel and axle*,
- child-safe knives used for chopping are *wedges*,
- cutting boards function as *inclined planes*, and
- spoons are *levers*.

Experimenting with simple machines and their effect on objects connects cooking activities to physics.

Mixing ingredients is also part of the cooking process. As children combine liquid and dry ingredients, they can immediately see a change in materials. Some of the changes that occur are reversible. For example, mixtures of raisins and cereal can be separated back into their component parts. Many other changes, however, are irreversible. An egg that has been scrambled cannot return to its original yolk and white formation. The addition of heat and cold also causes changes in materials that children can observe. For children, cooking is beginning chemistry.

Mathematics is also important in cooking activities. The measurement of ingredients provides young children with some of their first experiences in using standard measurement tools. Teachers can take advantage of cooking opportunities to allow children to compare measurements; for example, two ½ cups of water fill a 1-cup measure. Quantification is also a component of cooking. Children may need to count tablespoons, cups, or pieces of various ingredients that go into the mixture.

Children also use technology when cooking. In addition to simple machines, which are early examples of technology, children may use electric mixers, blenders, toaster ovens, electric skillets, freezers, and so forth.

STEM LEARNING IN THE BLOCK AREA

The block area is rich in STEM learning potential. First, children's experiences designing and creating block structures parallels the adult professions of architecture and construction engineering. In addition, the block area gives children innumerable opportunities to construct physical knowledge relationships. Children learn that broad, flat bases are stabler than tall, thin ones. They discover that four cylinders positioned in a rectangular formation provide a strong support for a flat roof or floor board. Many children develop the construction pattern of two parallel rectangular boards alternating with two more parallel boards placed on top of and perpendicular to the first two boards. This formation can be used to build tall, stable towers (see photo below).

Parallel rectangular structure

Children also experiment with **inclines**, one of the **simple machines**, and learn that vehicles move faster down slopes that are steeper. All of these discoveries are related to physics.

Geometry and measurement are also firmly embedded in the block area. Children can explore the properties and uses of geometric solids, such as cylinders and rectangular solids. They can also organize blocks by their shapes. As teachers engage with children in the block area, they can direct attention to these relationships and model important mathematical vocabulary. For example, the teacher might comment, "Your cylinder blocks must be very strong. They are supporting the rest of your building." Teachers can also model positional and directional terms, another important component of geometry. An example would be, "You have cylinder blocks on the bottom of your structure, long rectangular blocks in the middle, and smaller rectangular blocks at the top."

Children's first use of measurement is through direct comparison of objects. Unit blocks are constructed to show proportional lengths, so the block area is an excellent place to focus on measurement concepts. A double unit block (longest rectangular block) is twice as long as a unit block (middle-size rectangular block); a half-unit block (shortest rectangular block) is half as long as a unit block. Teachers can model these relationships. For example, if a child needs more unit blocks and none are available, the teacher can demonstrate that two half-unit blocks cover the same distance.

STEM LEARNING AT THE SENSORY TABLE

The sensory table provides a laboratory environment for studying earth science. Children spend hours exploring the properties of water and seem fascinated with the way water takes the shape of its container. As children pour water into a bottle, the water first covers the bottom of the container and then begins to move upward until it fills the entire bottle. At this point, the water overflows the bottle and flows down the sides, a process that young children watch endlessly. When clear tubes are added to the water table, children find that the water collects in the lower, curved part of the tubing. As they raise and lower the ends of the tube, children notice that the water repositions itself so that it always climbs evenly up both sides of the tube. Children discover that moving water has power. It can turn the gears on water wheels. When children squirt water from basters, the spray can move objects floating on the water. The properties and movement of water are important concepts in geology.

Dry materials behave differently from water. When children pour sand through a funnel, the sand creates a pile, something that water does not do. Children are often surprised when sand will no longer move through their funnel because a tower of sand is blocking the hole. When children pour sand into clear tubes, the sand does not move evenly up the sides the way water does; instead, it tends to clump at the bottom. Children are also fascinated with filtering dry materials. When pea gravel is mixed with sand, children can sift the sand through the holes in a colander, leaving the pebbles behind. This filtering of materials in the natural world is an important process in geology.

Mathematics also plays a role in carefully planned sensory table experiences. When seashells are added to the sensory table, children can group them by various attributes, including size, color, design, texture, shape, and type of shell. Sorting and classifying objects in this way is an important component of the algebra standard. To group the materials in a particular way, children must formulate and follow a general rule that determines the placement of each object. Deciding on groupings and determining the relationships within and among groups help children develop logical reasoning. There are many materials that children can sort and classify in the sensory table. The following are some examples:

- small stones that vary in color, size, and texture

- toy fish or boats of various types, colors, and sizes

- an assortment of plastic worms and insects

- rubber ducks that vary in details such as clothing, color, and size

Through repeated experiences with sorting and classifying, children learn that objects can be sorted in many different ways depending on the criteria used to determine the groups.

The sensory table also provides opportunities for children to model mathematical situations and engage in problem solving. Are there enough people to put one in each boat? How many people are needed to put two people in each boat? If five people get into a boat, will it still float? How can the boats be distributed so that everyone has the same amount? Effective teachers regularly pose questions such as these to stimulate children's mathematical thinking.

STEM LEARNING IN ART ACTIVITIES

Art connects to all three content standards in science: life science, earth science, and physics. To make a connection to life science, teachers may introduce plant materials for children to incorporate into their creations. For example, pressed leaves, dried grasses, and assorted seeds and nuts can be used for autumn collages. Pine needles, holly leaves, and pinecones can be added to winter activities. Feathers, flower petals, and colored eggshells can create spring creations. Using plant life for art experiences not only adds to children's creativity but also provides opportunities for teachers to talk about the materials the children are using and for children to examine the items more carefully.

Many of the art materials children regularly use are related to earth science. Children may not realize this unless teachers help them make the connection. The most obvious example is clay, which is composed of naturally occurring fine-grained *minerals*. Children discover that moist clay is pliable and can be manipulated into many different shapes, but once the clay has dried, it hardens and preserves its shape. Sand, salt, and chalk are other naturally occurring materials that are frequently used in art.

The tools that children use in art activities fall within the realm of physics. Scissors are a class-one double *lever*, in which the connecting point of the scissors acts as the *fulcrum*. As the object to be cut is moved closer to the fulcrum, the mechanical advantage increases so that even thick materials, such as cardboard, can be cut. The scissors' blades function as *wedges*, another *simple machine*. When children work with design scissors, in which the blades cut a variety of patterns, they discover the relationship between the shape of the scissors' blades and the shape of the line that is cut. Pencils, crayons, and markers are other examples of levers used in the art area. The closer the child's fingers are to the tip of the drawing tool, the easier it is to make a dark mark.

Yet another connection to physics comes from the mixing of colored pigments, including paints, crayons, and colored water. Historically, red, blue, and yellow have been regarded as the three primary colors, which when combined can produce the secondary colors of orange, green, and purple. Modern color theory, which is based on extensive scientific research, recognizes *magenta*, *cyan*, and yellow as the three primary colors. Regardless, through combining colored pigments in the art area, children learn that new colors can be created.

Mathematics is also an important component of art experiences, primarily through children's explorations of patterning, *symmetry*, and shapes. As children experiment with various colors of markers or beads, they often begin to alternate colors, thereby creating a pattern. These patterns should be acknowledged and described by teachers so that children can relate what they have created to the concept of a pattern. The teacher might say, "I see a pattern on your paper. The colors red, green, and blue keep repeating in the stripes you made. See? Red, green, blue, red, green, blue." Both parents and teachers are familiar with the balloon-head images that children produce when they begin to draw people—a large circle, a face, and four lines extending from the circle to represent arms and legs. One of the interesting aspects of these early drawings is that they show children's recognition of symmetry, a repetition of form on either side of a midline. Finally, when children transition into representational drawing, they often exhibit a design phase in which they draw geometric forms (see drawing below) and connect them. Eventually, these shapes evolve into recognizable figures of people (see drawing on page 64), buildings, plants, and animals.

Geometric forms as a bridge to representational art

A child's artwork with figures of people

STEM LEARNING IN MUSIC ACTIVITIES

Sound production, and therefore music, is closely related to physics. Through experiences with musical instruments, children learn that the material a sound-producing object is made from affects its sound in three ways: (1) *pitch*, (2) *dynamics*, and (3) *timbre* (pronounced *TAM-bur*). *Pitch* refers to how high or low a tone sounds (technically, the number of vibrations per second) and is directly related to the size of the object. Larger instruments produce lower pitches than smaller instruments. Children discover this relationship when they have the opportunity to create sounds with sets of objects that are identical except for size: triangles, wood blocks, chimes, cans, xylophone bars, and so forth.

Dynamics is how loudly or softly an instrument can be played. A plastic bottle maraca filled with sand sounds much softer than the same type of bottle filled with dried corn or pebbles, no matter how hard one shakes it. Similarly, a drum played with a wooden mallet sounds much louder than a drum played with a sponge-tipped mallet.

Timbre, or sound quality, is affected as well. For example, the previously described maraca filled with sand produces a swishing sound, while the maraca filled with dried corn creates a sharp, rattling sound. Metal, wooden, and plastic rattles each have a distinctive sound. The study of sound production is called *acoustics*, a special branch of physics.

Because pitch is directly related to size, measurement is also a component of activities designed to help children construct pitch relationships. Children's earliest form of measurement is through direct comparison of objects when the objects are all visible (Gelman and Ebeling 1989). Activities that include several sizes of the same instrument allow children to make these direct comparisons and to use early measurement vocabulary, such as *small, large, short,* and *long*. More-experienced children can use interlocking manipulative pieces, such as cubes or links, to quantify the length of the instruments.

GEOMETRIC GRILLED CHEESE

MATHEMATICS: GEOMETRY; PHYSICS

Materials

○ bread slices

○ cheese slices

○ illustrations of geometric shapes and child-safe knives, or cookie cutters in geometric shapes

○ toaster oven

Activity Description

This activity has a strong mathematics component. Children cut geometric shapes out of square cheese slices, arrange their shapes on bread, and toast them in a toaster oven. If children use plastic knives to cut the squares of cheese into other shapes, teachers may wish to have illustrations of geometric shapes available for children to use as models. As an alternative, children can use cookie cutters, which are readily available in standard geometric shapes. The toaster oven, which has a viewing window, can be positioned so that children cannot touch the hot surface but can still observe how the cheese and bread react to heat.

 ## Science Content

Heating results in **physical changes** to both the bread and the cheese. Although the bread still remains in solid form, it loses flexibility and becomes stiff to the touch. If white bread is used, the color changes to a shade of brown. The cheese may change briefly to semiliquid form and spread out over the bread. Teachers can discuss all of these changes with children.

 ## Mathematics Content

The mathematics content in this activity is geometry. The experience gives children a new way to interact with shapes. Some children may position their cheese shapes so that they are close together; they may find that as the cheese melts, their shapes combine to produce a new shape. For example, two triangles may combine to form a rhombus. This provides a good topic of conversation, since the composition and decomposition of geometric forms is an important concept in geometry.

 ## Connections to Technology

The toaster oven, which is critical in this cooking experience, is an example of how technology is used to produce heat.

Comments and Questions to Support Inquiry

• Do you think the bread will change when we heat it in the toaster oven? What about the cheese?

• Describe how your toast is different from the bread. How is it similar?

• Look at what happened to your hexagon-shaped cheese. It looks almost like a circle now.

CORNMEAL MUFFINS

LIFE SCIENCE, PHYSICS

Materials

- ○ several dried ears of corn
- ○ several pairs of tweezers
- ○ mortar and pestle (or small wooden bowl and 1½-inch cylindrical block)
- ○ 2 rectangular unit blocks
- ○ grain mill (available from cooking stores)
- ○ cornmeal mix, along with additional ingredients as indicated on the box

Activity Description

This activity allows children to follow the process of creating and cooking with cornmeal. On the first day of the activity, children can use tweezers to pluck kernels from dried ears of corn. In the process, they can observe how the corn kernels grow on the cob. If a stalk of corn is available, children can examine the entire plant. After one or two days of plucking corn, it is time to grind the corn kernels. Children can use and compare three methods:

1. Pounding the corn with a mortar and pestle
2. Crushing the corn between two blocks
3. Using a table-size grain mill

On the final day of the project, children can use purchased cornmeal to bake muffins.

Each stage in the process of creating and using cornmeal provides new opportunities for children to engage in scientific inquiry. As children remove kernels from the corn cobs, they can discuss the function of the tweezers and how they aid in the process of removing the kernels. During the corn-grinding phase, children can observe an irreversible physical change

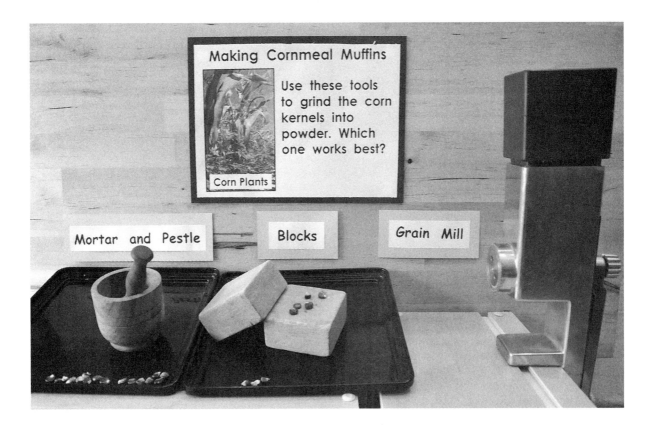

as the kernels are turned into a powder. Finally, during the cooking process, children can observe changes in materials as they mix ingredients and then bake the muffins.

Recipes for cornmeal muffins are included in most American cookbooks. Making cornbread or cornmeal muffins from a recipe allows children to see all of the ingredients that are needed. In contrast, prepackaged mixes already have the dry ingredients mixed, so children can't see the cornmeal separated from the flour, sugar, baking powder, and salt.

 ## Science Content

Throughout the process of making cornmeal, children use five types of *simple machines*. The tweezers used to pluck the corn kernels are a class-three *lever* because the effort (squeezing) is between the *fulcrum* (where the bars are joined) and the *load* (corn kernel). The pestle or the blocks used for pounding the corn are also class-three levers; in this case, the effort is force applied to the handle of the pestle or the block, the fulcrum is the elbow or wrist, and the load is the head of the pestle or the bottom of the block. The corn grinder employs several types of simple machines. The crank is a *wheel and axle*; a *screw* moves the corn through the body of the grinder; and *wedges*, or blades, cut up the corn.

 ## Mathematics Content

The mathematics content in this activity relates to measurement and quantification. During the baking process, children use standard measurement units such as cups and teaspoons. They also need to quantify the number of measurement units that are needed, such as 2 cups. Teachers can sequence the steps of the baking process as first, second, third, and so forth. This introduces children to the vocabulary and concept of *ordinal numbers* within a meaningful context.

 ## Connections to Technology and Engineering

The use of simple machines connects this activity to both technology and engineering. Use of the machines is itself an application of early technology. Application of the scientific principles involved in simple machines remains an important component of engineering, and engineers must be aware of the ways in which *force*, *load*, and outcome are related.

Comments and Questions to Support Inquiry

- What happened to the cornmeal after you put it through the grain mill? What made the corn turn to powder? Do you think there is a way to turn the powder back into kernels?

- Did the tweezers help you pull the corn kernels off the cob? How do the tweezers work?

- What do you think will happen to the cornmeal and flour when we add the milk?

- Take a close look at how high the muffin mix is in the muffin cups. After the muffins bake, we'll see if the mix is the same height as it is now.

LIMEADE AND LEMONADE

LIFE SCIENCE, PHYSICS

Materials

○ lemons, enough for each child to have half a lemon

○ limes, enough for each child to have half a lime

○ child-safe knives

○ 1 or more hand juicers (as pictured)

○ small cups, 2 per child

○ cold water

○ sugar

○ bowls, measuring cups and spoons, spoons for stirring

○ color photos of lemons and limes growing on trees (from Internet sources or books)

○ red and blue ice cubes (optional)

○ recipe chart

Activity Description

Many children have never had the opportunity to handle limes and lemons, although they may have seen them in the grocery store. This activity allows children to compare the outside and inside of limes and lemons, and to discuss the similarities and differences between the two fruits.

The most obvious difference is color. In addition, limes are usually smaller than lemons and have a taste that is even sourer than lemons. Before the limes and lemons are cut in half, children can predict whether they will be the same color on the inside as they are on the outside. Following are components of the fruits that children can observe:

• the number of sections inside, which children can count

• the presence and number of seeds

• the protective rinds that surround the interior fruit

• the juice

• the smell

• the taste

After children have had plenty of time to examine the lemons and limes, they can make individual servings of limeade and lemonade. If children work in pairs, one child can make the limeade and the other child can make the lemonade. The drinks can be poured into small cups so that each child can sample the two beverages. If desired, children can add an ice cube that has been colored with red or blue food coloring before freezing and observe the mixing of colors.

To make the limeade or lemonade, children first need to squeeze the juice from the fruits. Using a hand juicer gives children experience with a **simple machine** and allows them to see how the seeds are filtered away from the juice.

The following is a simple recipe for limeade:

- juice from half a lime
- ½ cup cold water
- 1 tablespoon sugar

 Science Content

Several science concepts are embedded in this activity. Exploration of the limes and lemons connects it to life science. Teachers should include photographs or books that show limes and lemons growing on trees as part of the activity.

Use of a hand juicer connects this experience to physics. The hand juicer consists of a series of ridges, or wedges, for squeezing the juice from citrus fruits, such as lemons, limes, and oranges. A *wedge* is one of the six classical simple machines. It consists of two small *inclines* that are joined together to create a narrow ridge. The wedges apply pressure to the fruit pulp and force the juice out of it.

Children may also notice that the sugar disappears, or dissolves, into the juice and water mixture. This dissolution of the sugar occurs when the crystal structure of its molecules breaks down, allowing the sugar to form a solution with the water-juice solvent.

 Mathematics Content

Geometry is a component of this activity. Both the limes and the lemons are elliptical solids. When the fruits are cut in half, the pulp is divided into sections that are rotationally symmetrical. This means that when the fruit is rotated a certain number of degrees around its central point, it looks the same as before it was turned. The *symmetry* is not perfect, as there are usually some slight variations in the sizes of the sections, but it is still an interesting pattern for children to observe.

Children may be very interested in counting the sections of the limes and lemons to see if each fruit has the same number of segments. Although ten is a typical number of sections in both limes and lemons, some may have more or fewer segments. Children may also want to count and compare the seeds in each lemon and lime. The results can be recorded on a chart, if desired, for later discussion. Quantifying and comparing are important parts of the investigative process, and they connect this activity to the number and operations content standard. Use of the recipe chart allows teachers to model *ordinal numbers* (first, second, and so forth) as they guide children through the sequence of steps.

Yet another mathematical component of this activity is measuring. During the process of using the ½-cup measure, children can experiment with pouring two ½ cups of water into a 1-cup measure. They can also pour 3 teaspoons into a tablespoon. If the lemonade is too sweet, the teacher can suggest using 2 teaspoons of sugar instead of 1 tablespoon.

 Connections to Technology

Technology is incorporated into this activity through use of the hand juicer.

Comments and Questions to Support Inquiry

- What do you notice that is similar about the inside of the lime and the lemon?
- Does the lemon have as many segments as the lime? Let's write down how many sections your lemon and lime have so that we can compare all of the lemons and limes.
- What happens when you push down harder on the juicer as you twist the lemon?

BAKING BREAD

LIFE SCIENCE, PHYSICS

Materials

- ○ bread recipe and ingredients
- ○ cooking utensils, including measuring cups and spoons, a large bowl, and loaf pans
- ○ oven

Activity Description

Baking bread allows children to observe many changes in materials as they combine ingredients and expose the dough to heat. Perhaps the most fascinating part of the experience for children is observing the reaction of the yeast, which puffs up the bread dough into a balloon-like dome. When children punch this dome, it quickly contracts.

There are many recipes for bread. Some types of bread need to rise two or even three times before they are baked, which takes several hours. While these recipes might work well in a full-day setting, teachers who have half-day classes may prefer a recipe that requires the dough to rise only once. One of the most interesting parts of the experience of baking bread is kneading the dough, which mixes the ingredients and stimulates the growth of the yeast. Kneading dough is a very tactile experience. Because

After rising

Before rising

After baking

the dough tends to be sticky, it is a messy but enjoyable experience. As the dough becomes too sticky to knead, small amounts of flour can be added to make it more workable. For teachers who want to avoid having to clean sticky fingers, the dough can be placed in a sturdy, gallon-size zip-top baggie before it is kneaded.

 ## Science Content

Baker's yeast is a critical component in bread because it makes the finished product less dense. Yeasts are microorganisms that are classified as *fungi*. When yeast is mixed with warm water and sugar, the yeast converts the sugar into carbon dioxide, which is why the mixture bubbles and expands. As the other ingredients are added to the mixture, this reaction continues, making the bread dough rise. Punching down the dough releases the carbon dioxide gas. The yeast dies when the dough is baked, leaving behind the tiny holes that make bread light and fluffy.

 ## Mathematics Content

Much of the math content in this activity comes from measuring the ingredients that go into the bread dough. Children can also visually compare the size of the bread dough before and after it rises.

 ## Connections to Technology

The main use of technology in this activity is the oven that is used to bake the bread.

Comments and Questions to Support Inquiry

- What does the yeast and water mixture look like? The yeast is producing carbon dioxide, which is what is making the bubbles.

- Watch what happens to the dome of bread dough when Annie punches it. Did you hear the air rushing out?

- Let's wait awhile and see if the bread dough makes a big balloon shape again. Do you think the yeast is still working?

- Look closely at your slice of bread. Can you see the air holes left behind by the yeast?

VEGETARIAN SOUP

LIFE SCIENCE, PHYSICS

Materials

- ○ variety of fresh vegetables
- ○ child-safe knives
- ○ small trays or cutting boards
- ○ vegetable juice
- ○ water
- ○ slow-cook pot, electric skillet, or hot plate

Activity Description

Cooking vegetable soup allows children to closely observe a variety of vegetables before and after they are cooked. Many children customarily eat vegetables that have already been processed. This activity allows them to see what green beans, peas, corn, cabbage, tomatoes, potatoes, and any other vegetables chosen for the soup look like when they come directly from the plant. Whatever vegetables are fresh and in season can be used. Small pasta shells can also be added to create a thicker soup.

Children can learn more from this activity if the vegetables are unprocessed. For example, corn can be shucked and then cut from the cob with a plastic knife, peas can be removed from their pods, and cabbage leaves can be peeled from the head. Onions are particularly interesting to examine because of their layered structure.

Teachers do not need a recipe to make vegetable soup. The children can help create their own. Water can be added to vegetable juice, such as V8 or tomato, to form the base of the soup. Children can then add vegetables to the mixture in the quantities desired. As they peel, trim, tear, and chop raw vegetables, children become more familiar with the structure of the food.

The soup can be heated slowly in the classroom, out of the reach of children, in a slow cooker or electric skillet. This activity can be repeated at various times during the year as different vegetables come into season and become available. If possible, teachers should have pictures of the vegetables growing on plants so that children can make this association. These can be downloaded from the Internet or found in garden books. If children grow vegetables in their own container garden (Activity 4.10), they can add their own vegetables to the soup.

Informational books about farms help children make connections between the food they see in stores and how it is grown. Six books by Nancy Dickmann, which comprise the World of Farming series, provide vivid photographs and simple text for young children and beginning readers: *Farm Animals, Farm Machines, Food from Farms, Jobs on a Farm, Plants on a Farm,* and *Seasons on a Farm.*

Science Content

A main goal of this activity is for children to compare the texture of vegetables before and after they are cooked. Teachers will want to direct children's attention toward the effect of heat on the vegetables. Cooking vegetable soup also draws children's attention to the plant parts that are used in the foods we eat. Some of the vegetables we eat, such as potatoes, carrots, and onions, are roots. In plants such as cabbage, the leaves are the parts that go into the soup; in contrast, we eat the flowers of cauliflower and broccoli. Adding this information to the discussion as children make the soup extends their vocabulary and science knowledge.

Mathematics Content

As part of the soup-making process, children will need to cut whole vegetables into smaller parts. Teachers can emphasize the fractional components involved. For example, teachers may need to cut whole potatoes into halves and then fourths before children can chop them into smaller pieces. Teachers should identify these fractional parts as they cut them. With other vegetables, such as cauliflower, children may be able to cut a whole piece into two parts. Teachers might say, "If you cut this flower in the middle, you'll have two halves that are the same size."

Connections to Technology and Engineering

The plastic knives used in this activity are examples of **wedges**, a **simple machine**. Heating the soup involves the use of modern technology. Agricultural engineers research how to grow higher-quality plants more productively. Nancy Dickmann's book *Farm Machines* helps children understand the extensive technology used on modern farms.

Comments and Questions to Support Inquiry

- Can you help cut up this cauliflower? What does it look like to you? Cauliflower is a flower we can eat.

- Crack open this pod, and see what's inside. How many peas were in your pod?

- The outside leaves of the cabbage are big. What do the leaves close to the center of the cabbage look like?

- How do the vegetables feel now that they've been cooked? Are they still hard and stiff?

BUILDING WITH INCLINES

PHYSICS

Materials

○ classroom blocks, organized in a separate area

○ wooden boards, ¼ inch thick and 4 inches wide, cut to lengths of 8, 12, 16, and 24 inches (or lengths desired by the teacher)

○ mesh shelf liner, coarse sandpaper, felt, and raised stickers

Activity Description

In this activity, all sorts of predesigned boards for *inclines* are introduced into the block area. The surfaces of the blocks vary so that children can notice the effects when they roll vehicles or slide objects down them. Because the boards also vary in length, children will notice that size differences can affect the slope, or steepness of the incline, depending on where they position the boards. For example, a 24-inch board creates a rather gentle slope when propped against a block that is 6 inches high, whereas an 8-inch board creates a much steeper slope when propped against the same 6-inch block. Children can experiment extensively with these incline boards as part of their construction activities.

The boards used in the photograph are cut from wood that is ¼ inch thick and 4 inches wide. The narrow thickness makes the boards easy to manipulate for experimental and design purposes; however, teachers can also alter regular wooden blocks for this activity. The following surfaces are taped or otherwise adhered to the wood: mesh shelf liner, course sandpaper, felt, and raised stickers to create speed bumps. Each of these surfaces is applied to incline boards of four different lengths: 8, 12, 18, and 24 inches. A set of unaltered, smooth wooden boards is also included. Teachers can take digital photographs of various constructions for further discussion or to include in a class book about inclines.

🔍 Science Content

When children prop boards against their block structures, they create a triangular formation in which the block structure is the height of the triangle, the floor is the base, and the incline board is the hypotenuse, or longest side of the triangle. As the angle between the incline board and the block structure increases, the steepness of the incline decreases, and objects move more slowly. Children will find that they can increase the steepness of an incline in two ways: (1) they can keep the same incline board but connect it to a higher part of the block structure, or (2) they can select a shorter incline board and prop it to the same point on their structure. Either of these changes strongly affects the movement of objects along the incline.

The other variable in this activity is the surface of the inclines. Both the softer surfaces and the rougher surfaces slow the movement of the vehicles.

 Mathematics Content

Mathematics and science are inextricably linked in this activity since the geometry of the incline formations explains, in large part, their effect on moving objects. As children build structures with inclines, teachers can trace the triangle that is formed by the blocks, the incline, and the floor. Teachers can also use hand gestures to show how the angle of the incline has increased or decreased. These logical-mathematical concepts take a long time to develop. Pointing out the geometric forms created by the structures draws children's attention to these important relationships within a context that is interesting to them.

  Connections to Technology and Engineering

Because the **inclined plane** is one of the six classical **simple machines**, it is an example of early technology. Understanding inclines is critical to civil and construction engineering. Children's books that show how roads and structures are built may draw attention to this connection. Some examples are *What Is a Plane?* by Lloyd G. Douglas, *Building a Road* by Henry Pluckrose, and *A Year at a Construction Site* by Nicholas Harris.

Comments and Questions to Support Inquiry

- I see you made your incline steeper by connecting the board to a higher point on your building.

- I can make a steep ramp from this lower point. I'll just use a shorter board.

- What happens to the speed of your car when it hits those speed bumps?

- Which surface makes the cars go the slowest?

- Look at the angle formed by your incline. You made your incline steeper by creating this smaller angle. See? (*Demonstrate with gestures.*)

BUILDING WITH PULLEYS

PHYSICS

Materials

- ○ classroom blocks
- ○ several sizes of pulleys
- ○ pipe cleaners or Velcro strips
- ○ cord or string that fits the pulleys
- ○ small baskets or buckets that have a handle

Activity Description

Although children encounter **pulleys** in their daily lives, such as when they ride an elevator or escalator, they usually cannot actually see the pulleys. Therefore, they have no knowledge of what pulleys are and how they work. In this activity, pulleys are introduced into the block area for children to explore as part of their construction activities. Self-adhering Velcro strips or long pipe cleaners are threaded through the eye of each pulley so that children can attach the pulleys to their block structures. Precut lengths of string, as well as a ball of string that children can cut themselves, are also available to thread through the wheels on the pulleys. Accessory materials include small buckets, baskets, or wooden boxes with handles for attaching to the pulleys.

If children have already had experiences with pulleys (perhaps through activities such as Activity 4.2, 4.6, or 4.7), they may already have ideas about how to use the pulleys without much help from the teacher. In other cases, the teacher may need to model some ways in which children can create vertical and horizontal pulley systems. Digital photographs of the children's designs can be used to create

a class pulley book in which children comment about their designs. This encourages children to rethink what they created and how it worked, an important part of the communication process.

 ## Science Content

A pulley is one of the six classical **simple machines**. It consists of a grooved wheel that is free to move around its axle, and a rope or cord that is threaded through the groove and attached to the object that one wishes to move. The purpose of a simple pulley is to change the direction of a **force** applied to an object. In a vertical pulley, when the cord is pulled downward, the object moves upward. In a horizontal pulley, a person pulling the rope toward himself can move the object away from himself.

The book *The New Way Things Work* by David Macaulay illustrates and explains pulleys. Although not written for young children, this book is a useful resource to help teachers understand mechanical inventions. In addition, the illustrations, particularly those of the pulley systems in an escalator and elevator, can help children understand how they work. *What Is a Pulley?* by Lloyd G. Douglas is written for young children and beginning readers. It includes vivid photographs of pulleys used in real-world contexts, such as on cranes and flagpoles.

 ## Mathematics Content

Understanding directional terms is an important component of geometry. Pulleys cause a change in direction, so use of directional terms should be an important goal in the conversations that accompany this activity. For example, teachers can talk about the relationship between pulling down to get an object to move up. *Up, down, toward, away from, nearer, farther, left,* and *right* are directional terms that should be modeled by teachers.

  ## Connections to Technology and Engineering

The pulley is itself an example of early technology. Understanding how pulleys work will help children later as they explore the use of pulleys in more complex technological innovations. Pulleys are used in mechanical and construction engineering, as well as in the machines employed in many types of manufacturing.

Comments and Questions to Support Inquiry

- Tell me how the elevator in your block building works. Which way do I have to pull the cord to make my person go up?

- This is a pulley. Let's attach it to your building and see how it works. We'll put the end of this string through the wheel on the pulley, and the bead will keep it from coming unthreaded. We'll tie the other end to this bucket. Now pull down on the bead and see what happens.

- I see you used the pulleys to connect your buildings. What a good idea. Now you can move things between the buildings.

NATURAL BUILDING MATERIALS

LIFE SCIENCE, PHYSICS

Materials

- ○ classroom blocks
- ○ wooden cylinders cut from branches
- ○ grapevine
- ○ assorted natural materials, such as bamboo, dried grasses, or bark

Activity Description

Adding natural materials to the block area enhances children's creativity and encourages experimentation. For this activity, wooden cylinders cut from branches, grapevines, bamboo, and other assorted natural materials are introduced into the block area. They provide new materials for children to explore, stimulate their imaginations, and lead to more complex and varied play themes.

Wooden cylinders that vary in length, width, and height are cut from tree branches, logs, and sticks for this activity. Shorter and wider sections can be used to build platforms or bases, while pieces that are longer and narrower create support columns. Wood that has started to decompose should be avoided because it will likely contain microorganisms that may also decompose the classroom carpet. A preservative, such

as polyurethane, can be applied to the wood pieces if desired.

Wild grapevine is common in many parts of the country. While it is an annoyance to gardeners, it is prized by many craftspeople for making arches and wreaths. Grapevine provides children with a somewhat pliable material to add to their creations. They may use it to connect buildings or make "rope" ladders. Wild grapevine is abundant in many rural and urban areas. It can also be purchased at craft or gardening stores. Grapevine can be kept pliable by soaking it in water.

Sales at craft stores are a good place to acquire bamboo and other natural materials to add to the block area. Long pieces of bamboo can be cut into smaller lengths.

Science Content

Placing natural materials in the block area helps children draw the connection between natural materials and the building trades. The wood sections allow children to see what trees look like on the inside and to better understand the relationship between the wood they see in their home and school environments and its original source. Children may wonder why the wood pieces are round (actually cylindrical) but the wood they see in floorboards is rectangular. Having a section of wood available that is cut vertically rather than horizontally can help children understand this relationship. As children examine the rings on the cut branches, teachers should point out that trees grow outward and not just upward.

Books such as *Houses and Homes* by Ann Morris can help children understand how natural materials are used to build homes around the world. The vines, bamboo, and other natural items that teachers add to the block area may be materials that children may have had little opportunity to handle. These experiences help children begin to realize how much of our lives are dependent on materials from the life sciences.

Mathematics Content

The wood samples used in this activity introduce children to cylinders in many different sizes and forms. Teachers can help children compare the cylinders and determine what characteristics they all have in common. This helps children move from the visual level of geometric understanding, in which they begin to recognize and name shapes, to the descriptive or analytic level, in which they begin to describe the properties of shapes (Van Hiele 1999). Children may notice the **concentric** circles in the wooden cylinders. With teacher support, they can count the rings to determine the age of the tree or branch that the sample came from.

Connections to Engineering

Block building is closely related to architecture and engineering. To successfully design and construct buildings, architects and engineers must understand the properties of materials and their effect on balance and stability.

Comments and Questions to Support Inquiry

- What can you do with these tall cylindrical branches?

- How many cylinders did it take to support your platform? What happens if you add a third cylinder?

- There are some long pieces of grapevine here. What can we do with them?

- The long grass looks like one of the pictures from the book. Where do you plan to use it in your building?

SOFT AND HARD BUILDING SURFACES

PHYSICS

Materials

○ classroom blocks

○ fabric, such as linen kitchen towels or bandannas

○ foam crafting material

○ cardboard

Activity Description

The strength and flexibility of building materials affect how they can be used for construction. For this activity, soft and semirigid materials, such as fabric, foam crafting material, and cardboard, are added to the block area. As with the use of natural materials in Block Activity 3.8, this introduction of new and varied materials into the block area stimulates children's creativity and enables them to experiment with concepts related to engineering.

Linen kitchen towels are the fabric used in this activity. The towels are relatively small and lightweight, which allows children to manipulate them easily. If children use the towels to make tents, they will quickly realize that tents also need a frame. Children are also likely to discover some construction problems that need to be solved when the towels are used to make roofs, such as their tendency to sag in the middle.

The foam crafting material is an interesting building medium for children. While it has enough rigidity to hold its shape when placed across blocks to make a roof, it can also be bent to form curved shapes, such as the dome for a building or a cylindrical silo. The cardboard has more rigidity than the foam. It can be propped against a block structure at an angle to form a lean-to, is sturdy enough to make a flat roof, and can be folded to create an angle, such as in a gable roof.

 ### Science Content

The rigidity, or stiffness of a material, refers to its ability to resist being deformed when *force* is applied to it.

 ### Mathematics Content

The rigidity of materials is related to the geometric forms it can take. Therefore, children are likely to notice that they can bend some of the more flexible materials into other shapes. Although the foam can be bent into a more circular form, it needs a counterforce, such as blocks pressing against its sides, to maintain this shape. While thin pieces of cardboard can be bent, thicker pieces tend to crease. When the cardboard and foam are creased to form an angle, the cardboard is better able to maintain this shape than the foam. While the fabric can be easily shaped into other forms, it cannot maintain its new shape without a framework for support.

 ### Connections to Engineering

Understanding the rigidity of materials is important in engineering. Children can begin to see this connection through their own experiments. For example, if they want to put a curved roof on a building, they need to use a material that has sufficient flexibility.

Comments and Questions to Support Inquiry

- Which material bends? Can you use it to put a curved roof on your barn?

- What can you do to keep the fabric from sagging in the middle?

- Jason draped the fabric over a tall block to make a tent. What does he need to do to make the tent longer?

- I want to build a gable roof like the one in this picture. Which material do you think I should use?

BUILDING WITH MIRRORS

PHYSICS

Materials

○ children's building blocks

○ blocks with mirrors mounted into frames, or small, unbreakable mirrors, such as those made for school lockers

Activity Description

Building blocks with mirrors are now commercially available from companies that sell early childhood materials. The blocks have hardwood frames that encase an unbreakable acrylic mirror. Some mirror blocks come in sets with different geometric shapes. The blocks give children the opportunity to experiment with light reflection by positioning the mirrors in different locations on their block structures. Children discover that the mirrors allow them to see things that they otherwise could not see because the objects reflected by the mirror are positioned behind or to the side of the child's position.

 ## Science Content

Light *reflection* refers to a change in direction of a light wave when it encounters a reflective surface such as a mirror. The angle at which a light wave strikes this surface is called the *angle of incidence*, and it is equal to the *angle of reflection*. The light reflection diagram helps explain these angles.

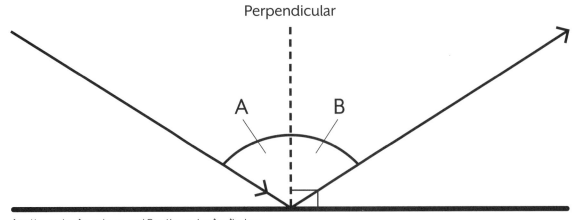

Perpendicular

A   B

A is the angle of incidence, and B is the angle of reflection.

Mathematics Content

In addition to experimenting with angles of reflection (or how they can position the mirrors to see various objects), children may also notice a special type of pattern called *reflective symmetry*. The reflected image of an object is identical to the object, but the components of the object appear in reverse order. Therefore, if a child places a triangular block in front of and to the left of a cube, in the mirror the triangle will appear behind and to the right of the cube. These observations are important to point out and discuss with children. Positioning terms are a component of the geometry standard.

 Connections to Technology and Engineering

Optics is the area of physics in which the properties of light are studied. The field of optical engineering focuses on applications from the study of optics, such as the design of telescopes, lenses, and microscopes. All of these applications involve technology.

Comments and Questions to Support Inquiry

- What can you see through the mirror block at the top of your building?

- If you turn your mirror block, can you see your friend's building?

- Where do you have to put your block in order to see the book area?

- I can see the door to the classroom reflected in the mirror block on your building even though I'm not facing the door. Now I can tell without turning around if anyone comes in.

SAILBOATS

EARTH SCIENCE, PHYSICS

Materials

○ small toy sailboats

○ several basters, bulb syringes, or straws

○ sensory table or tub of water

Activity Description

This activity allows children to experiment with wind power. Children use basters or straws to create wind and move small toy sailboats across the water table. In the process, they learn that both the *force* and the direction of the moving air affect the movement of the boats.

Small toy sailboats are available for little cost. Those used in the photograph were ordered online for less than one dollar per boat. A bulb syringe, used for cleaning mucus from an infant's nose, or a kitchen baster can be used to create puffs of air. Children may experiment with these tools and discover that they can also shoot water from them. Since moving water also creates a notable force, teachers can direct the children to use the water to move the boats. A variation of this activity is for children to blow air through straws to move the boats.

The sails on the toy boats must be stiff enough to cause resistance to the moving air. Cloth sails on inexpensive boats may be too floppy, but they can be replaced with sails that are cut from craft foam and sewn into place, as shown in the photograph. These sails have adequate rigidity.

 ## Science Content

Although moving air creates a force that can move objects, sailboats are propelled by the wind pushing directly against the sail only when the ship is moving downwind, or in the same direction that the wind is blowing. It is this force that children will be exploring in this activity. It is important for teachers to know,

however, that this is not the only force that affects the movement of sailboats.

When the ship is not moving directly with the wind, the sails are positioned to function like airplane wings. When the leading edge of the sail points into the wind, an area of low pressure is created on the side of the sail facing the wind, and an area of higher pressure is created on the side of the sail facing away from the wind. The area of higher pressure moves the sail toward the area of lower pressure, puffing the sail into the wind and pulling the boat along with it. This is one of the reasons that sailboats can move in directions other than just downwind.

Although young children cannot understand the concept of high and low pressure, teachers should not lead them to believe that sailboats move only because the wind pushes the sail. Teachers can simply say that sailboats can move toward the wind because the sails can also function like the wings on an airplane. The book *The Craft of Sail* by Jan Adkins can help teachers understand the physics involved in sailing. Although written for older children, the illustrations, combined with the teacher's descriptions, can help interested children begin to understand the scientific principles.

 ## Mathematics Content

The main mathematical connection in this activity is the use of directional terms, which is part of the geometry content standard. Vocabulary such as *near*, *far*, *toward*, and *away from* should be modeled by teachers to describe the movements of the boats. Teachers may also want to introduce the nautical terms *port* (toward the left side of the boat), *starboard* (toward the right side of the boat), *fore* (toward the front of the boat), and *aft* (toward the rear of the boat).

 ## Connections to Engineering

Shipbuilding is also referred to as naval engineering. People who build ships are called shipwrights. Building boats is one of the oldest forms of engineering.

Comments and Questions to Support Inquiry

- Tell me exactly what you did to make your sailboat move.

- What happens to the boat if you blow air onto this part (*gesture*) of the sail?

- Your boat is moving farther away from you and closer to Felipe.

- Can you make your boat move in a different direction?

❗ Misconception Alert

Do not tell children that sailboats move solely because the wind pushes the sail. This is true only when the sailboat is moving in the same direction that the wind is blowing. Sailboats can also move into the wind when the placement of the sails creates a lift effect, similar to the wings on an airplane. The water also pushes against a sailboat's keel, or centerboard, similar to the way the wind pushes against the sail.

PLUMBING PROBLEMS

PHYSICS, EARTH SCIENCE

Materials

- ○ clear plastic tubes
- ○ 45-degree and 90-degree elbow joints, tees, couplings, and caps
- ○ sensory table, initially filled with water and later with dry sand
- ○ cups for pouring

Activity Description

Many children have noticed pipes in their homes or school buildings, perhaps under the sink, in the bathroom, or in the basement. Most children have also been told not to flush toys, clothing, or sand down the toilet. This activity gives children the opportunity to discover why those admonitions are important.

Sections of clear tubes, 45-degree and 90-degree elbow joints, tees, couplings, and caps are placed in the water table along with cups to pour water or sand through the pipes. The tubes used in the photograph, which are used to store fluorescent lightbulbs, are sold in the fluorescent lights section of building supply stores. The technical name is "clear polycarbonate lamp guard for 48-inch T-12 fluorescent tubes." The tubes can be cut to various lengths. Elbow joints, couplings, and caps can be found in the plumbing department. For the first two days of the activity, colored water is added to the water table. Children can connect the pipes in a variety of ways and watch how the water moves through them. For the next two or three days, dry sand replaces the water in the table. As children pour the sand into the pipes, they can observe how it behaves when compared with the water. Children are likely to notice that sand sometimes clogs the 45-degree elbow joint and quickly backs up when it encounters the 90-degree elbow joint. The caps stop the flow of both water and sand.

PVC pipe can also be used for this activity, but since it is *opaque*, children cannot see the materials

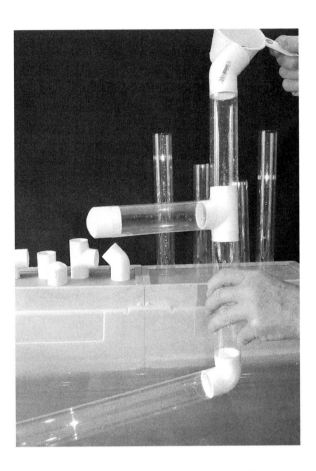

pass through the pipes. On the other hand, PVC pipe is more durable than fluorescent light tubes.

Science Content

One of the properties of liquids is that they flow. While solids maintain their shape unless broken, liquids do not. Instead, liquids flow to the lowest possible level and take the shape of their container. For this reason, liquids move through the elbow joints of the plumbing as long as the pipes are angled slightly downward. If two pipes are connected to an elbow joint to form a V shape, the water will move up both of the pipes to the same level.

Sand behaves differently from water because sand is composed of particles, which are solids. When sand is poured, it forms a cone-shaped mound. There is a maximum angle that this sand cone maintains. As more sand is poured onto a pile, the base of the cone spreads out to maintain this angle. Anyone who has built a sand pile has observed this phenomenon. This tendency of sand to form a pile causes it to clog the elbow joints in the plumbing.

 ## Mathematics Content

This activity is closely tied to the geometry standard. Use of the pipes and fittings allows children to create angles. Teachers can point out the lines formed by the straight pieces of pipe and the angle that is formed when the pipe is joined by the elbow joints or couplings.

 ## Connections to Engineering

Knowledge of the movement of water and how it can be controlled is essential in construction engineering. Keeping water from flowing onto roadways, installing plumbing in buildings, and diverting rainwater away from buildings are just a few of the water-related issues that construction engineers must confront. Some children may be interested in the book *Underground* by David Macaulay. It shows the many types of pipes, valves, and connections that lie beneath roads and buildings. Teachers will need to simplify the text.

Comments and Questions to Support Inquiry

- What happens to the water when it gets to the elbow joint? Can the water flow down the sideways pipe?

- Why doesn't the sand come out the side of the elbow joint? It looks like you have a plumbing problem!

- Look, I made a V shape with the pipes and the elbow joint. Pour some water into the pipe, and let's watch what happens.

- Let's look under the sink and see if we can find an elbow joint.

LIFE IN A POND

LIFE SCIENCE, EARTH SCIENCE

Materials

- ○ sensory table containing a small amount of water
- ○ rocks
- ○ sand
- ○ plastic aquarium plants
- ○ toy freshwater fish
- ○ toy forest animals

Activity Description

For this activity, a small amount of water is placed in the sensory table along with rocks, sand, plastic aquarium plants, toy freshwater fish, and toy forest animals that live near a pond. Sticks may be added so that beavers can build their lodges. Children can create habitats for the animals based on information from children's books. *Pond Life* by David Stewart is a good choice for older preschool and kindergarten children, while *Life in a Pond* by Carol K. Lindeen works well with young preschoolers. Both books have excellent illustrations.

Various types of animals live in and around ponds: *amphibians*, *reptiles*, fish, *invertebrates*, birds, and *mammals*. Amphibians are *vertebrates* that in most cases undergo *metamorphosis*, changing from water-breathing to air-breathing animals. Frogs, toads, and salamanders are examples. Reptiles may look similar to amphibians but breathe air through-out their lives. Turtles and garter snakes are reptiles that often live near ponds. Birds that live near pond environments include cranes, ducks, geese, and swans. Goldfish, catfish, and minnows are fish that

live in ponds. Mammals are air-breathing, vertebrate animals that have hair and nurse their young. Some mammals that live near ponds are raccoons, beavers, and opossums. Finally, a number of invertebrates are important inhabitants of pond communities. These include dragonflies, flies, spiders, and worms. Packages of inexpensive toy forest animals, which include many of the animals listed above, are sold in craft and toy stores. Stores that sell fishing supplies often have packages of plastic worms and insects that are typically used for bait.

 ## Science Content

The pond ecology provides a wide variety of animals with the environment they need to survive. Beavers are plant eaters, and raccoons and opossums are *omnivores*, meaning that they eat both plants and animals. Most turtles are omnivores, and garter snakes eat fish, frogs, and insects. Toads and frogs primarily eat invertebrates, such as insects and worms. Geese primarily consume grasses, and ducks live on plants, worms, and snails. Swans consume mostly plants but sometimes eat fish. Some children may be fascinated with pond animals and have many questions, so it is helpful to have informational books on hand. The book *Pond Life* by George K. Reid is a good guidebook for teachers. *Plants in Different Habitats* by Bobbie Kalman and Rebecca Sjonger includes color photographs of freshwater plants and simple text.

 ## Mathematics Content

There is good math potential in this activity. Children will need to sort and classify the animals as they decide where to place them in the various pond habitats. Sorting and classifying is part of the algebra standard. Once the animals are sorted, children may want to quantify them and compare how many of each type they have. This connects the activity to number and operations and data analysis.

 ## Connections to Technology

As children present questions about pond life, Internet searches can be helpful. There are many sites devoted to this topic.

Comments and Questions to Support Inquiry

- Here's a beaver. What do you think it needs for its home? Should I look in the book area for information about beavers?

- Can you find some animals that live in the water and some animals that mostly live on the land?

- Here come the ducks. They want to go for a swim. What do you think they will eat for their breakfast?

- There are a lot of insects that live around a pond. I wonder why they are important.

> ### ❗ Misconception Alert
>
> Animals that live in saltwater are not the same as animals that live in freshwater. Including sea animals in the pond habitat would be confusing to children and reinforce misconceptions about saltwater and freshwater animals.

WATER SLIDES

PHYSICS, EARTH SCIENCE

Materials

○ vinyl gutter, cut into 18-inch sections

○ small plastic people

○ cups for pouring

○ sensory table or plastic tub partially filled with water

Activity Description

The effects of moving water and *inclines* are combined in this activity through experiments with water slides. Most children have had previous experiences with slides in the motor room or on the playground. Some may have played on water slides at home or at swimming pools and water parks. This activity gives children the chance to create their own water park in the sensory table.

The water slides used in this center are created from pieces of vinyl gutter. From a standard 10-foot length of gutter (priced at just over six dollars), four 18-inch sections are cut, and the edges sanded. Children can prop the gutters against the sides of the water table to create slopes that vary in steepness. They can then pour water down the chutes to send toy people sliding into the water. As the steepness of the slope increases, so does the speed of the flowing water and the toy people it carries with it.

 ## Science Content

Children may have already experimented with inclines of varying slopes, such as those in Activities 2.2, 3.6, and 4.5. Based on those explorations, they may realize that increasing the steepness of an incline causes objects rolling down the ramp to move faster. Will the same be true for water? Children will be eager to experiment and find out. Teachers can help them explore the parameters. When the water slides are almost horizontal, the water moves very slowly;

when the slides are steep, the water moves down in a swift gush.

 ## Mathematics Content

This activity allows children to explore lines, as created by the slides, that are horizontal, vertical, and at various angles in between. It is therefore connected to geometry. After several days of experimenting, children may want to measure the time it takes for the toy people to reach the bottom of each incline. A *metronome*, a device used by musicians, produces sound and light at regular intervals that children can count to measure the elapsed time. This connects the activity to the measurement standard.

 ### Connections to Technology and Engineering

Hydropower is power that is harnessed from the *force* of moving water. Historically, energy from water wheels was used to grind grain, run machinery, and irrigate crops. Today hydropower is important in generating electricity. Understanding the power of moving water is therefore important to various types of engineering, such as mechanical and electrical, and the technology that is connected to these fields. Use of a metronome connects this activity directly to technology.

Comments and Questions to Support Inquiry

- My toy person is Grandpa. He wants to go down a slow water slide. How should I position my slide so that Grandpa moves slowly?

- Pour some water down this chute, and see what happens to your toy person.

- Is there a way to position the slide so that the water doesn't flow but stays still?

- What happens when the slide is really steep?

GEOLOGY SHAKES

EARTH SCIENCE

Materials

- ○ sensory table, or long plastic storage box
- ○ board, about 6 inches wide and slightly longer than the sensory table or storage box
- ○ containers of pebbles, sand, and water
- ○ clear plastic containers, preferably with lids

Activity Description

For this activity, a board is placed across the top of the water table, and containers of pebbles, sand, and water are set inside the table. Children create concoctions by mixing scoopfuls of the pebbles, sand, and water in clear plastic containers. If lids are available, children can shake up their geology shakes before setting them on the board; otherwise, they can stir the mixtures. As children spend time filling additional containers, changes begin to occur in the mixtures setting on the board. The once dark brown water quickly begins to lighten in color.

Young children love mixing things, so it is good to have plenty of replacement materials on hand. Save some of the mixtures for at least a week. Children will notice that overnight the water becomes increasingly clear, and this process continues for several days. They may also observe a rim of sand between the sand and pebble mixture at the bottom of the jar and the water at the top.

During this activity, the contents of used containers can be dumped into the body of the water table, and the containers can be rinsed at the sink to be ready for the next group of experimenters. On the following day, children can use colanders to sift the pebbles from the sand, a filtering process that is also an excellent science activity.

 ## Science Content

The purpose of this activity is for children to explore the process of **sedimentation**, which is the tendency for particles to settle out of the fluid in which they are suspended. In geology, sedimentation results in the formation of **sedimentary rocks**. Moving water picks up sediment and deposits it when it reaches some kind of barrier, such as the curve in a creek or river, or a tree that has fallen across the water.

In this activity, three materials are sorted through the **forces** of nature. Gravity causes the heavier pebbles to sink to the bottom of the container, which displaces the water and some of the sand. Because the sand is heavier than the water, it forms a layer on top of the pebbles and fills in the gaps between rocks, leaving the gradually clearing water on the top.

 ## Mathematics Content

Children may want to create recipes for their geology shakes, such as two scoops of pebbles, one scoop of sand, and three scoops of water. These recipes can be written on note cards and attached to the containers for later comparison. This variation in the activity introduces the mathematical concepts of quantification and measuring, while also increasing the scientific potential.

 ## Connections to Engineering

Understanding the process of sedimentation and the properties of various materials is important in civil and construction engineering. Building a road or a house on a base that could easily be eroded by water could lead to serious problems.

Comments and Questions to Support Inquiry

- This geology shake is completely brown. I'm going to set this sand timer on the board next to the container. When the sand runs out, let me know. That will be in five minutes, and I want to see how this geology shake looks then.

- I thought you put the water in first. How did the water get up to the top?

- If we put a lot of pebbles in this container, do you think the water will still end up at the top?

- If you want to shake the container again, that's all right. We'll see if the same thing happens again, and the pebbles go to the bottom.

- I see a line forming in between the bottom layer and the water. What do you think is causing that line?

CREATING "TOPS" FOR TOPS

PHYSICS

Materials

○ compact discs

○ colored permanent markers

○ corrugated cardboard, cut into 1-inch diameter circles

○ short pencils, about 3 inches in length

○ glue

Activity Description

A wide variety of toy tops are available for children to experiment with. In this activity, children can create their own tops, along with interchangeable surfaces for the tops. Compact discs form the base of the tops. Children can use permanent markers to create designs on the reflective silver surface of the discs. Prior to the start of the activity, teachers can create spindles for the tops by cutting 1-inch diameter circles from corrugated cardboard and poking 3-inch-long pencils through the cardboard. Once children have decorated their tops, the pencils are inserted through the hole in the disc, and the cardboard circles are glued to the bottom of the disc. After the glue has dried, children can spin their tops and watch as the rapid rotation alters the appearance of their designs.

Teachers may want to ask parents to donate compact discs that come as advertisements in the mail. Television stations may also donate discs that are going to be thrown away. Compact discs are inexpensive to purchase in bulk: about fourteen dollars for one hundred discs, which is only fourteen cents per disc. A school can purchase a box for teachers to

share, or teachers can combine their resources and purchase a box.

On subsequent days, children can create a variety of different surfaces to add to their tops by decorating precut paper circles, the same size as the discs, with holes punched in their centers. If the tops are rotated on a piece of white paper, the pencil spindles will leave spiral marks on the paper. If teachers do not want the spindles to leave marks, they can cover the pencil tips with a thin coating of glue.

 ## Science Content

Tops are toys that can balance when rotating around an axis. This movement is called the *gyroscopic effect*. When tops are first spun, they tend to wobble until the axis becomes securely balanced. After the top has rotated successfully for a period of time, it begins to lose momentum and once again wobble. One of the reasons that tops are fascinating to watch is that they create interesting optical effects. For example, a series of widely spaced dots may look like a solid line when the top is rotating rapidly.

 ## Mathematics Content

The mathematical content of this activity relates to the circular shape of the discs, and the lines and shapes produced by the rotating tops.

  ## Connections to Technology and Engineering

Tops are closely related to *gyroscopes*, which measure and maintain orientation, or position, in three-dimensional space. Some modern technical applications of gyroscopes include smartphones, electronic game systems, and compasses. Gyroscopes are therefore used in electrical, mechanical, and aeronautical engineering.

Comments and Questions to Support Inquiry

- I see a face on your top. What do you think the face will look like when you spin the top?

- I see circular red and blue lines on your top when you spin it. What did you draw on your top that produces those lines when your top turns?

- I'm going to color half of this circle blue and half of it yellow. I want to see if the colors look the same when I spin the top.

- Does your triangle still look like a triangle when the top is turning?

NATURE'S IMPRINTS

LIFE SCIENCE

Materials

- ○ variety of weeds, wildflowers, grasses, and other plants
- ○ nonfiction books about plants
- ○ magnifying glass
- ○ tempera paint
- ○ sponge brushes
- ○ paint brayers (paint rollers)
- ○ paper
- ○ camera

Activity Description

The structure of plant parts, such as leaves and petals, is much more visible to children when paint impressions are created. In this activity, children sponge paint onto plant parts and press them onto paper to create imprints. A class book is created showing a photo of each child's plant and the collage of imprints it created.

A variety of "found" plants can be used for this activity. Although commonly referred to as weeds, various grasses, wildflowers, vines, and shrubs are very interesting to children. Some plants that are generally free for the taking are dandelions, cattails, honeysuckle, cornflowers, Queen Anne's lace, wild grapevine, and milkweed. Cut or pull the plants that are to be used the day before they are needed and keep them in water until class. Photographs of the plants, for use in the class book, can be taken before the activity begins.

As children sponge paint onto various parts of their plants, teachers can talk about those parts and why they are important to the plant. Children can cut or pull their plants apart to make them easier to

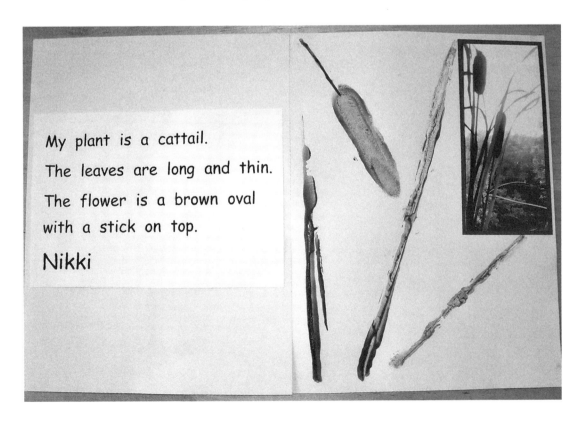

My plant is a cattail.
The leaves are long and thin.
The flower is a brown oval
with a stick on top.

Nikki

manage. The plant parts should be assembled on the paper with the paint side down. Carefully place another sheet of paper or a lightweight piece of cardboard over the plants. Children can roll brayers (paint rollers) over the top sheet to create uniform paint impressions of the plants on the bottom paper. Thicker sections of plants, such as cattails or milkweed pods, can simply be pressed onto the paper.

It is important to have several children's books available in the classroom to use as references during this project. Although written for primary-grade students, *Plants in Different Habitats* by Bobbie Kalman and Rebecca Sjonger offers clear, beautiful illustrations of plants and answers many questions that children may have.

 ## Science Content

The plants included in this activity are categorized as green plants, a group that includes trees, shrubs, flowers, grasses, and ferns. They can be further classified as **vascular plants** because they have a system of leaves, stem, and roots. These plants use light and carbon dioxide to synthesize food through a process known as **photosynthesis**.

As children examine and paint various parts of the plants, teachers can point out that the leaves are where the plant makes food. Children may notice that leaves are attached to the plant with a stalk, which is called a **petiole**. The veins in the leaf transport water and nutrients. If plants are uprooted, children can examine their root structure. The roots anchor the plant in the ground and take in water and nutrients from the soil. The flower is the part of the plant that makes seeds.

 ## Mathematics Content

Teachers can direct children's attention to the geometry apparent in the structure of plants. Leaves are often symmetrical, in which one side of the leaf is the mirror image of the other. Flowers tend to be rotationally symmetrical, with the petals organized around the center of the flower. If the flower is turned a certain number of degrees (depending on the number of petals), it looks the same as before it was rotated.

 ## Connections to Technology

The digital photographs that are included on each child's plant page help children connect the various parts of the plant that they used to create imprints to the plant as a whole. Magnifying glasses can help children examine the plant structures in greater detail.

Comments and Questions to Support Inquiry

- Look at all the lines in your leaf print. Those are the leaf's veins. They take water to other parts of the leaf.

- The roots of your plant make an interesting design on your picture. I see thick parts and parts that look like hairs. Those hairs move water to the main part of the root and up into the plant.

- Your flower print is symmetrical. The petals are all attached to a center point.

CREATING FOSSILS

EARTH SCIENCE

Materials

○ self-hardening clay

○ playdough rollers

○ seashells

Activity Description

Children who have the opportunity to examine *fossils* (Activity 2.11) will notice that many contain the imprint of ancient shells, or shells that have turned to stone. In this activity, children can create their own fossils with self-hardening clay. The clay is first smoothed with rollers. Children then press seashells into the clay to create an imprint. After the clay dries, it will resemble the imprints created in stone over millions of years. If desired, the clay can be trimmed into squares before it dries to form clay tiles.

Children's books such as *Fossils Tell of Long Ago* by Aliki will help children connect the fossils of the past with the seashells of today.

Bags of seashells can be purchased inexpensively at craft stores. Children's books that show beautiful photographs of seashells and identify them are available in libraries. *The Shell Book* by Barbara Hirsch Lember is one example. After the tiles have hardened, children can reexamine them and try to find the shells that fit into their molds. This reinforces the important idea that fossils preserve the form of the original creature.

Science Content

Fossils are the preserved remains or impressions of plants or animals that died millions of years ago and have turned to stone. Fossils form when the remains of a plant or animal are covered with sediment soon after the organism dies. In some cases, groundwater filled with *minerals* filters into small cavities in the plant or animal and over time hardens into stone. In other cases, the remains of the organism completely dissolve, and a mold is left behind.

Mathematics Content

Many seashells have symmetrical designs. Shells such as scallops show bilateral symmetry; if a line is drawn down the center of the shell, one side is the mirror

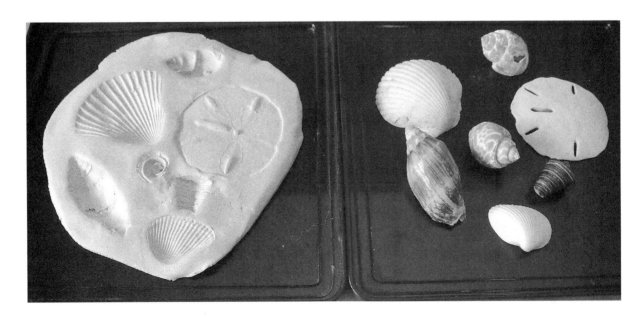

image of the other. Other shells have a spiral design that forms a special type of pattern known as a *Fibonacci sequence*, which appears often in nature. The shapes and symmetry of the shells align this activity to geometry.

As children try to fit shells into their hardened molds, they will need to turn, slide, and flip the shells. These are called geometric transformations. A turn means that a shape is rotated a certain number of degrees. In a slide, all points on the shape move as a unit when it is repositioned. Finally, a flip shows the mirror image, or reflection, of an object.

  ### Connections to Technology and Engineering

Paleontologists use special technology and engineering methods to remove and preserve fossils. The book *Digging Up Dinosaurs* by Aliki describes this process for children.

Comments and Questions to Support Inquiry

- I can see an imprint of this spiral shell in your clay. Do you want to press the top part of the shell into the clay and see what it looks like?

- Here is your clay tile from earlier this week. Can you find the shells that fit into the molds on your tile? It's like a puzzle, isn't it?

- Can you see the ridges on the shell in your clay mold?

- If you turn the starfish, does it fit exactly into the mold?

PENDULUM SALT PRINTS

PHYSICS

Materials

- ○ 2 pieces of wood, 16 by 1½ by ¾ inches
- ○ 1 piece of wood, 12 by 1½ by ¾ inches
- ○ 1 piece of wood, 18 by 12 by ½ inches
- ○ screw eye
- ○ glue gun
- ○ small plastic bottle
- ○ cord
- ○ salt
- ○ glue
- ○ paper
- ○ colored chalk

Activity Description

Children who have had previous experiences with *pendulums* (Activity 2.5) may be interested in the path that the swinging pendulum follows. For this activity, colored salt dripping from a suspended bottle allows children to view and preserve the elliptical path of a pendulum.

A pendulum is a weight suspended from a fixed point from which it is free to move. A pendulum frame can be as simple as a child's chair with a hook screwed into the bottom to hold the pendulum cord. The frame from an infant gym makes an excellent support for a pendulum. The teacher-made pendulum in the photograph is created by screwing together two side pieces of wood, 16 by 1½ by ¾ inches, to a top piece of wood, 12 by 1½ by ¾ inches. The sides are then screwed to a base made from plywood, 18 by 12 by ½ inches, and a screw eye is inserted into the center of the top board to hold the pendulum cord.

The pendulum bob, or weight, is a small plastic bottle with a flip-top lid to release the salt. The lower half of the bottle is cut off. A hot glue gun is used to melt holes through opposite sides of the bottle near the cutoff edge. A cord is threaded through these holes and tied to the hook on the pendulum frame.

The table salt used in the activity is inexpensive and can be quickly colored by rubbing colored chalk over it.

To implement the activity, glue that has been heavily diluted with water is brushed over a piece of black construction paper sized to fit under the frame. The pendulum bottle is partially filled with salt, which drips out as the pendulum swings. Teachers need to pretest the pendulum before the activity is implemented with children. If the salt drips out too fast, the hole can be made smaller by placing tape over a portion of it. The diluted glue preserves the elliptical path created by the dripping salt.

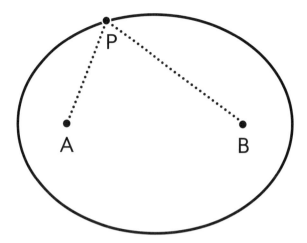

As point P moves around the ellipse, the sum of the length of lines AP and BP remains the same.

An ellipse is not the same as an oval. An oval does not have a precise mathematical definition but can generally be described as egg-shaped, as the Latin derivation of the word implies.

 ## Science Content

The swinging pendulum often follows an elliptical path because it is initially given a slight sideways motion when the weight is released.

 ## Mathematics Content

Children have many opportunities to view ellipses in this activity. An ellipse looks like an elongated circle. While a circle is a two-dimensional geometric form in which all points are the same distance from a single fixed point in the center, an ellipse has two fixed points (foci). If lines are drawn from any point on the ellipse to these foci, the sum of the length of these two lines is always the same.

 ## Connections to Technology and Engineering

The pendulum is an example of technology that has been used for centuries in clocks and continues to be used for scientific research. Understanding the mathematics of curves such as ellipses is important in the technical drawing required of engineers.

Comments and Questions to Support Inquiry

- What does the path created by the pendulum look like?

- Now that your picture is dry, let's trace the salt path with our fingers.

- Where do you see curved lines in your picture? Are there any straight lines?

SNOWFLAKE PROJECTIONS

EARTH SCIENCE

Materials

○ easel

○ overhead or LCD projector

○ snowflake image

○ colored pencils or markers

Activity Description

Because snowflakes are so tiny, it is difficult for children to observe their symmetrical configuration. In this activity, the image of a small plastic snowflake is projected onto easel paper. Children can trace the intricate design and discuss the hexagonal formation. Experiences such as this may lead children to create their own symmetrical designs.

Small plastic snowflake ornaments or garlands are commonly available during the winter holiday season. Teachers should choose snowflakes that reflect the forms of real snowflakes, preferably with a hexagonal formation.

For this activity, a small plastic snowflake is placed on an overhead projector so that a large version of the image appears on the classroom easel. An LCD

projector can also be used to project a PowerPoint image of a snowflake.

Children can use colored pencils or markers to trace the image. In the process, they become more aware of the **symmetry**, or repeating designs, that occur on each arm of the snowflake.

 ## Science Content

Snowflakes begin as ice crystals that grow in structure as water molecules in the air collect on their surface. Snowflakes typically exhibit a hexagonal, symmetrical form because their crystal formation is sixfold. Most snowflakes are not completely symmetrical, however, due to slight variations that occur in the environment as they fall. In addition, not all snowflakes have six sides. Snowflakes with three, twelve, and even eighteen sides have been photographed. Teachers may enjoy reading the book *The Snowflake: Winter's Secret Beauty* by Kenneth Libbrecht and can share Patricia Rasmussen's amazing photographs with children.

 ## Mathematics Content

Working with snowflake images gives children experience with hexagonal formations, a shape they encounter less frequently than circles, triangles, and squares. The activity also provides experience with **symmetry**, an important concept in both geometry and science.

 ## Connections to Technology

The use of an overhead or LCD projector to enlarge the snowflake image is a practical application of technology for this activity. Children may want to place other objects on the projector and see how their images appear when enlarged.

Comments and Questions to Support Inquiry

- How would you describe the snowflake on your paper?

- How many arms does the snowflake have?

- Does the same design appear on all of the arms of the snowflake?

- Look how small the snowflake on the projector is compared with the image on your paper. Projectors make objects look bigger.

WATER CAN BAND

PHYSICS; MATHEMATICS: ALGEBRA

Materials

- ○ several sizes of metal cans with lids, such as empty paint or spice cans
- ○ spoons
- ○ small pitcher of water
- ○ several small blocks and 1-inch cubes
- ○ tape or video recorder

Activity Description

Children create interesting percussion sounds and patterns for this activity. First, children use *levers* to pry the lids off of several sizes of cans. Next, they add water to the cans and listen to the unusual sounds

that are produced when they tap the cans. Finally, children use the water cans to create sound patterns, which the teacher can record for later listening.

The cans used in this activity have metal lids that seal tightly, such as metal spice containers, some coffee or tea containers, and empty paint cans. (Unused empty paint cans in both gallon and quart sizes can be purchased at building supply stores.) To open the cans, children use spoons to pry up the lids. The spoons function as *levers*, one of the six classical *simple machines*. Next, children add varying amounts of water to the cans and replace the lids.

Before children begin playing the water drums, place a square wooden building block under the larger cans and a 1-inch cube under the smaller cans. Elevating the cans allows them to vibrate more freely

Glissando Cans
1. Pry the lids off the cans.
2. Add water to the cans.
3. How do they sound when You tap them?

and produce a more resonant, distinctive sound. As children tap the cans with their spoons, they will hear an eerie *glissando* sound, which is a sliding up and down in *pitch*. Children will also notice that the larger cans produce a lower sound than the smaller cans. After children have had ample time to experiment with the cans, teachers can help them create patterns such as the following:

- cans played in order from smallest to largest
- cans played in order from largest to smallest
- large–small; large–small
- small–small–large–large; small–small–large–large
- large–large–small–small; large–large–small–small
- large–medium–small; large–medium–small

Teachers may choose to make video or audio recordings of the children's patterns as an additional component of this activity. Viewing and listening to the recordings reinforce both the scientific and mathematical concepts explored in the activity.

Science Content

Children are presented with three science concepts in this activity. First, the spoons that are used to pry open the cans are class-one levers because the *fulcrum* (the point where the spoon touches the rim of the can) is in between the *force* (the handle of the spoon, which is pressed down) and the *load* (the lid). Children could not open the cans without this useful tool. Second, children can hear the difference between the sounds produced by larger cans and those produced by smaller cans. Smaller vibrating objects produce a higher sound than larger objects. Finally, the water column in the cans is also moving.

As the cans vibrate, the water moves in waves, which constantly change in height and create the glissando effect.

Mathematics Content

This activity provides another way for children to create and extend patterns. Many children recognize and remember patterns more easily when sound and movement are involved rather than just visual symbols, such as colors or shapes.

Connections to Technology

The *lever* used to pry open the cans is an example of early technology that we still use in our everyday lives. Making video or audio recordings of the patterns children create is a modern application of technology.

Comments and Questions to Support Inquiry

- Can you use this spoon to help you get the lid off of the can? It looks like there's a groove around the lid.
- Listen to how the sound goes up and down when you tap the can.
- How does the sound of the little can compare to the sound of the big can?
- If I want to make a really high sound, which can should I play?
- Let's make a pattern by going back and forth between these two cans.

NATURE'S MARACAS

LIFE SCIENCE

Materials

○ dried ornamental gourds

○ dried lotus pods

○ dried locust pods

Activity Description

Several types of natural materials make interesting maracas. Ornamental gourds, which are often displayed in classrooms in the fall, can be dried by laying them in a cool place where they have ample air circulation. Once they are fully dried and hard, tap the gourds lightly against a table to release the seeds from the dried fibers of pulp. The gourds make a pleasant sound when children shake them. Larger gourds can also be dried. They can be purchased at farmers' markets in the fall. An interesting musical instrument that is made from a large, dried gourd is the *shekere* (pronounced *SHAY-ker-ray*) from West Africa. For this instrument, the gourd is hollowed out to create resonance, and the sound comes from a net of beads, shells, or beans that surrounds the gourd and rattles against it. It is interesting for children to compare the sound of rattling coming from inside a gourd to the sound of rattling from outside the gourd. Shekeres can be found in African import stores and in music education and early childhood catalogs.

Another plant that produces a natural maraca is the lotus, a flowering water plant that is native to tropical Asian countries and Australia. The seed pods from this plant are popular for autumn floral displays and can be found in craft stores. The seeds are clearly visible through holes in the dried pods; this allows children to see what is creating the rattling sound.

Some trees produce seed pods that make natural maracas when dried. The honey locust tree, which is common in the eastern half of the United States, produces a profusion of long seed pods that are dark brown when they drop to the ground. The seed pods make a soft, rattling sound when shaken. Although locust maracas do not last very long, it is interesting for children to see how this tree protects its seeds, which are clearly visible when the pod cracks open. Children can compare the sounds and shapes of the natural maracas and use them to create sound patterns. For example, half of the class might play dried gourds, and the other half locust pods. With the teacher directing, they might play the following patterns:

gourds–gourds–locust–locust–locust;
gourds–gourds–locust–locust–locust

locust–locust–gourds–gourds;
locust–locust–gourds–gourds

Children can also use the natural maracas to accompany songs.

 Science Content

The use of natural maracas draws attention to the life cycle of the plants that they come from. Gourds are closely related to pumpkins and follow the same growth pattern. Children's books that trace the development of pumpkins, such as *From Seed to Pumpkin* by Wendy Pfeffer, help children understand this natural cycle. Seeds from the gourds used as maracas can grow the next generation of plants.

 Mathematics Content

Children may be interested in estimating the number of seeds that are in a dried gourd or locust pod. After the maraca has served its musical purpose, it can be cut open, and children can count the seeds. They can compare the actual number of seeds to the estimates they made.

Comments and Questions to Support Inquiry

- What do you think is making that rattling sound inside the maraca?

- Which maraca has the loudest sound? The locust pod is really long, but it doesn't sound very loud.

- Which sound do you like the best? Why?

- Do you think there are more seeds in the locust pod or the gourd? We'll open them both in a few days and find out.

RATTLE DRUMS

PHYSICS

Materials

- ○ 3 clear plastic food containers, approximately 7 by 5 by 1½ inches
- ○ plastic beads
- ○ metal washers
- ○ rice
- ○ glue
- ○ 3 wooden spoons

Activity Description

A snare drum is a type of drum with cords stretched across its bottom surface that rattle when the head of the drum is struck. In this activity, a rattling sound is also produced when drums are tapped, but the rattles come from inside the drums.

Three different drums are created from clear plastic food containers, approximately 7 by 5 by 1½ inches. Each drum has a different type of material inside: plastic beads, metal washers, or rice. After the materials have been placed inside the containers, the lids can be glued shut to prevent spillage.

The drums sound best if they are suspended when played. Children can hold the drums by the handle on the food container, or the drums can be suspended from a peg board divider or shelf back. Children will discover that the sounds produced by each drum vary. The washers create a loud, metallic sound. The rattle of the beads is a little softer and more muffled. The rice produces a soft swishing

sound. Children can use the drums to create rhythmic patterns to accompany favorite songs. Wooden spoons make good mallets for these drums.

Science Content

The material that is used in a musical instrument affects two aspects of the sound: the tone quality, or *timbre*, and how loud the instrument sounds, or its *dynamics*. *Acoustics* is the branch of physics that deals with sound vibrations, and musical acoustics focuses, in part, on the sounds produced by instruments.

Mathematics Content

Once children have explored the scientific aspects of the rattle drums, they can turn their attention to creating music with them. Teachers can model examples of rhythmic patterns that children can play using the drums, and children can also create their own patterns. In the examples below, the drum with washers is labeled **W**, the drum with beads is labeled **B**, and the drum with rice is labeled **R.**

{W RR} {W RR} {W RR} {W RR}

{W B R (silence)} {W B R (silence)}

{WW B B RR} {WW B B RR}

Connections to Technology and Engineering

Although this activity does not specifically connect to technology and engineering, the study of how sounds can be produced, manipulated, and recorded is an important branch of both of these areas.

Comments and Questions to Support Inquiry

- Tap each of these drums, and see what kind of sound it makes.

- Which sound would you play if you didn't want to wake up your baby sister?

- I'm going to play a pattern on the drums. See if you can play the same pattern.

- Now you play a pattern, and I'll try to copy it. Tell me if I get it right.

- Which drum should I play to make a loud sound? Why do you think the drum with screws has the loudest sound?

PIPES AND PITCHES

PHYSICS

Materials

○ steel pipe, ¾ inch in diameter, cut to lengths of 11, 9, and 7 inches

○ steel pipe, 1¼, ¾, and ½ inches in diameter, all cut to lengths of 10 inches

○ wooden mallet (see instructions below)

○ cord, fishing line, or pipe cleaners

○ 6 cup hooks

Activity Description

What happens to the sound when chimes are the same width but vary in length? What if the chimes are all the same length but vary in width? This activity gives children the opportunity to answer those questions through their own experimentation. There are two sets of teacher-made chimes in this activity. The first set of chimes is made from ¾-inch steel pipe, cut to lengths of 11, 9, and 7 inches. The second set of chimes is made from steel pipes that are 1¼, ¾, and ½ inches wide, all cut to lengths of 10 inches. The ends of the pipes should be sanded or filed so that they are not sharp. Two small holes are drilled through opposite sides of each pipe, about 1 inch from the top, so that the pipes can be suspended with cord, fishing line, or pipe cleaners. Each set of pipes is suspended from hooks on a small frame. As an alternative, the pipes can be grouped by set and suspended by U hooks from a peg board divider or shelf back.

Grouping the chimes in sets is important because it allows the children to focus on changes in sound caused by variation in one of the dimensions, either

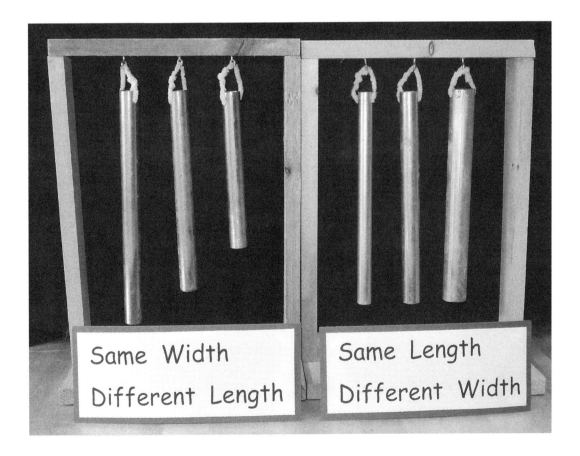

length or width. The pipes can be purchased in hardware or building supply stores. The set of ¾-inch pipes can be made for less than five dollars. Since three different pipes are needed for the set that varies in width, and since pipes typically come in 10-foot lengths, several teachers may want to combine resources and share the pipes. Pipes often need to be cut for use in construction jobs. For this reason, teachers who know building contractors or plumbers may want to ask if leftover pieces that would normally be thrown away can be saved for them.

Teachers can reuse the frames from Activity 2.4 or 2.5 to suspend the chimes in this activity, or they can make separate frames for the chimes (see Activity 2.4 for a materials list). The sides of the frames in the photograph are 14 by 2 by 1 inches, and the top and bottom are 12 by 2 by 1 inches. The baseboard is 12 by 7 by 1 inches. The pipes are suspended from cup hooks and spaced so that they can vibrate freely. The mallet is made from a 7-inch-long dowel glued into a wooden bead with a hole that is the same diameter as the dowel.

The chimes can be placed in the music, science, or STEM center in the classroom for repeated experimentation by the children. Children should be guided to carefully listen to the sounds produced by each bar. Then they can begin to create sound patterns with the chimes. The teacher might create a pattern for a child to play and then ask the child to create a pattern for the teacher or another child to repeat.

Science Content

Size variations in both the length and the width of a vibrating object change the **pitch**, or how high or low the instrument sounds. For children to construct this relationship, the pipes should be carefully grouped based on variations in either length or width. Teachers will need to supply the terms *high* and *low* for the relative pitches produced by the chimes. Low-sounding tones have fewer vibrations per second than higher-sounding tones.

Mathematics Content

Several mathematical concepts are embedded in this activity. Bars that are arranged according to size are seriated, an important concept related to the algebra standard. If the bars are periodically rearranged, many young children will quickly put them back in order according to size. Children also explore two types of measurement comparisons in this activity: length and width, or in this case, diameter. Since all of the bars can be seen and felt, children can use direct comparison to make measurement judgments. If children are interested, they can also use interlocking manipulative pieces, such as cubes or plastic inchworms, to measure the pipes. Patterning is the third mathematical concept supported by this activity.

Connections to Technology and Engineering

As discussed in other music and sound-related activities in this book, the study of how sounds can be produced, manipulated, and recorded is an important branch of both acoustical engineering and sound technologies.

Comments and Questions to Support Inquiry

- What is different about these pipes? What is the same?

- Do the pipes that have different lengths sound the same or different from one another?

- These pipes are all the same length. Do they sound the same? Since they are all the same length, why do you think they sound different?

BIRDSONG PATTERNS

LIFE SCIENCE; MATHEMATICS: ALGEBRA

Materials

○ Audubon plush toy birds with recorded birdsongs

Activity Description

Songbirds sing in patterns that children can learn to recognize and repeat. In this activity, children listen to the recorded sounds of birdsongs in Audubon toy birds. They use hand signs, singing, and clapping to repeat the patterns.

The Audubon birds used in this activity are plush replicas of common songbirds. By squeezing the birds, children activate a microchip that plays the authentic sound of each species, as recorded by the Cornell Lab of Ornithology. Some bird songs are melodic, a short tune that repeats. To help children remember and represent the melodic patterns, teachers can model the standard vocal syllables from music along with their corresponding hand signs, called Kodály (pronounced *KOH-dye*) hand signals. Both are represented in table 3.25. Other birds emit only a single tone but in a pronounced rhythmic pattern. Children can clap the patterns produced by birds whose songs are strictly rhythmic with no melody.

Great horned owl

Black-capped chickadee

On the first day in which the activity is implemented, teachers should introduce two birds whose songs are quite different, one with a melodic pattern and the other with a rhythmic pattern. The black-capped chickadee is an excellent choice for day one, because the bird's song alternates between the musical tones sol and mi, which are easy for children to sing. As the children listen to the recorded song, they can join in with the teacher and use their hands to represent sol and mi. Next, children can listen to the song of the great horned owl, which is a single **pitch** with a distinctive pattern of long and short sounds. They can then clap this pattern with the teacher. As a final component of the first day's experience, the teacher can hide the two birds in a bag. As children listen to the bird songs, most will find that they can already distinguish between the two birds. On subsequent days, additional birds can be added to the activity. The Audubon birds used in this activity are sold in bookstores, toy stores, and museums.

Table 3.25: Representations of Musical Patterns in Bird Songs

AUDUBON BIRD	BIRD AND SONG	REPRESENTATION
	Black-capped chickadee	
	Great horned owl	hoo HOO hoo hoo (steady beats) clap clap (sh) (sh) clap (sh) clap (sh)
	Northern cardinal	
	Blue jay	jeer jeer jeer jeer jeer jeer (steady beats) clap clap clap clap clap clap
	Western meadowlark	

Science Content

Although each species of songbird has a specific recognizable song, the songs may vary based on time of year and circumstance. In addition, many songbirds are able to invent or learn new song variations. These may then be passed on to other birds of their species.

Patterns are important elements of both mathematics and science. Understanding systems, order, and organization is a unifying concept of the National Science Education Standards (National Research Council 1996), and patterns are a key element in this regard.

 ## Mathematics Content

In mathematics, recognizing, describing, and extending patterns are considered key concepts for young children and are included in national standards (National Council of Teachers of Mathematics 2000). However, constructing the concept of a pattern as a repeating element can be difficult for young children. This activity introduces the concept of patterning through multiple modes of learning—auditory, visual, vocal, and movement-related—which addresses learning differences among children and reinforces the important idea that patterns can be represented through many different symbol systems.

 ## Connections to Technology

The ability to play back the recorded bird calls is an obvious use of technology in this activity. Teachers and children can also hear the recorded sounds of birds on the Cornell University website: www.allaboutbirds.org/guide/search.aspx.

Comments and Questions to Support Inquiry

- You were able to keep singing the chickadee's song pattern even after the recording stopped playing.

- We need four claps for the owl's pattern—short, long, short, short.

- Can you sing the pattern this bird makes?

- I'm going to hide the birds in this bag. See if you can tell which bird is singing just by listening to its pattern.

STEM Outdoors

Sean and Amanda each carried a pumpkin from their classroom to the outside playground. When they reached the teeter-totter, they placed their pumpkins into boxes that the teacher had taped to opposite ends of the teeter-totter. Slowly, Sean's side of the teeter-totter moved downward.

"My pumpkin's heavier!" exclaimed Sean.

"No, it isn't," Amanda disagreed. "My side is heavier. It went up."

"I wonder how we can figure this out," mused the teacher. "How can we know for sure whether the heavier side goes down or up?"

"I know," said Mike, who had been watching the experiment. "Sean is heavier than his pumpkin, so he should sit on one end of the teeter-totter and put the pumpkin on the other end. If Sean's end goes down, we know that the side that is heavier goes down."

The teacher removed the box from one end of the teeter-totter so that Sean could sit on it. His end of the teeter-totter quickly moved down to the ground.

"Okay," said Amanda. "You're right. The side that goes down is heavier."

• • •

A teeter-totter is essentially a balance scale, and young children are often confused about which side is heavier. Children are accustomed to the idea that tall things, such as grown-ups, are heavier. Because the side of the teeter-totter that goes up is farther from the ground and therefore looks taller, children reason that it is also the heavier side. In the vignette above, the children were able to conduct their own experiment to determine whose assumption was correct.

Introducing STEM activities into outdoor environments is important for three reasons:

1. Children are in contact with the natural environment, which opens up opportunities to explore plants, animals, and natural phenomena that are not available in the classroom.

2. Children can use their whole bodies to explore materials, which helps them understand the physical properties of objects in new ways.

3. Activities that are too messy to conduct inside can be performed outside.

CONTACT WITH NATURE

Even in urban environments, outdoor play brings children into contact with nature. Children can feel the breeze and watch how it moves objects, sometimes swirling leaves into mini-tornadoes or causing papers to race across the ground. They can harness this wind power to conduct their own experiments, such as watching the movement of balloons (Activity 4.1) or observing the effect of wind on outdoor chimes (Activity 4.8). When children are playing outside, they notice phenomena created by sunlight coming into contact with various surfaces. They can explore shadows (Activity 4.3) and *reflections*. Children can also watch the effects of water. They may notice how water is absorbed by the doll clothes they are washing and then evaporates when the clothes are hung up to dry (Activity 4.6). They can add water to the sandbox and observe how it changes the consistency of the sand. Children can make tracks by walking or riding their tricycles through puddles, and watch how the water seeps into the ground.

In outdoor environments children can observe and investigate plant growth. They may pick dandelions and notice the parts of the plant. They might observe differences between moss and grass. Even on concrete playgrounds plants find a way to grow through the cracks. On playgrounds where there is no space to garden, children can create container gardens with plants that are easy to transport from the classroom (Activity 4.10). They can also watch neighborhood animals, such as birds, squirrels, and insects, and may find ways to interact with them, as by filling a bird feeder (Activity 4.2) or observing what foods ants like to eat (Activity 4.4). Time spent in scientific investigations on the playground helps children understand the ebb and flow of life around them.

LARGE-MOTOR EXPLORATIONS

Outside play equipment is often large enough to allow children to use their whole bodies as part of the exploration process. Children can swing from a tire swing and become a human *pendulum*. They feel the up and down motion of a balanced teeter-totter. These experiences may help them better understand science equipment that they use in the classroom, such as pendulums and balance scales. In the outside area, children can use *pulleys* to hoist objects far beyond the height they can reach (Activities 4.2 and 4.7). They can roll objects up or down *inclines* that are too large to use in the classroom (Activity 4.5). They can feel the extra effort needed to pull a wagon behind their tricycle.

Children may learn more about the importance of *simple machines* from these play experiences than from interacting with smaller versions that are used in the classroom. For example, while pulleys may be fun to play with inside, they are really needed in the outside area to hoist the bird feeder beyond the reach of neighborhood cats (Activity 4.2). They learn that the *wheel and axle* on the tricycle, which allows them to use the pedals to move forward (Activity 4.9), works much better than trying to scoot along by pushing down on the ground.

EXPLORING MESSY MATERIALS

A third benefit of outdoor STEM experiences is the lack of inhibition that comes from working in an environment where spills do not matter. Children can mix colors on a large surface (Activity 4.11), hang dripping clothes up to dry, and perhaps best of all, play with bubbles (Activities 4.12, 4,13, and 4.14). The activities in this chapter help teachers utilize outdoor time to foster scientific inquiry.

BALLOONS ALOFT

EARTH SCIENCE, PHYSICS

Materials

○ package of balloons

○ straws

Activity Description

Most children are familiar with balloons. They may tie them to a string and run, with the balloon trailing behind, or tap the balloon with their hands and try to keep it from falling to the ground. In this activity, children are encouraged to use the *force* of moving air, which they create by blowing through straws, to keep their balloons aloft. Even a small amount of air can send the balloons soaring. When children play with balloons outside, they may also notice how breezes blowing on the playground move the balloons in particular directions.

Some children become upset when their balloon pops and the wonderful toy is ruined. As balloons will definitely hit the ground and pop during this activity, teachers are encouraged to have a number of extra balloons in reserve. Then children can experiment with the balloons without fear of breaking them.

NOTE: Some children are allergic to vinyl, which is often used in balloons. Check for any allergies before doing this activity with children. Balloons are also a choking hazard for younger children. Keep any unused or burst balloons safely away from younger children.

Science Content

Moving air creates a force that can move objects. Although balloons can float temporarily, eventually they fall to the ground because of gravity. Moving air, however, can have enough force to keep balloons aloft much longer.

Mathematics Content

The mathematical content of this activity is mainly related to directional terms, which are part of geometry. Children will notice balloons rising as they blow air beneath them, and falling when they stop blowing air. Balloons will also change their lateral direction based on what part of the balloon is impacted by the moving air.

Connections to Technology and Engineering

For centuries the energy of moving air has been captured by windmills and converted to mechanical energy, which can then be used to grind grain, pump water, or run other equipment. Today wind turbines are used to produce electricity.

Comments and Questions to Support Inquiry

- What's keeping your balloon up in the air?

- Can you make your balloon go back and forth between you and Emma?

- What direction does your balloon float if you don't blow on it? The wind must be moving your balloon.

- Where do you have to blow on your balloon to make it go toward me?

FEED THE BIRDS PULLEY

LIFE SCIENCE, PHYSICS

Materials

- ○ bird feeder
- ○ 2-inch diameter pulley
- ○ birdseed
- ○ children's binoculars
- ○ nonfiction picture books of birds
- ○ digital camera or camcorder (optional)

Activity Description

A bird feeder is an excellent way to direct children's attention to the various species of birds that live in their program's neighborhood. Children are much more aware of and interested in birds if they can take part in caring for them. To make the bird feeder accessible to children but also keep the birds safe from predators, the bird feeder is attached to a pulley mounted to a tree branch, an outcropping of the building, or another high location on the playground. Children can lower the feeder each day, add food for the birds, and then raise the feeder to a safe height. The rope can then be tied to a hook to keep the feeder in place until the next day.

It is helpful if the bird feeder can be positioned so that it is visible from the classroom. The birds may be more likely to visit the feeder when there are no children on the playground. Children's binoculars can be placed near the classroom windows so that children can closely observe the birds from inside the room. Books that identify birds can be placed in the same area so that children can learn to name the types of birds that visit their feeder.

 ## Science Content

A **pulley** is one of the six simple machines. It consists of a grooved wheel that can move freely on its axle. A rope threaded through the grooves of the wheel is

attached to the object that one wishes to move. The purpose of the pulley is to change the direction of the **force** applied to the rope. When children pull down on the rope attached to the bird feeder, the feeder moves upward to a height beyond where the children can reach. Conversely, when children release the rope, gravity pulls the bird feeder down so that they can refill it. Pulleys are inexpensive and readily available in hardware or building supply stores.

A bird feeder lures birds from the local environment to a place where children can more easily observe them. Informational books for children, such as *About Birds: A Guide for Children* by Cathryn Sill, can increase children's knowledge and understanding of the birds in their neighborhood.

Mathematics Content

If a ⅛ cup is used to fill the feeder, children can take turns and count each unit as it is added. After eight children have added their birdseed, teachers can point out that they have put 1 full cup into the feeder. Later, perhaps at the sensory table, children can experiment with adding ⅛ cup of birdseed to a 1-cup measure. The bird-feeding activity therefore connects to number and operations and to measurement. As children use the pulley, they experience the directional changes of down and up. Directionality is part of geometry.

 Connections to Technology and Engineering

The pulley is itself an application of technology. Another useful technological addition to this activity is several pairs of children's binoculars, which enable children to observe the birds more closely from inside the classroom and thus experience the effects of magnification. Teachers and children can also take photos or videos of the birds visiting the feeder if a digital camera or video recorder is available.

Pulleys are often used in construction and civil engineering, from the trucks and machinery that are needed to construct buildings and roads to the pulleys used in elevators and escalators. Children can see examples of pulleys in children's books about construction, such as *Machines at Work* by Byron Barton, *Building a Road* by Henry Pluckrose, and *A Year at a Construction Site* by Nicholas Harris.

Comments and Questions to Support Inquiry

- Let's look in this book to identify the birds at our feeder. Can you find a gray bird with a black head like the bird that is eating now?

- How many birds are eating at the feeder right now?

- Let go of the rope just slightly and watch what happens to the feeder.

- Pull on the rope until the feeder is almost up to the tree branch. I'm glad we have the pulley. We wouldn't be able to put the bird feeder up high enough without it.

- When you pull down on the rope, which way does the bird feeder go?

TRACING SHADOWS

EARTH SCIENCE

Materials

○ sidewalk chalk

○ digital camera (optional)

Activity Description

Shadows can be very deceiving, which is perhaps why children find them so interesting. Shadows change in size and position. Sometimes they appear on the wall, and sometimes they are on the ground. One moment a shadow seems to be following a child around, and the next moment it vanishes. This activity helps young children gain a context for when and where shadows occur, and learn what factors affect their appearance.

This activity should take place on a sunny day when it is not too close to noon. Children can work in pairs. While one child stands still, another child can use sidewalk chalk to trace her partner's shadow. Children can take turns posing for shadow drawings and tracing shadows for their friends.

The appropriate children's names should be written inside the shadow outlines so that children can return to them at various times during the day and compare their current shadow to the shadow outline that was previously traced.

Science Content

A shadow is an area that cannot be reached by a light source because an object is blocking the light. The shadow's image is a reverse projection of the object that is blocking the light. Therefore, if a child who is creating a shadow lifts his right hand, the shadow will appear to lift its left hand. The length of a shadow that is created by the sun increases as the angle between the sun and the earth decreases. For this reason, shadows are long early in the morning, steadily decrease in length until noon, and then gradually increase until they are again quite long before sunset.

 ## Mathematics Content

The mathematics content in this activity relates to measurement. Children can compare the length of their shadows at various times during the day to the size of the outline that is drawn on the sidewalk. Measurement terms such as *little*, *big*, *longer*, and *shorter* can be used during these observations.

 ## Connections to Technology

Teachers may wish to take digital photographs of children tracing the shadows of their peers. Later, when the shadows are either larger or smaller than the lines, the photos may help children verify that originally the shadow was within the chalk lines.

Comments and Questions to Support Inquiry

- What happened to your shadow? Is it the same size as it was when your friend traced it this morning?

- Do you remember where the sun was this morning? Is it in the same place now? Remember to just glance up—don't look right at the sun.

- Let's trace shadows again tomorrow. Do you think the same thing will happen?

- Look. If I stand here, part of my shadow is on the ground, and part is on the wall.

THE ANTS COME MARCHING

LIFE SCIENCE

Materials

○ 4 lids from small plastic containers

○ small amounts of sugar, cheese, crackers, and water

○ magnetic board

○ note cards

○ labels for the materials, placed in each lid

○ digital camera (optional)

Activity Description

Ants are part of most people's environments, whether they live in urban, suburban, or rural areas. Children notice ants on the sidewalk, in the grass, and sometimes on trees or plants. The movement of ants often seems haphazard. This activity helps children learn more about materials that attract ants.

Children can help the teacher place small amounts of various foods in shallow lids that are labeled with the type of food each contains. Sugar (sweet), cheese (protein), and crackers (carbohydrate) are good choices because they represent different types of food. Water can be placed in a fourth dish. The dishes should be located in a part of the playground where they will not be stepped on or disturbed—perhaps just outside the fence. At various times during the day, small groups of children can return to the dishes and count how many ants are in each. The observations can be discussed during group time.

If digital photographs are taken of each observation, they can be projected onto the wall or a screen during a group discussion. After counting the ants, children can put the foods in order for each observation based on the number of ants that appeared on each food lid.

A magnetic board may be particularly useful for organizing the data. The foods can be listed on note cards, which can be displayed on the magnetic board as the data are analyzed. If desired, prints of the photographs can be mounted next to the appropriate labels.

 Mathematics Content

Because this investigation focuses on which foods ants like the best, quantification of the ants on the various food trays is critical. Some children may make a perceptual comparison to determine which food plate has the most ants, while other children may attempt to count the ants. Regardless of strategy, this experience supports the development of number sense. Later, when the foods are ordered according to the number of ants on the lids, children work within the mathematical area of data analysis.

 Connections to Technology

Digital photography and later projection of the images enhance this activity because the photographs preserve the children's observations. In addition, it is easier to count the ants in the photographs because they appear larger and don't move around, as in real-time observations. Setting the camera to record the date and time of each photograph also preserves the precise time of the observation.

Comments and Questions to Support Inquiry

- Look at all the ants that showed up to eat. Which food lid has the most ants on it? Which has the fewest?

- We have six observations of our ants to look at, some from yesterday and some from today. Let's chart how many ants are on each food lid for each observation.

- Now let's put the foods in order on the magnetic board for each observation. Did the same food have the most ants each time?

Science Content

One of the ways in which scientists learn about animals is through careful observation. In this case, the children are conducting an experiment in addition to making observations because they have introduced specific items into the environment of the ants. Children may observe ants carrying rather large pieces of food. Ants can lift objects that weigh twenty times their weight.

Some children may be interested in learning more about ants. The children's book *Ants* by Melissa Stewart combines vivid photographs with an appropriate amount of text for young children.

LARGE VARIABLE-SLOPE RAMPS

PHYSICS

Materials

○ collapsible clothes rack

○ several lightweight pieces of wood, 48 by 12 by ¼ inches

○ strip of wood, 12 inches long, for each incline

○ wood glue

○ sturdy trucks or cars

○ sidewalk chalk

Activity Description

The outside area is an excellent venue for children to study large variable-slope *inclines*. In this activity, the frame to support the inclines is a collapsible clothes rack, which can be easily transported outdoors each day. The ramps consist of lightweight wood, 48 by 12 by ¼ inches, with a strip of wood glued to the back of each board approximately 2 inches from the top. This allows children to hook the ramps over the bars on the frame. Because the wood is so light in weight, it can easily be repositioned by the children. They can roll sturdy trucks down the inclines and compare how the slope affects the speed of the truck and how far it travels. Because children can work on either side of the clothes frame, four is an ideal number of ramps to maximize participation.

On the first few days that the ramps are introduced, children are likely to be mainly interested in manipulating the inclines and racing the trucks. Later in the week, children may become more interested in measuring the distance the trucks travel. An easy way to help children conduct these measurements is to draw chalk lines on the pavement at 1-foot intervals. Children can count the number of lines the trucks cross to gauge how far they have traveled.

Science Content

An **inclined plane** is one of the six classical **simple machines**. It allows individuals to slide or roll objects from one level to another, which requires less **force** than lifting them. The more gradual the slope of an incline, the less force that is needed to move an object up the incline, because the force is distributed over a greater distance. The speed at which an object moves down an incline is related to the steepness, or slope, of the incline, as is the distance it travels.

 ## Mathematics Content

Racing trucks is an exciting way for children to think about measurement. In this activity, the lines that are drawn on the pavement at regular intervals provide uniform units for children to quantify as they measure distance. These lines are much less confusing than the many lines and symbols that appear on standard yardsticks and measuring tapes. For this reason, pre-drawn lines provide a transition for later understanding of standard measurement tools.

  ## Connections to Technology and Engineering

Because an incline is one of the six simple machines, this activity allows children to explore one of the earliest types of technology. The relationship between the angle of an incline and the speed at which objects roll down it is critical to the field of civil engineering, which includes the design and building of roads.

Comments and Questions to Support Inquiry

- Does the truck that gets to the bottom first also go the farthest?

- How did Linda get her car to go so far? Where did she put the ramp?

- Is it possible to make the ramp so steep that it no longer works well? What happens to the truck when the ramp is too steep?

- When we record the distance the trucks travel, which part of the truck should we look at? We want to be sure we all measure the same way so we can compare our measurements.

- If the truck is in between the lines, how should we notate that on our measurement sheet?

LAUNDRY DAY: HORIZONTAL PULLEY

PHYSICS

Materials

- ○ clothesline
- ○ 2 pulleys
- ○ doll clothes
- ○ clothespins
- ○ bucket of water

Activity Description

Children love to wash doll clothes. In this activity, a clothesline is attached to two pulleys mounted along a fence. As children finish washing each item, they can attach it to the clothesline with clothespins and use the pulley system to move the clothes out of the way, making room for the next item to be washed.

 ## Science Content

There are two types of **simple machines** used in this activity. The first is the **pulley**, which in this activity is used to move objects horizontally. By pulling one of the ropes toward themselves, children can move the clothes hanging on the other rope away from themselves.

The second type of simple machine used in this activity is a double **lever**, used in the pinch-style clothespins. A lever is a bar that rests on a pivot point, called the **fulcrum**. In this case, two bars are joined at the fulcrum with a spring mechanism. By applying **force** to one end of the bars (pinching), the other end is forced open. The spring causes the clothespin to snap shut when the force is released.

Mathematics Content

Focusing on two types of mathematical content enhances this activity. Although the primary objective is to help children understand the function and purpose of a pulley, the use of directional terms, such as *left, right, toward, away from, closer,* and *farther away,* is an important aspect of the activity. Quantification can also be incorporated into the experience. Children can compare the number of items of clothing that are hanging from the clothesline to the number of clothespins that are used. This may involve use of either **one-to-one correspondence** or counting strategies.

Connections to Technology and Engineering

Pulleys are an example of technology that has been used by humans for thousands of years and continue to be an important component of many types of machinery. Children may notice pulleys on cranes, sailboats, and tow trucks. Pulleys are used in both mechanical and construction engineering.

Comments and Questions to Support Inquiry

- Why did the clothes move to the left when I pulled to the right? What makes that happen?

- I'm glad the clothesline is attached to pulleys. Now we don't have to walk across the yard to hang up our wet doll clothes.

- What happens when you pull the rope toward you?

- Do we have more doll clothes or more clothespins on our clothesline? How can we find out for sure?

RAISE THE FLAG: VERTICAL PULLEY

PHYSICS

Materials

- ○ dowel or broomstick, approximately 1 inch in diameter and 5 feet long
- ○ piece of 1-inch-thick wood, 20 by 12 inches
- ○ wood glue
- ○ 2 small pulleys
- ○ 2 small cup hooks
- ○ rope or cord
- ○ neutral-colored bandanna
- ○ fabric markers

Activity Description

This activity offers children another opportunity to observe the workings of a *pulley*. The flagpole is made from a 5-foot length of dowel, 1 inch in diameter. (An old wooden broomstick will serve the purpose.) The baseboard is a 20-by-12-inch piece of 1-inch-thick wood. The dowel is inserted into a 1-inch hole in the baseboard and glued. Cup hooks are mounted near the top and bottom of the pole, and the pulleys are hung on the hooks. The cord is then threaded through the pulleys and tied.

Children can design individual or class flags and use the pulley to raise them during outside time. A bandanna that is a neutral color makes a good background for the flags, and fabric markers can be used for the lettering and designs. The flags can be easily attached to the rope with chip-bag clips. Through their frequent experiences with the pulley, children learn that by pulling down on the rope, they can make the flag go up.

Science Content

This activity incorporates a vertical pulley mechanism such as that used in Activity 4.2, so the scientific content remains the same. In this application, however, children are physically closer to the pulley, so they can observe it more closely. Occasionally, the frame can be laid on the ground so that children can handle the pulley and examine it more carefully. The pulley frame can also be used inside the classroom.

Mathematics Content

The pulley on the flagpole allows the vertical position of the flag to be changed. Observations and conversations regarding the movement of the flag incorporate knowledge of position and direction, as well as the language that describes them. These are components of the geometry standard. If desired, teachers can mark 1-foot intervals along the pole. This allows children to measure the distance the flag travels as it moves up and down the pole.

 Connections to Technology and Engineering

This activity gives children the opportunity to experiment with an early form of technology because the pulley is one of the six **simple machines**. Pulleys are widely used in machinery and in the trucks and equipment used for construction. Photographs in children's books can help children make the connection between the type of pulley they are using and the many other uses of pulleys.

Comments and Questions to Support Inquiry

- It's your turn to raise the flag. Can you make it go to the top of the pole? Could you have reached the top of the pole without the pulley?

- When I clap my hands, stop moving the flag, and we'll measure how high it has traveled so far.

- Let's count backward while Daniel lowers the flag. Watch for each time the flag crosses a line on the pole.

- Could we use a pulley if we needed to lower something into a hole?

CREATING WIND CHIMES

EARTH SCIENCE, PHYSICS

Materials

○ thick stick, approximately 12 inches long, for each child

○ selection of metal, wooden, and natural objects, as described in the activity

○ cord or wire

Activity Description

Many natural objects make lovely sounds when they are tapped together. In this activity, children discover that the *force* of moving air has the power to move objects, which can create sounds when the objects touch one another. To make wind chimes, children can select various sizes of metal washers, brass hoops, seashells, bells, pieces of bamboo, small sections of metal pipe, and sticks or wooden dowels. They can even include shapes or letters made from self-hardening clay. Brass hoops, seashells, bells, and bamboo are available in craft stores, and metal washers and steel pipe can be found in hardware or building supply stores. Long pieces of bamboo, dowels, and metal pipes can be cut to various lengths and sanded to remove sharp edges. Holes can then be drilled through the pieces so that they can be suspended. Small holes can even be carefully drilled through seashells.

A major goal of this activity is for children to observe the difference in the sounds that various materials create. This is related to both the size and the material of the object. Plenty of time should be allocated for children to gently tap objects and listen to the sounds they create. To create pleasing sounds, the objects must be able to vibrate freely. For this reason, teachers should tie loops of wire or string through the objects before the activity begins. Children can hold these loops to suspend the objects while they gently tap them with a pencil or stick. After children have selected the objects they want to use for their chimes, they can attach their chimes to a stick. The wind chimes can then be hung in places on the playground where they can move freely in the wind.

Science Content

The material that an object is made from affects its tone quality, which is called **timbre** in music. This is why a violin and flute sound different from one another even when they play the same notes. Another physical property that affects sound is the size of the vibrating object. Larger objects produce lower tones than smaller objects even if they are otherwise identical. All of these variations in sound are encompassed in the scientific area of **acoustics**.

Another science concept explored in this activity is the force of moving air. While children can't see air, they can feel its movement when a breeze blows. The wind chimes give children another way to measure the force of moving air, since the chimes jingle louder when the wind is stronger.

Mathematics Content

Children have many opportunities in this activity to compare the size and shapes of objects, which connects this learning experience to measurement and geometry.

 Connections to Technology and Engineering

Technology is increasingly being used to harness wind power. Engineers have designed wind turbines to maximize the power that moving air can generate. Some children may have seen wind farms with thousands of wind turbines. Photographs of older windmills and more modern wind turbines can be found on the Internet.

Comments and Questions to Support Inquiry

- The bamboo and the pipe are the same length, but they make different sounds. Why do you think that is?

- I want my wind chime to make quiet sounds. What materials do you think I should use?

- Close your eyes for a minute while I play the long pipe and the short pipe. See if you can tell which one I'm playing.

- Our wind chimes were loud yesterday. Why don't we hear them today?

TRICYCLE TRACKS

EARTH SCIENCE, PHYSICS

Materials

○ tricycles, or other riding toys

○ tub of water

○ towels

Activity Description

Teachers can vary the standard tricycle-riding experience by creating a wet area for children to ride through. If there is no depression in the pavement to hold water and create a puddle, old bath towels can be used for the activity. Keep wet towels nearby in a tub of water. When children ride over a towel that is placed on the pavement, they can view the tracks produced by their tricycle, something that is usually not visible to them. Three parallel lines should emerge. Children should notice that no matter what direction they travel, the lines stay consistently the same distance apart. Also, the wet lines grow gradually fainter and disappear as all of the water is transferred from the tricycle tires to the pavement.

Science Content

One of the properties of water is the ability to stick well to other materials. This is called *adhesion*. When water comes in contact with other surfaces, its adhesive properties are stronger than its *cohesive properties*, which would tend to hold it together. Children

notice this adhesive property of water. They like to step in puddles and make footprints, or dip their fingers in water and draw designs. Teachers can point out that when the tricycle rolls over the wet towel, some of the water transfers to the tires. In contrast, when the tricycle rolls over a dry towel or a piece of cardboard, it does not make tracks.

 Mathematics Content

This activity gives children an opportunity to create and observe parallel lines, an important concept in geometry. Parallel lines are lines that never cross, or intersect, as long as they continue in the same direction. The wheels on the tricycle are a fixed distance apart, so the lines they create also remain a fixed distance apart.

  Connections to Technology and Engineering

Children may be surprised that the round tricycle wheels create straight lines. The tracks produced by the water allow them to observe this outcome, which in turn may draw their attention to the **wheel and axle** mechanism of the tricycle. The wheel and axle is a historic technological innovation that remains an important part of our lives. Tricycles themselves are, in fact, a form of technology!

Comments and Questions to Support Inquiry

- How many parallel lines did your tricycle make?

- How did you make three lines? I only see two wheels on the back of your tricycle.

- If one line curves, do the other lines curve too?

- Can you make tire tracks by riding over this piece of cardboard?

- Here's a dry towel. Try riding over it, and see if you make tire tracks.

CONTAINER GARDEN

LIFE SCIENCE

Materials

- ○ rolling cart
- ○ flowerpots
- ○ potting soil
- ○ seeds or seedlings
- ○ water
- ○ fertilizer
- ○ digital camera

Activity Description

Watching plants grow is an important learning experience for young children. Unfortunately, growing experiences at school are often limited to planting a seed and taking it home as soon as it sprouts. Many programs, particularly those in urban environments, may not have a safe place for children to grow a garden and watch the plants over time. A container garden can solve this dilemma. Vegetables and flowers can be planted in pots and rolled outside each day to receive the necessary amount of sunlight. They can be returned to the building at the end of the day. Plants can be planted earlier in the spring when they are housed in containers, because they can be taken inside at night so that they won't suffer frost damage.

Teachers have a wide range of options for what to plant in container gardens. Seed packages usually have growth rates listed, so teachers can select plants that will reach maturity during the school year. It is helpful to plant seedlings as well as seeds so that children can observe the root structures before the plants are transferred to a permanent pot. Green

beans are particularly fast growers. The beans are ready to eat within fifty days. Pots can be rolled out to the playground on a cart, or children can carefully transport them in canvas bags with handles.

 ### Science Content

Children gain much more knowledge about plant growth when they can observe plants over an extended period. Language related to the growth, parts, structure, and use of plants can be repeated over time until children begin to use the new vocabulary themselves. It is particularly exciting for children to realize that they can grow their own food. In today's world, most children do not have the opportunity to observe vegetables while they are growing, so they have little connection with the growth process necessary to produce the food they eat.

 ### Mathematics Content

Mathematical language is an important part of the conversations that revolve around container gardens. Children can compare the sizes of various plants, look for **symmetry** in their leaves, and notice whether they grow vertically, such as sunflowers, or horizontally, such as pumpkin vines. Children can also record and later graph the number of vegetables each plant produces. They can also measure the growth of plants over time.

  ### Connections to Technology and Engineering

Teachers can introduce technology by taking regular digital photographs of the plants. This helps children remember their growth cycle. Children's comments and observations can be included with the photographs in a PowerPoint presentation that is burned on discs to share with parents. As children water and fertilize the plants, teachers can explain that agricultural engineers study and develop techniques and materials to help plants grow better. Nancy Dickmann's children's books *Farm Machines*, *Food from Farms*, and *Jobs on a Farm* can help children understand this connection.

Comments and Questions to Support Inquiry

- Here's a photo of our pumpkin plant when it had flowers. Look at the plant now. There's something else growing where the flowers used to be.

- How many beans are hanging from our green bean plant? Let's count again tomorrow and see if we have the same number of green beans.

- Which one of our plants is the tallest?

SPRAYING THE RAINBOW

PHYSICS

Materials

○ large piece of white paper, or white sheet

○ red, blue, and yellow food coloring

○ spray bottles

○ water

Activity Description

For this activity, children can experiment with color mixing on a large surface. Large pieces of fabric or paper are mounted to an outdoor wall or fence. As children spray water colored with red, blue, and yellow food coloring onto these surfaces, they discover the new colors that are created. Children can also observe the movement of the water, particularly if the background material is relatively absorbent.

Although easel paper can be used for this activity, fabric is a better choice because it absorbs some of the water and allows children to observe how the colors spread out across the fabric. A white sheet makes an excellent backdrop for the colored water, but light-colored burlap, cotton, or muslin can also be used. By conducting this activity outside, worries about spills and cleanup are minimized.

Science Content

Two science concepts are embedded in this activity. The first is the effect of mixing colored pigments—in this case red, blue, and yellow. While these are conventionally referred to as the three primary colors, meaning that in various combinations they can produce all other colors, this predates contemporary color theory. The actual primary colors are **magenta**, **cyan** (pronounced *SIGH-an*), and yellow. Perception of color occurs because the colored water (or paint, crayons, and other pigments) subtracts (absorbs) certain wavelengths of light and reflects the remaining wavelengths. Children will notice that when blue and red overlap, a shade of purple is produced. Yellow and blue produce a shade of green, and yellow and red produce a shade of orange.

The second science concept that children can observe in this activity is **capillary action**, which is the ability of a liquid to flow against the **force** of gravity to occupy the narrow spaces between fibers. Children may notice that the colors spread out in all directions from the original concentration of colored water.

✚ Mathematics Content

Children will notice changes in the area of the backdrop that is colored as they spray water onto it. As the area that has color increases, the area that is white decreases; however, the entire area of the backdrop remains the same. While this concept seems obvious to adults, it may not be to children. As the colored portion of the backdrop increases, children may think that the area of the paper or sheet itself has also changed. Concepts of area are a component of geometry.

  Connections to Technology and Engineering

The spray bottles employ a pump, which is a simple but important example of technology. When children pull the trigger on the spray bottle, the area inside the head of the bottle is reduced, and water is forced out. When the trigger is released, the area inside the head of the bottle expands, and new water moves up a tube inside the bottle to fill this empty space. More information about how spray bottles work can be found on the website www.howstuffworks.com.

Understanding capillary action is important in agricultural engineering, where maintaining adequate soil moisture is often critical. Children can watch this capillary action when they soak up water with a sponge, drip juice on a napkin, or pour water into plant containers.

Comments and Questions to Support Inquiry

- Watch the blue water fan out across the sheet. It's moving in all directions.

- What happened at this spot on the sheet, where the red water and blue water touched each other?

- I see green on the fabric, but there is no green water in any of the bottles. How did you make the color green?

- Do you think the fabric will still have all of these colors after it dries out?

❗ Misconception Alert

Modern color theory has determined that the primary colors for mixing pigments, such as paint or ink, are magenta, cyan, and yellow, rather than the conventionally recognized colors of red, blue, and yellow.

BUBBLE CLUSTERS

PHYSICS

Materials

- ○ several bowls
- ○ dish-washing liquid
- ○ water
- ○ straws
- ○ digital camera

Activity Description

Clusters of bubbles form when children blow air through a straw into a bowl containing a small amount of soapy water. While children are initially interested in the size of the bubble clusters they can produce, they can be directed to look at the geometric shapes created by the interlocking bubbles once the initial excitement ebbs.

Children also like to pop the bubbles. If they insert a dry finger into the bubbles, the bubbles quickly pop; however, if they moisten a finger by first dipping it into some bubble solution, the finger can pass through the bubbles without popping them. Children are also fascinated by the colors and reflections created by bubbles.

All that is required to make the bubble solution is a squirt of liquid dish-washing soap added to a bowl containing a small amount of water. A towel placed underneath the bowls can absorb any spills. For young children, who may suck soapy water up through the straw, simply use a safety pin to poke a hole near the top of the straw. Children will still be able to blow air through the straw, but they will not be able to suck up the liquid.

Science Content

Because children are blowing air into the water through their straws, they are likely to determine that air is filling the inside of the bubbles. The water forms a film that encases the bubble because of the *surface* *tension* of the water. The soap helps keep the bubble intact longer by strengthening the weakest parts of the bubble.

The colors produced by bubbles are due to light, which reflects from both the outer and inner surfaces. The colors change as a result of the various thicknesses of the bubble film, combined with the interference caused by the various reflected wavelengths.

Mathematics Content

Geometry is a major component of bubble experiments. Single bubbles are spherical because a sphere is the minimal area needed to enclose a given volume. The interconnecting bubbles in a cluster produce many domed hexagonal (six-sided) and pentagonal (five-sided) shapes. Children may also observe rectangular and triangular forms. A plane is created where two bubbles merge.

Connections to Technology and Engineering

Although the geometric shapes produced by bubbles can be clearly observed, the bubbles usually do not last long. Digital photographs of the children's bubble clusters preserve the bubble images, allowing children as much time as needed to count the sides of the shapes.

Comments and Questions to Support Inquiry

- What happens when you blow air into the soapy water?

- I'm going to take photographs of some of the bubble clusters so that we can count the shapes produced by the bubbles. Then we can make a bubble shape chart.

- The bubbles are *iridescent*. The colors seem to change as I look at them from different angles.

- What happens when you touch a bubble? Now dip your finger in this bowl of bubble solution, and try again. What happened this time?

CREATING BUBBLE WANDS

PHYSICS

Materials

○ pipe cleaners

○ assorted objects with closed and open perimeters

○ bubble solution, or dish-washing liquid and water

○ bowls

Activity Description

In this activity, children use pipe cleaners and many different found objects to create bubble wands. Two questions are the focus of the children's explorations:

1. Since bubbles are round (spherical), do bubble wands have to be round?

2. What are the necessary characteristics of a bubble wand?

In response to the first question, many children may predict that bubble wands have to be round, because the bubble wands that come with commercial bottles of bubble solution are usually round, and free-floating bubbles have a spherical shape. With regard to the second question, children may not be able to form a prediction until they have performed their experiments. They may have had too little experience to make a prediction.

Large bottles of bubble solution are inexpensive and readily available except during the winter months in cold climates. Teachers may find that it is cost-effective to just buy commercial bubble solution. On the other hand, bubble solution can be easily made from 1 cup of liquid dish-washing detergent combined with enough water to make a gallon of solution. A tablespoon of glycerin added to the solution will make the bubbles last longer but is not necessary.

Teachers should encourage children to create various shapes of bubble wands with the pipe cleaners and test them out. Children may want to record their

results by drawing a picture of the shape of the bubble wand and the shape of the bubble it produced. The found objects should include materials that have closed and open edges, since closed perimeters are needed to create bubbles. Here are some examples of closed- and open-perimeter items.

Closed perimeter:

- bottle cap loop
- slotted spoon
- mesh strainer
- key ring
- stretch headband (continuous loop)
- children's scissors (handle)
- small flowerpot with a hole in the bottom
- can, with both top and bottom removed
- belt buckle
- cookie cutter
- plastic vegetable basket (square holes)

Open perimeter:

- fork
- comb
- plastic headband
- baby link, from a set of interlocking links
- horseshoe
- tweezers
- cup hook
- U-bolt

 ### Science Content

The air inside a bubble pushes out against all points on the surface of the bubble with equal pressure. This is why single bubbles always assume a spherical shape, regardless of the shape of the bubble blower, after they are blown into the air and are no longer constrained by the frame.

 ### Mathematics Content

Geometry is a focus of this activity as children create various shapes of bubble wands to try out. Children also become aware of open and closed lines since a closed perimeter is necessary to create a bubble wand.

Connections to Technology

Bubble technology is used in products as diverse as shaving cream and firefighting foam. Recently, air bubbles have been used to contain oil spills. Bubbles are forced under the water. As they rise to the surface, they create an air-bubble curtain that the oil cannot pass, separating the oil from the water.

Comments and Questions to Support Inquiry

- What do the bubbles look like when you blow through the mesh strainer?
- Why does the stretch headband make a bubble, but the plastic headband doesn't?
- Jamie made a square bubble blower. Let's watch him blow a bubble and see what shape the bubble is.

INSIDE A BUBBLE

PHYSICS

Materials

○ child's wading pool or washtub

○ several gallons of bubble solution

○ plastic hoop, such as a hula hoop, large enough to fit around a child

○ digital camera or video recorder

Activity Description

This activity gives children the exciting opportunity to observe the world from inside a bubble. The bubble solution is poured into a large plastic or metal container, such as a baby wading pool, a washtub, or a large storage container. The bubble is created with a plastic hoop that is large enough to fit easily over the child but small enough to fit inside the tub. An adult pulls the hoop out of the solution and lifts it vertically until the bubble wall extends above the child's head. It is helpful if another adult is standing by to take a photograph or video of the extraordinary event.

 ## Science Content

In this activity, a cylindrical bubble wall is created that surrounds the child. Children can observe the bubble film from this unique position. The activity illustrates the stretchy nature of bubble film. Additional information about the physical properties of bubbles is included in Activities 4.12 and 4.13.

 ## Mathematics Content

This activity illustrates the creation of a cylinder, a three-dimensional geometric form, starting with the circular bubble frame at the bottom that extends upward to create curved walls. As children carefully turn their heads, they can see that the inner wall of the cylinder is curved in each direction. Children on

the outside of the bubble can view a large cylinder being formed.

 ## Connections to Technology

Using a digital camera or video recorder connects the activity to technology. Other uses of bubble technology are described in Activity 4.13.

Comments and Questions to Support Inquiry

• What does the world look like when you're inside a bubble?

• What had to happen to make the cylinder taller?

• Do you think we could make a bubble that is tall enough to cover a grown-up?

STEM in a Project-Centered Curriculum

The kindergarten class was excited when they arrived at school on Monday. A large pumpkin was placed in the center of the science table, just inside the classroom. There was a sign on the wall behind the pumpkin. "It says, 'What is inside the pumpkin?'" said Morgan, who could read. Some of the children had seen pumpkins before in the grocery store, but most of them had never seen the inside of a pumpkin.

"You have all week to think about what could be inside the pumpkin," said Mr. James, their teacher. "You can write your guesses on the clipboard on the science table. On Friday, we'll open up the pumpkin and find out what is really inside."

By Friday, there were a wide variety of responses on the prediction sheet. Only a few children predicted seeds and "gooey stuff." Several children thought there might be candy inside, because their only association with pumpkins was Halloween. The children were amazed at all of the seeds they found inside the pumpkin. They took turns separating the seeds from the pulp and rinsing them in water. At group time, the class counted the seeds. Then the teacher asked them what they wanted to do with the seeds. Several children immediately said that they wanted to plant them.

"You can't plant them now," said Anya. "It's too cold outside."

"We could save them and plant them next spring," suggested Mr. James.

"Could we plant them in pots and put them by the big window?" asked Garth.

Mr. James considered this suggestion. The back wall of the classroom was mostly windows, and since it faced south, it would let in lots of light. "Why don't we try Garth's idea?" he suggested. "We can plant some of the seeds right now and see if they grow. We can even plant a few outside and see if Anya is right that it's too cold for them to grow. We can also save some to plant in the spring if the seeds don't grow well now."

The children were enthusiastic about this idea. They soon started a conversation about what the pumpkin plants would look like.

"I think the seeds will grow into trees, and then the trees will grow pumpkins," said Danny.

"No, we'll see green leaves come up, but the pumpkin will be under the ground," argued Cody. "It's like potatoes. You can't see them because they grow under the ground."

"It could just be like a flower," said Sarah. "It grows a plant, and then the pumpkin grows on the plant like a flower."

"That would never work," Cody explained. "The pumpkin is too big. It would knock the plant down."

Mr. James was pleased with this conversation because it showed the connections the children were making to what they already knew. It seemed that a pumpkin project was now under way. He quickly scrapped his journal-writing plan for the afternoon and instead suggested that the children draw a picture of the plant they thought might grow from the pumpkin seed. Over the next few weeks, they would continue to make drawings of the plants as they sprouted, which would improve their observational skills and help them visualize and remember their learning. He would also adjust the math inquiry and problem-solving activities to center around pumpkins, and the growing plants would allow the children to begin exploring measurement concepts. During lunch, he mused to a colleague, "I always plan planting activities for the spring, but now is when my class is interested in seeds, because they just discovered where pumpkin seeds come from. It will be interesting to see where this new project goes."

· · ·

INTRODUCTION TO PROJECT WORK

Many teachers are familiar with the concept of an emergent curriculum in which the interests and ideas of particular children or groups influence curriculum decisions in the classroom. For example, if a group of children were particularly interested in trains, then the teacher might integrate books and manipulative materials related to trains into the curriculum. The teacher might also transform the dramatic play area into a train or train station. Projects take emergent curriculum a significant step further. In project work, children become involved in extensive, in-depth investigations of questions that inspire their curiosity. The teacher serves as a facilitator who through careful comments and questions helps children focus and evaluate their thinking. The teacher provides materials and time for children to experiment, create, and observe. And, importantly, the teacher documents learning for ongoing reflection.

The inspiration for the current worldwide interest in preschool and kindergarten project work comes from the Reggio Emilia Schools in Italy (Edwards, Gandini, and Forman 1998). For the past several decades, early childhood educators have been inspired and amazed by the extraordinary exhibits of projects that have emerged from these schools. Countless books and articles have been written, and educators from the Reggio schools regularly conduct seminars throughout the world to help teachers and administrators adapt key aspects of Reggio educational practice to their own situations.

One focus of the Reggio approach to learning is investigative projects, which can be undertaken by a few children, a group of students, or an entire class. These projects may be brief in duration or last for an extended time, depending on the interest of the children involved. Projects may evolve from questions that children have, such as "What is a crowd?" or from ideas introduced by the teacher. In one well-known example, when a school needed a new table, the children were charged with informing the carpenter of the dimensions required for the table. This led to the extensive exploration and construction of measurement concepts (Reggio Children 1997).

The pumpkin scenario described in the vignette at the beginning of this chapter is an example of a project that arose from the interests and questions of the children. Although the teacher intentionally focused their attention on inquiry through his initial prediction activity, he did not expect the discovery of pumpkin seeds to lead to a project. It was the intense interest of the children that propelled an interesting science activity into an investigative project. The ice project (Project 5.1) is similar. It grew from the interest of a group of children in creating a skating rink for the playground into a project that eventually involved the entire class in the investigation of how to make ice.

Other projects may be introduced by the teacher but follow a course determined by the children. An example is the tree project (Project 5.2). The teacher introduced the project based on children's typical interest in seasonal changes but never expected that the children would want to build their own tree. Incorporation of the graphic arts into this project resulted in a greater understanding of the makeup of a real tree.

INTEGRATING STEM INTO GROUP PROJECTS

STEM is a natural component of project work because both focus on inquiry. As children investigate questions that interest them, they naturally ask questions based on their hypotheses, experiment with materials, observe the results, and communicate information. This is all part of scientific inquiry. Some projects have science content at their core, such as investigations involving weather, plants, animals, or mechanics. Other projects may seem unrelated to either science or mathematics but incorporate these disciplines as children become involved in the investigative and creative process. An example is the movie project (Project 5.3). In making props and set designs for their movie, children encounter problems related to physics, construction engineering, and measurement. In addition, the entire project revolves around technology. Thus, this creative endeavor encompasses all of the STEM disciplines.

THE PROCESS OF IMPLEMENTATION

Implementation of projects varies based on the goals of the project and the needs of the children. It is the responsibility of the teacher to direct a course of action and help children focus their thoughts. During the course of an investigation, interests may emerge and change. For example, during the tree project documented in this chapter, the attention of the children was diverted to spiders

for several days when one spun a web on the tree that the children were observing. Sometimes the initial goal of the children may remain unmet. For example, in the ice project, the children's original goal was to build a skating rink. However, during the course of the project, the children became so engrossed with figuring out how to make ice and were so satisfied with eventually achieving this objective that they never returned to their original goal of creating a skating rink.

Teachers are perhaps never busier than when they are supporting a class project. An important part of the teacher's role is to help document the children's learning. Photographs and transcriptions of the children's comments must be assembled and displayed so that they are available to the children for ongoing reflection. Being able to review what has already been done, as well as the outcomes, is an important part of the investigative process for both scientists and children. In addition, teachers must accumulate materials for each day's activities. Because the trajectory of a project is in constant flux, teachers sometimes need a couple days of breathing space before the investigations can continue. If the course of a project is adequately documented, children can quickly return to their investigations after a short break.

Perhaps most importantly, teachers need time to reflect. By regularly examining children's work, ideally with one or more colleagues, teachers can speculate about what children actually understand. Then they can consider activities or materials that can be introduced to move children forward in their thinking. The reflective process often seems undervalued in our high-speed society, but it is considered absolutely essential by Reggio Emilia educators.

The process of implementation varies from project to project in this chapter. Whereas the quilt project (Project 5.4) was largely teacher-led, the ice project was primarily determined by the course of the children's daily investigations. The sections on implementation that are included with each project serve as a framework for implementation based on the educational goals and emerging needs of each project.

ICE

A large and unexpected snowstorm blanketed the city just as the Winter Olympic Games were beginning to be telecast. The juxtaposition of these two events created a great deal of discussion at the two preschool classroom lunch tables, which were situated in front of full-length windows. The children at one table asked their teacher if they could make an ice-skating rink, to which the teacher agreed. She asked them, however, how they would make the ice. This question generated an amazing array of responses.

Takuo: "Use flour, salt, and spaghetti sauce to make it stick."

Jenny: "Put water out in the cold."

Uzma: "I know one thing. We can put the chalk in the snow."

Felipé: "Put water and snow in a bowl, and put it in the freezer. It will be in one big piece."

Sophie: "Put water, milk, and snow in the bowl, and stir it up, and put it in the thing with holes in it [ice cube tray]."

Tina: "Put water in the freezer, and it makes ice."

Joey: "Put the water on the paper."

The nature of these responses revealed a wide range of understanding of a science concept that adults might assume young children already know. After all, all of the children had had numerous experiences with ice in cold drinks, and some had clearly seen adults put ice cube trays into the freezer. Nevertheless, the visual perceptions of many of the children clouded their understanding of the true nature of ice and led to some astonishing suggestions. One thing was clear from the conversations: the children were quite excited about the idea of making ice and had many ideas that they wanted to test.

• • •

Project Description

Because there was such widespread interest in making ice, the teacher decided that this project should include the entire class. It also seemed like a project that could be covered rather quickly, perhaps within one to one and a half weeks. Carrying out the children's experiments would obviously be a major focus of the process, but the teacher also hoped to incorporate art materials to help children express their interest in ice.

Phases of Implementation

Day 1—Planning: On the first day of the project, the teacher met with children in small groups to discuss their ideas for how to make ice. The teacher promised to bring all of the requested ingredients to school on the following day so that the children could carry out their experiments. Many of the older children had specific ideas about what materials they wanted

to combine in their attempt to make ice, which the teacher carefully wrote down. Other children were content to listen at this phase of the project.

Day 2 —Experiment Day: As promised, the teacher had assembled all of the necessary ingredients for the class experiments. All of the children took part in this phase of the project. They met in small groups with either the teacher or the teacher's assistant, who kept careful notes about what the children did and said. Below are the notes from some of the class members.

Takuo mixed flour, salt, and spaghetti sauce. Then he said, "I think I need to add cold water. Now I have a good idea for the ice. Put it in the refrigerator."

Brandon said, "First you get some water, and then you get some sauce, and then some milk. Put it outside." He also added salt and sugar for good measure.

Sophie mixed water and milk. Originally she had wanted to add snow, but there was no snow left on the playground because a work crew had shoveled it all away. "Now I want some of that other stuff," she said. Sophie added some salt and put her bowl in the refrigerator. Sophie's friend Tina told her it looked like ice milk. "I have to keep stirring it," Sophie replied.

Jenny put water in a bowl and put it outside. She was afraid that children on the playground would disturb it, so she added a sign that said, "This is mine. Don't touch it."

Felipé also decided to use spaghetti sauce because there was no snow left. He added water, stirred the mixture, and put it in the freezer.

Joey put water on a piece of paper. Then he added milk and spaghetti sauce. (By this time, the spaghetti sauce had become quite popular with some of the experimenters.) "It tastes like spaghetti sauce," Joey said as he carried his experiment outside.

Andre said, "I think we gotta put some water in the bowl first, then some milk, then some salt." Andre then added spaghetti sauce. "It's turning into a milkshake!" he said. Andre put his experiment in the freezer.

Brandon, who had put his experiment outside, discovered that it had not changed much. "Maybe it rained, and that's why it didn't make ice," he decided.

Andre retrieved his experiment from the freezer. It had gotten hard. The teacher asked him if it looked like ice. "No," Andre replied. "It looks like ice cream."

Felipé's experiment ended up in the refrigerator instead of the freezer by mistake. Andre told Felipé that he had made soup. "Put it in the freezer," Felipé replied. "It will turn to ice faster."

Sophie was not sure if hers was ice or not. Brandon said, "No, it doesn't look like ice." Sophie added water and stirred some more. Then she put it back in the refrigerator.

Joey looked at his experiment and said, "It's not ice. It's spaghetti."

Jenny brought her bowl in from outside. "Maybe it got too warm," she said. "I should have put it in the freezer."

Takuo said, "Mine's orange! It's not ice." (The oil from the spaghetti sauce had risen to the top of the bowl, and the mixture looked very different from the previous day.)

Day 3—Experiment Results: The following day, during group time, the children took turns retrieving their experiments and discussing the results. Although the children were excited and eager to discover what had become of their experiments, they were remarkably nonchalant about the unexpected outcomes. Previously, the teacher had discussed the reality that many scientific experiments do not turn out as planned and that scientists use this information as a learning tool to guide future work.

Day 4—Ice Storm: The following day, nature produced an educational contribution to the ice project—an ice storm. Shortly after lunch, the children bundled up and went outside to experience the ice falling from the sky. With mouths wide open and hands held up to the sky, they tasted and felt the tiny kernels of ice. After returning to the classroom, the children used Q-tips with pastel and silver paints to draw pictures of the ice.

Day 5—Snow and Ice: In reflecting on the children's comments about making ice, the teacher realized that they were confused about the difference between snow and ice. While the children realized that the two were connected, they were not sure how snow differed from ice. On the previous day, the children had observed ice falling from the sky as small pellets, so now seemed a good time to focus their attention on the composition of snow. The teacher placed two small plastic snowflakes on an overhead projector so that an enlarged image of each appeared on two of the class easels. The children were fascinated with the process of projection as well as the intricate detail in the snowflake designs. They used colored pencils and markers to trace these symmetrical shapes onto easel paper.

Day 6—Playing with Ice: Now well into their second week of the ice project, the children seemed to have reached an impasse in their quest to make ice. The teacher's assistant suggested that they might learn something about ice from playing with ice cubes. This idea was quickly adopted by the class. The children worked in small groups, playing with ice cubes that had been placed on trays. The following are excerpts from the conversations the children had with one another and their teacher as they handled the ice cubes.

Andre exclaimed, "It's made of snow. These ice cubes are sticky."

Brandon discovered water on his hands. "There's water in the ice," he declared.

Andre added, "Squeeze it, and water comes out. It's too cold and really sticky."

Then Brian made another discovery about the ice. "If you bounce it, it'll crack," he told his group.

Catherine added, "Every ice cube is cold."

Everyone thought Andre's ice cubes were the best. His had melted the most.

Then the teacher asked a few questions. "Has anyone found any spaghetti in the ice cubes?" The group response was "no." Her next question was, "Has anyone found any flour in the ice cubes?" Again the group answered "no." Finally, the teacher asked, "Has there been any salt in the ice cubes?" Once again the answer was "no." (Note that these were the ingredients that many children had used in their ice experiments.)

Brandon then noticed a white color in the middle of an ice cube and thought it might be sugar. Andre thought he saw snow in his ice cube. Tina said, "It looks like a fish in there."

Next the children began to suck the ice cubes. Catherine said, "I'm sucking the water out."

Andre said, "It's totally cold."

Catherine added, "We want to eat the ice."

"Mine can spin," Andre discovered. He twirled his ice cube on the tray.

The teacher asked, "Is there anything on your trays besides water?" "No," Takuo answered. Then the teacher asked Tina if a fish had come out of her ice. "No," Tina replied.

"The ice is turning into water," Andre observed.

"Because it's hot," Jenny added.

Based on their explorations, the group eventually decided that they could make ice by putting just water into the freezer. This, of course, worked. The next day, everyone in the class made ice.

Celebration: Although the children never completed their initial desire to make a hockey rink, they were satisfied that they had discovered how to make ice. To mark the successful conclusion of the ice project, the teacher hosted a party for the children and their families. The children came in their pajamas, drank hot chocolate and ate doughnuts, and painted with ice cubes that had been colored with food coloring before freezing. The parents shared in the festivities and read the documentation panels that described the progress of the project with photographs and the children's own words.

Integration of STEM Learning

The ice project occurred long before STEM learning became an important trend in education. Nevertheless, it reflects the integration of curricula that has been recognized as best practice in early childhood for many years, as well as the impact of emergent curriculum. The idea for the project came directly from the interest of the children and falls under the content standards now designated as earth and space science and physical science.

STEM learning is exemplified in this project through the focus on scientific inquiry. When the children asked if they could make an ice rink, the teacher gave them the responsibility of figuring out how it could be done. The children formed hypotheses about how to make ice based on their prior experiences. Takuo knew that ice often has a white color, so he reasoned that white ingredients, such as flour and salt, might be involved. Knowing that ice sticks together,

he proposed spaghetti sauce as a sticky substance to help the ice cling to itself. Other children quickly picked up on the idea of white ingredients combined with spaghetti sauce. Jenny, who was the oldest child in the class, and Felipé both had hypotheses that were almost correct, although Felipé was confused about the difference between ice and snow.

The children were diligent in carrying out their experiments and pragmatic about the results. They accepted less than positive outcomes and communicated with one another throughout the project. The children's experiences and observations as they played with ice cubes, combined with the insightful questions posed by their teacher, led them to correctly infer that they could reverse the process of ice turning to water by refreezing the water. Forming a hypothesis, experimenting, observing, communicating, and developing inferences are all components of scientific inquiry.

The teacher and the teacher's assistant played key roles in the STEM learning process. They documented the children's thinking so that the children could remember their hypotheses when they conducted their experiments and could return to the reasoning that led to their conclusions. During the children's experiences with ice cubes, the comments and questions of the teacher and assistant kept the children focused on the components of the ice. Without their directed comments and questions, the children might not have reached the conclusion that ice is composed solely of water. The table below shows the STEM components from the ice project.

Table 5.1: Integration of STEM Components in the Ice Project

⌕ SCIENCE	⭘ TECHNOLOGY	⚙ ENGINEERING	➕ MATHEMATICS
Earth science— freezing/thawing Mixtures and changes in materials Solids and liquids Scientific inquiry	Freezer Overhead projector	Not a component of this project	Patterns and *symmetry* in snowflakes Measurement of ingredients

TREES

The tree project began after several children noticed a documentation panel from the previous year hanging in the hallway outside their classroom. They were excited to discover several of their siblings or friends in the photographs on this panel. In the photo, the children were examining a tree with beautiful pink blossoms on the playground. Later, when the children went outside to play, the teacher directed them to the same tree and asked what they noticed.

Olivia, Miriam, and Eli all replied, "It's green."

Olivia then added confidently, "It will be pink again."

Taking her cue from the responses of the children, the teacher then asked, "What color do you think the tree will be tomorrow?"

"Blue," predicted Miriam.

"Red," said Jack.

"Yellow," thought Olivia.

The teacher took a photograph of the children standing under the tree so that they could compare how the tree looked each day.

By the following day, more children had become interested in the lone tree on the playground. Although the tree was still green, children made confident predictions about the color they thought the leaves would be on the following day. Three children predicted green, and others predicted black, pink, orange, red, blue, and light blue. In addition, during group time the children decided that they would like to make a tree for inside the classroom. It was clear that a project had begun.

. . .

Project Description

The tree project unfolded on two fronts: (1) daily observations of the tree on the playground, and (2) the construction of a tree for inside the classroom. The teacher created an observation notebook to document changes that might occur in the playground tree. Children could write or dictate what they noticed each day and their predictions for the following day. In addition, the teacher included daily photographs of the tree and samples of the leaves.

Simultaneously, the children began planning and constructing their own tree for inside the classroom. To support children's learning, the teacher created a tree discovery area in the science center. She added cross sections of wood for the children to examine, various types of bark, a small sapling, a basket of leaves, photographs of trees, and related children's books. The class also took a field trip during the project to a local park, where they collected and examined the shapes of leaves, collected nuts to sort and

classify, and joined hands to measure the circumference of a large oak tree.

Phases of Implementation

NOTE: The days listed below indicate days in which the class was in session and working on the project, not calendar days. The class met four days per week.

Day 1—Planning: On the first day of the project, the teacher met with a group of interested children to discuss the building of a tree. Various ideas were presented, but the children decided that paper was too flimsy and pipes were too heavy. They decided to use cardboard boxes for the trunk of the tree and wrapping paper tubes for the branches.

Day 2—Timber!: Construction of the tree began on the second day and initially went well. Working in small groups that rotated as children visited and returned from the school motor room, the children

Measuring a tree

transformed the boxes into cylindrical shapes and taped them together to form the trunk. With help from the teacher, they cut holes for the branches and inserted the paper tubes. When the children decided they were ready, the teacher let go of the tree, which immediately fell to the ground. Stunned, the children began discussing the problem with their tree design.

The teacher noted that the tree on the playground did not seem to have any trouble standing up. The children had frequently pushed on it, and it never fell over.

Suddenly Sean had a revelation. "Our tree needs roots," he announced. "Roots help the tree stand up."

The children quickly agreed that Sean must be right. They, too, had noticed roots growing from the bottom of trees and descending into the ground.

Unfortunately, they could not cut a hole in the floor of the classroom to insert roots to support the tree. However, the children quickly came up with another idea. They cut strips of cardboard from remaining boxes, taped them to the tree, and then taped the opposite ends to the floor. The tree now stood up without falling.

Day 3—Trees Are Not Hollow: As soon as Laura and David arrived at school the next day, they ran to the book area and picked up plush baby owls and a toy squirrel that coordinated with two classroom books. They carried the animals to the class tree.

"These animals live in trees," Laura told the teacher. "Can you cut a hole in the tree so we can put them in?"

Making a tree

The teacher agreed and cut a hole in the spot indicated by the children. By now, several other children had come over to observe. David and Laura put the squirrel and owls into the hole in the tree, and the animals immediately fell to the floor inside.

"Oh no!" exclaimed Laura. "We lost them."

"I guess a tree has a middle," observed David.

Everyone agreed that the animals had to be rescued, so the tree was uprooted and the animals recovered. The teacher brought over a cross section of wood from the science area so that the children could observe what was inside the bark on the tree. After some discussion, the children decided to pile up boxes inside the tree to hold the animals.

Days 4–6: On subsequent days, the children worked at completing their tree. Before painting it, they carefully observed the colors and formations of the bark on the tree outside. Several children noticed bumps on the bark that had an orange tinge. After the tree was painted, these children used orange construction paper to re-create these bumps and taped them to the tree.

The children made leaves in a variety of ways. Some children rubbed colored crayons over actual tree leaves and cut them out. Other children drew or painted leaves. So that the children could better observe the detail in leaves, the teacher introduced self-hardening clay, which the children used to create leaf tiles. They rolled the clay into thin slabs, placed the leaves on the clay, and used cylindrical blocks to roll and press down on the leaves. When the leaves were removed from the clay, children could observe the intricate web of lines created by the veins in the leaves and their symmetrical shape.

Day 6—A Visitor: Meanwhile, daily observations of the tree on the playground had continued. On the sixth day, Biyu noticed something new on the tree. "There's something sticky there," she said, "and I don't like it." It was a spider web, complete with a large orange and green spider. The children quickly became fascinated with the spider, and for several days it became the focus of their attention. The teacher let them spray water onto the web so that they could observe the details better. The mist did not disturb the spider or the web, but it made the web clearly visible.

Days 14–18: Gradually, the children noticed that leaves on the top of the tree had begun to change color. Then, on day 14, children were excited to observe major changes in the tree.

David said, "It's yellow. It turned colors."

Miriam observed, "It looks like it's turned to colors."

Cindy, a child with physical and language delays, reported, "Leaves fell. Leaves came down."

By day 18, the children noted that most of the leaves had fallen from the tree onto the ground. Many of the children concluded that the tree had died. Although the current phase of the tree project was now over, it was obvious to the teacher that it would need to be revisited in the spring, when buds would appear and pink blossoms would again cover the tree. The observation notebook and photographs of the children interacting with the tree would provide a tool for them to recall how the tree had changed during the fall and was now changing again.

Celebration: Following the completion of the tree project, the class held an evening celebration for their families. Leaf-shaped cookies were served, and the teacher shared a PowerPoint presentation that documented each phase of the project. Then the parents had a surprise of their own. They presented the class with a beautiful bonsai tree so that they could continue to care for and learn about trees in the classroom.

Integration of STEM Learning

The tree project was an outgrowth of children's questions regarding the changing colors of the tree on their playground. It provided an excellent opportunity for children to engage in scientific inquiry related to what is now the life science content standard. As part of their desire to build a lifelike model of a tree, the children encountered problems that led to their discovery of two important components of real trees. First, they realized that trees need roots, in part to provide support. Later they learned that trees have a solid core. Because children developed these concepts through solving a real-life problem, they are more likely to remember what they learned. While this project primarily revolved around science explorations, it also contained important elements of mathematics, technology, and engineering, which are documented in the table below.

Table 5.2: Integration of STEM Components in the Trees Project

🔍 SCIENCE	⚙ TECHNOLOGY	⚙ ENGINEERING	➕ MATHEMATICS
Life science—composition of trees Exploring changes in trees over time Spiders and webs	Digital photography PowerPoint and projector	Structural concepts related to balance and stability	Patterns and *symmetry* in leaves Measurement of circumference

CLASS MOVIE

Ben and Elizabeth were excited. Their class was going to make its own movie, and they had decided that their characters would be superheroes. As part of the movie, they were going to fly a spaceship that they had built out of cardboard boxes, tubes, and paper. Their dilemma was how to make it appear that the spaceship was flying. Their teacher sat down with them to think about this problem.

"Remember that the spaceship doesn't really have to fly," the teacher commented. "It just has to look like it's flying."

"But you can see the floor under the spaceship," said Elizabeth. "When people see the floor, they'll know the spaceship isn't really flying."

"And another problem is that our spaceship doesn't move," added Ben.

"So it seems like you have two problems," the teacher summarized. "You need to make the spaceship move, and it needs to look like it's flying. Let's work on one problem at a time. How could you make the spaceship move?"

"Someone could push it," suggested Elizabeth.

"I know," Ben suddenly exclaimed. "We could put it on the wagon from the motor room. Then someone could pull the wagon, and it would look like the spaceship is moving on its own."

"Good idea," agreed the teacher, "but how will we keep the people who are watching the movie from seeing the person who is pulling the wagon?"

"Just hold the camera on the spaceship so they can't see the person pulling the wagon," Ben replied.

"Well," answered the teacher, "if I hold the camera so that the person doesn't show, why can't I also hold the camera so that the floor doesn't show? Should we try it and see?"

Ben and Elizabeth eagerly agreed. They placed their spaceship on top of the wagon, and the teacher lay on the floor, level with the spaceship, and videotaped from that angle. Sure enough, the floor did not show except in the distance.

"I think that will work," Ben declared, but Elizabeth still was not sure.

"You could still see a little bit of the carpet," she said.

"Well, can you make the carpet look like the sky?" the teacher asked.

"Yes!" Elizabeth exclaimed. "We can use that blue paper on the big roll and make some clouds." Elizabeth and Ben eagerly began the next phase of their movie preparation—creating the sky.

• • •

Project Description

For twenty years, preschool and kindergarten children in the author's class created an annual class movie. Over this span of time, technology advanced from reel-to-reel tape recordings to video and finally digital recordings. The first class movie was the teacher's attempt to help children understand the difference between reality and the pretend stories and special effects they regularly saw on television and in movies. The hope was that when children acted out roles they had created for themselves and later viewed their actions via recording technology, they would gain some understanding of the process that went into creating television shows and movies.

Children in succeeding classes often had siblings or friends who had participated in previous movie projects. Several would always ask if they, too, would be allowed to make a movie. Soon the yearly movie event was an expected and eagerly anticipated part of the curriculum.

Each year the teacher followed approximately the same procedure for the movie project. Children would begin by selecting roles. Next, a group

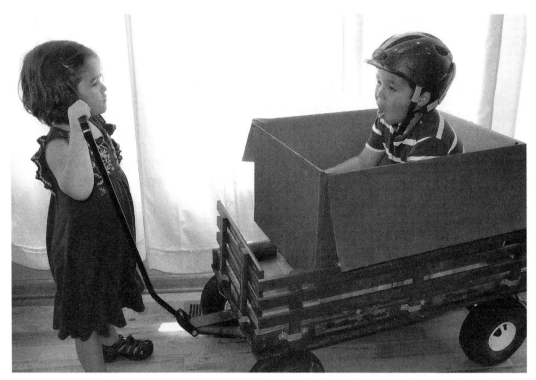

Making a spaceship fly

of interested children would write the story for the movie. During the following days, children would create set designs and costumes. Finally, the teacher would narrate and record the story as the children acted it out. The following descriptions are a synthesis of material from several of these movie projects.

Phases of Implementation

Step 1—Selecting Characters: Each child was allowed to select his or her own character for the movie. Choices often included several princesses, an array of superheroes, and assorted animals. The only rule for the movie was that no character could be killed. Once the characters had been chosen, the teacher created a chart that listed each child's name next to his or her character. This was posted in the classroom for referral.

Step 2—Creating the Story: On the second day of the movie project, interested children gathered at a table with the teacher to write the story. The teacher facilitated this process with leading questions, such as the following:

- How do you think the story should start?

- Where are the characters living?

- What is _____ doing at the beginning of the story?

- What happens next?

- What will the _____ do in the movie?

As the children worked together to create the story, the teacher wrote down their words, periodically reading the story back to them to keep it fresh in their minds. After the first draft of the story was completed, the teacher read it to the children in the class to make sure they were satisfied with their character's activities in the movie. Sometimes revisions were needed to make everyone happy. Then the story was read to the whole class during group time.

Step 3—Creating Set Designs: The children decided what set and props they needed for their movie, and how they would construct them. Large boxes, pieces of cardboard, rolls of poster paper, and donated fabric were often used. During this phase of the movie-making process, the STEM curriculum began to assume a major role in the project. The following examples, taken from several class movies, demonstrate the application of science learning to the creation of sets and props.

- CASTLE DRAWBRIDGE: A kindergarten class constructed a large castle out of an assortment of large boxes, complete with two towers. The children then decided that their castle needed a drawbridge. The children cut apart and taped together sections of packing boxes to build the drawbridge ramp. The problem was how to raise and lower the bridge, as this was an important part of the movie. Since the children had had prior experience with **pulleys** in the science area of their classroom, they understood that pulling down on the rope of a pulley could make an object go up. Several inventive children inserted a dowel rod through holes in the two towers so that it extended between them. Then they attached long pieces of twine to the far corners of the drawbridge. With help from adults, the children looped this cord over the dowel rod so that it essentially functioned like a pulley. When the castle guards pulled down on the ropes, the drawbridge was pulled up to block the gate. By loosening the ropes, the guards could lower the bridge over the pretend moat.

- FIRE-BREATHING DRAGON: A preschool class created a fire-breathing dragon as the villain in

A fire-breathing dragon

their movie. The dragon was made with large balloons covered in pieces of green paper to look like scales. The problem for this group was how to make the dragon look like it was breathing fire.

Eventually, several children decided to modify blow toys recently used as birthday party favors. This type of toy has a paper tube that is coiled, but when air is blown into the mouthpiece, the tube inflates, which causes it to straighten and pop out of its coiled position. The children created flames out of red paper and attached them to the tube of one of these blowers. During the filming of the movie, a child hid behind the dragon and blew the "flaming" birthday blower, which indeed looked like fire coming out of the dragon's head.

- SUPER SOAKERS: In the aforementioned dragon movie, three boys wanted to fight the dragon with super soakers. The teacher agreed, as long as the boys made their own soakers. One of the ground rules for the movie production was that the children would make all of the props and costumes out of found or donated materials. No costumes or props could be purchased. The boys had had previous experiences with pumps at the class water table. Applying this knowledge, they collected two-liter bottles to hold the water and inserted pumps from the water table into the tops of the bottles, where they were securely taped. These constituted their water cannons, which they successfully employed against the fire-breathing dragon.

- MAGIC CARPETS: In yet another movie project, several princesses wanted to fly on magic carpets. With the help of some friends, the girls decided that the carpets could be placed on the top of the class water table. The table was on casters, which would roll, and it had a sturdy wooden top. To make the table look like it was up in the sky, the children covered the front of it with blue poster paper. They then created clouds out of some foamy packing material from the storage room. During the filming of the movie, the princesses perched on their carpets, safely aboard the water table, while several children and an adult, who were hidden from view, pushed it across the room.

Step 4—Costumes: Before the cameras could roll, costumes needed to be made. Over the years, the teacher became more confident in the ability of the children to make their own costumes, and she turned more and more of the responsibility over to them.

This allowed the children to experiment with creating models, measuring, sewing, and coloring fabric—activities that integrated mathematics and science and involved problem solving, as the following show:

Learning to use a pattern

- LUKE SKYWALKER'S ARMOR: In the exciting, action-packed movie that involved the dragon, Sam decided to take on the role of Luke Skywalker. The teacher found a book for children titled *The Making of Star Wars*, which she brought to class for him to use as he designed his costume. Looking carefully at photographs in the book, Sam traced around his arms and legs to create a pattern. He then cut the pieces of armor out of easel paper. Unfortunately, when he taped the pieces together and tried them on, they quickly tore. Undaunted by the unsatisfactory result of his long effort, Sam accompanied the teacher to the school storage room, where they rummaged through miscellaneous donated items. Soon Sam spied a large roll of thin packing foam, approximately 5 inches wide. He carried it back to the classroom, where his friends helped him wind the foam around his arms, legs, and body. The foam was flexible when he moved, and did not tear. Sam had found the perfect material for his armor.

- CAT MASK: Lucie was fascinated with cats, so it was no surprise when she decided to portray a cat for her class's movie. She also loved the color pink, so naturally she wanted to be a pink cat. Apart from the color, however, Lucie wanted to look like a real cat. To provide her with an array of appropriate models, the teacher brought a book of cat photographs to class. Lucie was fascinated with the book and pored over it before finally selecting a cat to use as a model. She carefully drew the cat's face on pink paper and cut it out. Looking into a mirror, Lucie measured the mask against her face. It fit perfectly. Lucie looked like an adorable pink kitty.

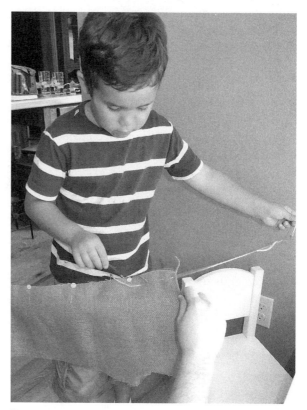

Sewing a costume

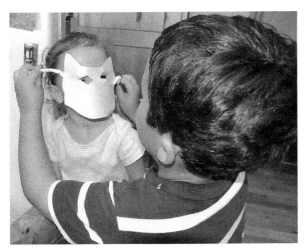
A pink kitty

- COLORING FABRIC: Several children wanted to be orange tigers for their class movie. The teacher had yellow and red burlap, which the children intended to use to sew tiger costumes, but they were not satisfied with the color choices. Tigers had to be orange. Unfortunately, there was no orange burlap to be found. "What can you do to make the burlap orange?" the teacher asked them. Several interesting ideas quickly emerged. Sarah suggested that they place the red burlap on top of the yellow burlap, because she knew that mixing red and yellow paint at the easel produced orange. The children experimented with this idea, but only the color of fabric on top showed. Next, Dwayne and Amit suggested that they paint the yellow burlap with red paint, because "red and yellow make orange." Dwayne tried painting his piece of yellow burlap with red water-color paint, and Amit tried painting his with red tempera paint, but the results for both boys were unsatisfactory—red burlap, not orange.

  The teacher commented that their ideas were good even though they had not yet worked. She then asked the group if they had mixed colors with any other materials. Carol quickly had an idea. "Water," she said. "We mixed colored water." Her idea was to spray the burlap with red water. The teacher gave Carol a spray bottle, which she filled with water and a few drops of red food coloring. When Carol sprayed the water onto the yellow burlap, it immediately turned orange. The children were ecstatic. Soon they had clipped all of the

yellow burlap to the outside fence and were busy spraying it with red water. The fabric color crisis had been solved.

- SEWING PANTS: In addition to three tigers, one of the class movies also included the previously mentioned pink cat and a green rabbit. This particular class had had considerable experience sewing with large needles and burlap, first creating sampler quilts and later sewing burlap squares together to make purses and bags. The teacher decided that they were ready to use a simple pants pattern for their costumes. She brought several pattern sizes to class, which the children held next to themselves to determine the appropriate size. The teacher showed the children how to lay the pattern pieces on the fabric, and the children cut them out. Then, with a student teacher helping to hold the pieces of fabric together, the children sewed the seams. When they eagerly tried on their pants, they fit quite well.

- MEASURING GOWNS: Many children needed gowns for their characters' costumes. Like burlap, tulle is a loosely woven fabric that is inexpensive and easy for children to sew. For this reason, the teacher brought yards of tulle netting to class for gown- and cape-making projects. The children helped one another measure the required length by holding the fabric up to their bodies and cutting. They then used large plastic needles to gather the top of the fabric to form gowns and capes.

Step 5—Filming the Movie: Once all of the preparations had been completed, the children assembled the sets and props and donned their costumes. This was often near the end of the second week of the project. By this time, the children were very familiar with the movie's story. The teacher simultaneously read the story and filmed the children's actions, which allowed her to judge how long to let a scene last. In between scenes, the teacher could stop the camera while the sets were rearranged and the appropriate children assembled "on set." As soon as the filming of the movie was completed, the whole class watched it. This enabled the children to compare what they had just done with how it looked on the screen. Recall that this was a major goal of the project. Children knew that the carpets on the table were not really flying, although they might appear to do so. They had constructed the monster themselves, so they knew it was not real. They also understood all the steps that were necessary to create their movie.

Celebration: Later an evening party was held so that the children's families and friends could see their movie. While the refreshments were served, the teacher highlighted all of the curriculum areas that were bound together by the movie, and described how the children used their thinking skills to solve major challenges in making it. Copies of the movie were distributed to all of the families.

Integration of STEM Learning

When children's ideas and learning are placed at the center of the movie project, inquiry becomes the guiding force. Children must apply scientific knowledge and extend their learning in order to solve problems, such as how to raise and lower a drawbridge, make a carpet appear to fly, and change the color of fabric. Children may need to make models or patterns, in much the same way as is required of engineers, and they develop measurement concepts as they progress through the creative process and bring their ideas to fruition.

Table 5.3: Integration of STEM Components in the Class Movie Project

🔍 SCIENCE	💡 TECHNOLOGY	⚙️ ENGINEERING	➕ MATHEMATICS
Physical science— use of **simple machines**, such as **pulleys** and wheels Exploring air and water pressure Exploration of materials Mixing pigments to change color	Video technology is a central focus	Structural concepts related to balance and stability (when building sets) Creating patterns and models	Measurement concepts

QUILTS

Tony carefully placed a sequence of beads on the table in front of him—red, blue, red, blue, red, blue. His class was creating a colorful burlap quilt, and he wanted to sew a pattern with the beads. After lining up his beads, Tony carefully threaded them onto a large plastic needle and inserted the needle into his burlap. To his surprise, the beads made a hump on the fabric.

"You made a hill," observed Samantha.

"It looks like a roller coaster," Tony exclaimed. "I think I'll make Kings Island." Soon Tony was adding hills of beads throughout his burlap square.

"That's interesting," commented his teacher. "What do you have to do to make a really tall bump, Tony?" she asked.

Tony looked carefully at the hills on his fabric. "I need to put the needle back in close to where it came out," Tony answered. "Then the beads go up in the air."

"I see," said the teacher. "So what if you want a really long hill, like this one? Then what do you do?"

Tony again examined his sewing square. "Then I have to put the needle in the burlap farther away from where it came out," Tony explained.

"Do you think you have more beads on this tall hill or the long hill?" the teacher asked.

"The long hill," Tony immediately answered. Then he began counting his beads, twelve for the long hill and thirteen for the tall hill. "Wow," said Tony. "The tall hill has more."

• • •

Project Description

The quilt project was another yearly tradition in the author's class, and quilts from previous years adorned the walls of the classroom and the halls of the school. They preserved the history of children who had previously attended the school, and they sparked interest in each successive class to create their own remembrances. As part of the quilt project, children created a variety of types of quilts. Some, such as the burlap quilt in the opening vignette, were sewn, while others were created with paper. A family quilt, in which each family created its own quilt square, was the culmination of the project.

The quilt project served, in part, to connect many areas of the curriculum. An assortment of excellent children's books presented quilt traditions from many cultures. Mathematics was embedded throughout the project as children worked with geometric shapes, combining them to form new shapes. Patterning, quantification, and measurement were also components of the project. Most importantly, the quilt project gave children the opportunity to

Class sampler quilt

represent their ideas through many different media and to work both independently and as part of a community.

Phases of Implementation

Phase 1—Sewing: Because quilts are traditionally sewn, the first phase of the project focused on developing basic sewing techniques. The most common stitch for hand sewing involves pushing the needle through the fabric from one side and pulling it back up through the opposite side, which creates a down-and-up pattern. Since safety is a concern for young children, and since they are still developing hand strength and fine-motor coordination, large plastic needles designed for children were used for the project.

Sewing on burlap

On the first day of the sewing phase, children used these needles, threaded with yarn, to sew on Styrofoam disposable plates. (Children can easily poke plastic needles through the plates, and unlike fabric, the Styrofoam will not bunch up if children pull the stitches tightly.) The teacher threaded the needles and tied a knot in a double strand of yarn, which prevented the needle from unthreading. With these materials, the children had the freedom to experiment and become familiar with the sewing process. Geometry and measurement were embedded in the activity as the teacher referred to positions on the plate, such as top, bottom, and edge, and helped the children compare long and short stitches. Children

sewed on Styrofoam plates for several days, first in small groups as a special activity, and later as a choice activity in the art area.

The next step in the sewing process was to begin sewing on fabric. Burlap was selected because the wide weave of this fabric allows children to easily insert a needle. In addition, burlap is inexpensive and available in a variety of colors. The teacher knew from prior experience that young children were often unsuccessful in sewing activities because they pulled the stitches too tightly and wrapped the needle around the edge of the fabric. As one child lamented, "Everything I try to sew turns into a ball." For this reason, the burlap squares were held in place by 7-inch embroidery hoops. The burlap was precut into 8-inch squares by the teacher, who also pulled out strands to create a fringed border for the finished product. The teacher worked with several children at a time at the special activity table as they learned the up-and-down pattern of sewing. It was now necessary to implement this technique, because if children wrapped the yarn around the edge of the fabric, the burlap could not be removed from the hoop. Naturally, there were many wraparound mistakes during this learning process, which the teacher could easily fix by reversing the direction of the needle and pulling out the offending stitches. It became a standing joke that "so-and-so" had wrapped the yarn around the hoop again. Children sometimes chanted the down-and-up pattern to help themselves and their friends. Eventually, children mastered the technique and were pleased with their sewing samples. The burlap was removed from the hoops so that the children could take it home.

After another day of sewing practice, beads with large holes were introduced. (Inexpensive plastic beads with holes that a large plastic needle can pass through are available at craft stores. Sequins and spangles can also be used.) Children now needed to learn to differentiate between the front and back of their sewing; otherwise, beads would end up on the wrong side of the fabric and not be visible when it was displayed. They also needed to learn the technique of adding one or more beads to the needle before taking a stitch. Children spent several days honing their technique, gradually adding in elements of their own creativity as they became comfortable with the medium.

Quilt square sewn on burlap

Finally, the class was ready to create a group quilt. Each child selected a color of burlap and an assortment of beads for his or her quilt square. When all the squares were finished, the teacher sewed them together, with the fringe facing out to create texture on the quilt. Each child's name was printed with puffy print on the appropriate square, and the quilt was displayed in the classroom.

Phase 2—Story Quilts: Story quilts are a specific type of quilt used by artists in many cultures to tell a story, commemorate an event, or even convey a message. For example, in the United States story quilts were used to give directions to enslaved people fleeing to northern states. Because children often like to tell stories about their drawings or discuss what they have created, this phase of the quilt project began with children drawing on story paper and then dictating or writing their reflections. (Story paper is blank at the top and lined at the bottom.) Creating a story or reflection to accompany their artwork helped children understand that art can convey a message. After they had created several samples, children chose one to contribute to a class story quilt. They then selected rectangular shapes precut from wallpaper samples to form a border for their quilt square. The individual story quilts were laminated, assembled into a giant class story quilt, and displayed in the school hallway. At the end of the year, children took their individual story quilts home.

The teacher also wanted the children to have the opportunity to create a fabric story quilt. For this phase of the project, children used fabric markers to draw on squares of white cotton fabric.

Sample of a story quilt square drawn on fabric

These squares were sewn together by the teacher, with contrasting fabric in between the squares, to create a second type of class story quilt. As in most traditional story quilts, in this version the story had to emerge from the artwork itself, since there was no accompanying text.

Phase 3—Geometric Quilts: Many traditional quilts have distinctive geometric designs, in which shapes are combined to produce a composite shape. For example, a pattern known as the Ohio Star incorporates squares and triangles to produce a star shape for each quilt square. During the beginning of this stage of the project, which occurred simultaneously with the sewing and drawing phases, children used a felt board and flannel shapes to copy and create quilt patterns. A similar activity occurred at the water table, where children placed moist foam blocks on Plexiglas easels to combine shapes into larger images. Children also used tangrams and similar manipulative toys to create pictures out of geometric shapes.

After about two weeks of free exploration, children created geometric quilt samples by positioning geometric shapes, which had been precut from self-adhering felt, onto a fabric base.

Sample squares from a geometric quilt

Children could also cut out their own shapes if desired. Once children had decided on the design they wanted to use, the backing was removed from the fabric so that the shapes could be permanently mounted. The following day, children followed a similar procedure with other types of fabric. Children could select shapes with a variety of colors, shapes, and textures for their creations. The teacher then used a heat-bond material and a hot iron to permanently mount each child's design onto fabric. The fabric squares were adhered to a backing to create a class geometry quilt. Children could discuss the individual shapes they used to compose larger shapes in their designs.

draw, glue, or sew designs onto their squares. Often, families chose to include items that represented not only their family but also their culture. African trade beads, fabric from various countries, miniature flags, and other special symbols adorned these family quilts, which were then displayed in the school.

Celebration: At the conclusion of the quilt project, families were invited for a potluck dinner. Families could view the various quilts completed by the class along with photographs of the children constructing them. Art materials were available for children and their families to make their own quilt squares.

Phase 4—Family Quilts: At the end of the quilt project, each family participated by creating a quilt square for a class family quilt.

During some years, a packet of materials was sent home to each family, and the squares were created outside of class. During other years, the families made their quilt squares at an evening class party to culminate the quilt project. In either case, white felt was used for the family quilt squares. Families could

Samples from a family quilt

Integration of STEM and Other Curricular Learning

Mathematics is the STEM area most heavily represented in the quilt project, since quilts by their very nature are often highly geometric. Throughout the project, children composed and decomposed geometric shapes in many areas of the curriculum, including the art, sensory, and manipulative areas. The art area included divided trays with shapes cut from various papers and fabric that children could use for free exploration. As a choice activity, children created individual quilts by gluing these shapes into designs on 12-by-18-inch construction paper. Foam shapes and blocks were an excellent medium for children to use in the water table. When moist, they adhere to plastic trays or easels. Illustrations of geometric quilt designs were laminated and hung on the wall in the sensory area for inspiration. Finally, an assortment of blocks and manipulative materials allowed children to make connections between the shapes used in traditional school materials and use of the same shapes in art and quilt designs.

Although not as heavily represented as mathematics in this project, science was also a component. Through working with many different fabrics and papers, children could compare and describe their textures and other characteristics. For example, they noticed that corduroy has raised lines and is a thick fabric, while satin is glossy, smooth, and much thinner. Children also found that some fabrics, such as chiffon, are **transparent**. They could see right through it. On the other hand, knitted fabric is **translucent**, and therefore partially obscures an image behind it. When children tried to look through **opaque** fabrics, such as denim and velvet, they could not see anything. Science was also represented as children experimented with various ways to adhere fabrics. They discovered that while some fabrics were easy to sew, it was difficult to penetrate denser materials, such as leather. Although the children could not fully comprehend the process of adhering fabrics through heat, they did observe that while iron-on adhesives are not sticky in their original state, they can permanently adhere fabrics when a hot iron is applied.

The quilt project also included strong ties to literacy. A wide variety of children's books that depicted quilt traditions from many different cultures were read to the children. Children also dictated and re-read stories from their own story quilts. Family values were supported as all families shared in a community class quilt. The following is a list of children's books used in the quilt project:

- *The Quilt* by Ann Jonas
- *Before I Was Born* by Harriet Ziefert
- *The Keeping Quilt* by Patricia Polacco
- *Luka's Quilt* by Georgia Guback
- *The Patchwork Quilt* by Valerie Flournoy
- *The Quilt Story* by Tony Johnston
- *Something from Nothing* by Phoebe Gilman
- *Sweet Clara and the Freedom Quilt* by Deborah Hopkinson
- *Charlie Needs a Cloak* by Tomie dePaola
- *Abuela's Weave* by Omar S. Castañeda
- *Texas Star* by Barbara Hancock Cole

Table 5.4: Integration of STEM Components in the Quilts Project

🔍 SCIENCE	💡 TECHNOLOGY	⚙️ ENGINEERING	➕ MATHEMATICS
Comparison of the characteristics of various materials Exploration of **adhesion** properties	Applications of heat, through ironing and laminating materials	Not a component of this project	Composing and decomposing geometric shapes Measurement concepts

6

Quick STEM Activities

In the distance, the teacher heard a fire truck's siren gradually becoming louder. He quickly assembled the children from his kindergarten class, who were playing on two large climbers on the playground. "Listen!" he said as the children gathered around. "We're going to listen for how the siren sounds as the fire truck goes by." As the children listened intently, they heard the fire siren not only get louder but also slide upward in **pitch**. *As the truck passed by, the siren glided downward in pitch and gradually became softer. The teacher used his hand to graph the upward and downward movement of the tone of the siren as the fire truck passed by. Then he and the children used their hands and voices to copy the sound of the siren.*

• • •

Teachers often lament that they do not have enough time to cover all of the requirements for their grade level. The above vignette illustrates, however, that important learning can take place when teachers capitalize on opportunities that occur throughout the day. The changing pitch of the fire truck siren, apparent to the observers but not to anyone riding on the truck, is an example of the **Doppler effect**. Because the truck is moving in the same direction as the sound waves emitted by the siren, the distance between the sound waves becomes shorter as the truck approaches. Shorter sound waves produce higher pitches. The reverse happens as the truck moves away from the observer. Although preschool and kindergarten children are not old enough to understand why the Doppler effect occurs, they can hear how it sounds. The next time the children hear a siren, some of them may again listen for the Doppler effect to occur.

Outstanding teachers take advantage of every available learning opportunity. Three simple guidelines can help even the busiest teachers greatly increase the instructional time they devote to STEM education:

1. STEM is everywhere.
2. Use all the available time.
3. Discussion matters.

STEM IS EVERYWHERE

When teachers become aware of the possibilities for teaching STEM, opportunities to explore the integration of science and mathematics, both through inquiry and applications to technology and engineering, abound in the school environment. Often, a simple addition or change of materials that are regularly used can result in new learning opportunities. For example, it is quick and easy to create a "puddle" outside by filling an aluminum baking dish with a small amount of water. Children can moisten the bottom of their shoes by stepping into the water and then observe the footprints they create on the pavement. They can also compare the designs in their footprints to the actual grooves in the soles of their shoes. This simple and quick addition to the outside environment allows children to explore the relationship between the grooves on the soles of their shoes and the water prints they create. It causes them to focus their attention, make observations, and think. The adhesive property of water is a topic they may formally study in science someday. Nevertheless, the interest and learning begin with the experiences they have as young children.

Another way to increase STEM learning opportunities is to make a simple alteration to a material that is commonly used. Small glasses that are routinely used for juice or milk can occasionally be marked into two equal sections with plastic tape. This creates an opportunity for teachers to discuss measurement and fractional parts of the glass as children consume the liquid. For example, the teacher might say, "When your juice gets down to this line, you will have drunk half the glass. Let me know when you get there." Over time, the teacher might introduce thirds and fourths in this manner. The topic of fractions is difficult for many students when they encounter it in elementary school. Simple experiences such as this, in which the teacher takes a few minutes to apply tape to glasses at snacktime, can provide a foundation for children to build upon in their later learning.

Many of the tools that are commonly used in the kitchen create excellent science experiences. They allow children to experience technological innovations that often involve **simple machines**. A commonly used cheese grater employs a cylindrical grater in a plastic case. When the handle is turned, the cheese passes over the serrated grater and emerges as fine strands. Many schools routinely serve cheese cubes or slices for snack. If teachers introduce a cheese grater such as the type just described, children can experience the working of two types of simple machines: the grater, which is a combination of many small

wedges, and a **wheel and axle**, which moves the cheese through the grater. This simple addition to a common classroom routine creates opportunities for experimentation, observation, and discussion.

USE ALL THE AVAILABLE TIME

Children spend considerable parts of the school day in activities that are not typically designated as "learning" times. These include the following:

- transitions between activities
- playground time
- movement to various areas of the school, such as the lunchroom
- arrival and departure
- eating times, such as breakfast, snack, and lunch
- hand washing

Time spent in these necessary routines is also time that could incorporate learning.

Consider what children might observe as they walk down the hallway. Perhaps the teacher decides to focus on positional terms in geometry. Children can look for what is above them, below them, and on their right and left sides. If they must turn corners or move up and down stairs, the teacher can model directional terms such as *left*, *right*, *straight ahead*, *up*, and *down*. Some children may want to draw maps of the trip from the classroom to the lunchroom to help parents or other visitors find their way.

On another day, the teacher might decide to focus on the construction of the school building, including the materials that are used in the hallway and lunchroom. Children could take brief moments to examine the smoothness and patterns in linoleum and the texture and shape of cinder blocks. They might observe the **reflections** from glass windows or showcases, identify the shapes of door frames and windows, and feel the coolness and smoothness of metal railings. On other days, observations might include a search for parallel or intersecting lines or lines that are vertical or horizontal. Children might quantify the number of cinder blocks along the wall from the kindergarten room to the stairway. They might go on a hunt for light sources, such as windows and lighting fixtures, or on a shape hunt. All of this learning, whether it involves generating new ideas or reinforcing existing knowledge, is STEM based, *and* it occurs during time that otherwise might be wasted in terms of learning.

If so much learning can take place during walks to the lunchroom, consider the learning opportunities that might occur while children eat. Some of the food is cooked and may have undergone a **physical** or **chemical change**. Comparisons can be made between food items in their raw and cooked forms. Some food has noticeable measurement characteristics. For example, children can compare the lengths of green beans or carrots. Children may not realize the source of the food they are eating. Because some children may not know that applesauce actually comes from apples, the teacher might share a book about making applesauce while the children eat. By simply looking at the lunch menu for each week, the teacher can plan math and science discussions related to the food.

Similar learning opportunities occur during routines throughout the day. While this chapter highlights some of the possibilities, teachers can discover many other opportunities within their own classrooms and school environments.

DISCUSSION MATTERS

The conversation that accompanies all STEM activities is particularly important to how well young children learn. Through their comments and questions, teachers can focus children's attention on the relationship between the children's actions and the ensuing results. In addition, teachers can encourage components of scientific inquiry and greatly increase the vocabulary and communication skills of children. The following are examples of comments or questions that might stimulate children's thinking in the footprint, juice glass, and cheese grating activities previously discussed.

Water Footprints

- What made the triangle-shaped marks in your footprint?

- Do you think your shoes will make the same footprints as Jeremy's shoes?

- How many steps can you take before we can't see your footprints anymore?

Fractional Juice Glass

- Have you reached the halfway mark on your juice glass yet?

- Your juice level is down to the mark. That means half of your juice is gone.

- Your glass is empty. You drank the whole glass of juice.

Cheese Grater

- What is cutting the cheese into such small pieces?

- What happens when you turn the crank?

- Did as much cheese come out of the grater as you put in? Let's look inside and see if any cheese is still in the grater.

The activities that follow illustrate simple additions or changes to the environment that can increase opportunities for STEM learning.

APPLE CORER AND DIVIDER

PHYSICS, LIFE SCIENCE

Materials

○ apple corer and divider

○ apples

Activity Description

Preschool and kindergarten classrooms are busy places, but most have places in their schedules allocated for snack or lunch. This is time that can be used for science and math learning opportunities. Many of the tools that are routinely used in the kitchen would be recognized in physics as *simple machines*. Such is the case with this activity. Rather than serving precut apple slices, teachers can ask for whole apples to be sent to the classroom. They can then use a simple kitchen tool called an apple corer and divider to quickly cut the apple into sections. Children watch in amazement as the metal wedges instantly separate the apple into eight sections and remove the core.

Integrating Science

Cutting the apple is only the beginning of the learning opportunities presented by the apple corer. One topic of discussion might be the properties of the apple itself. Children can talk about the difference between the color of the apple on the outside and the inside. They can pass the core around, examine it, and count the pips, or seeds. Children may notice the stem that held the apple to the tree. The teacher might even want to share a book about how apples grow.

On another occasion the conversation might center around the apple corer and divider itself. With the teacher's close supervision, children can take turns using the tool and feeling the amount of pressure they must exert to cut through the apple.

As part of the conversation, the teacher can ask what other tools people use to cut apples. Some children will likely mention knives. Both the apple corer and knives are examples of **wedges**, one of the six simple machines.

 Integrating Mathematics

The apple-slicing situation also provides interesting math problems to discuss. How many pieces of apple are there? Is that enough for everyone at the table to have one piece? Can everyone have two pieces? Teachers can also discuss the shapes of the pieces of apple and introduce the idea of fractional parts of the whole apple.

Table 6.1: STEM Components in the Apple Corer and Divider Activity

SCIENCE	TECHNOLOGY	ENGINEERING	MATHEMATICS
Exploring apples Using a simple machine	The apple corer is composed of wedges and is therefore an example of technology.	Wedges are an integral part of machines used in many types of engineering.	Counting Division Fractions Shapes Problem solving

SLOPING WATER TABLE

EARTH SCIENCE, PHYSICS

Materials

○ water table

○ blocks to raise 2 legs of the table

Activity Description

A simple way to encourage scientific inquiry in young children is to occasionally elevate one end of the water table. This causes the water to flow to the nonelevated end, confounding the assumptions of young children. They are eager to figure out what causes the water to behave in this way.

 ## Integrating Science

Having the water table positioned at a slight angle rather than horizontally introduces to children the idea of how water flows in the natural world. As children experiment by trying to add water to the end of the table that does not have any, they notice that the water constantly flows to the other end and pools there. Some children may wish to place small toys, such as plastic turtles, at the dry end of the table and watch the toys wash down the slope as they pour water over them. This illustrates that moving water has the power to move objects as it flows. Later the

Water tub raised at one end

teacher can remove the **wedges** that are elevating one end of the table, and the children can observe how the water quickly distributes itself evenly throughout the table.

 ## Integrating Mathematics

As children try to discover why all of the water moves to one end of the table, someone will probably notice that the legs at one end of the table are propped. This creates an angle, which causes the flat surface of the water table to slope. By placing a yardstick along the top of the water table but parallel to the floor, teachers can show children the angle that is created. Angles are an important aspect of geometry.

Table 6.2: STEM Components in the Sloping Water Table Activity

🔍 SCIENCE	💡 TECHNOLOGY	⚙️ ENGINEERING	➕ MATHEMATICS
Exploring water flow and the force of moving water	The force of flowing water is used to power many types of technology.	Engineers must understand slope and how water will flow when they build roads and buildings.	Angles in geometry

WINDOW PRISM

PHYSICS, EARTH AND SPACE SCIENCE

Materials

○ window prism

Activity Description

An inexpensive prism hung in a window that lets in sunlight will produce rainbowlike images that move around the classroom. Children can look at the colors and patterns and try to determine what is producing them. Over time and with teacher support, they may notice that the rainbowlike images seem to appear in particular parts of the classroom at particular times of the day. For example, they may notice that a rainbow image appears on the wall near the water table before snack but moves to a shelf in the block area by lunchtime.

Integrating Science

Teachers can help children experiment with the rainbow images. For example, they may ask children to stand in front of, next to, and behind the images and notice any changes. Children may discover that when someone stands in between the image and the window, the image disappears. With teacher guidance, children may infer that light from the window is related to the images and eventually discover the prism. After children realize that the rainbowlike image is related to the prism, they can position the prism in various places and look for the results.

A whole scientific investigation begins with a simple prism hung in the window.

Integrating Mathematics

Spatial reasoning and the understanding of positional terms are important concepts in geometry. This scientific investigation focuses on the position of the sun, the prism, and children's bodies. The use of positional terms by the teacher integrates important vocabulary from geometry into an interesting and meaningful situation.

Table 6.3: STEM Components in the Window Prism Activity

🔍 SCIENCE	💡 TECHNOLOGY	⚙ ENGINEERING	➕ MATHEMATICS
Exploring the effect of light shining through a prism	Prisms are used in *optics*, including eyeglasses and telescopes.	Prisms are used in optical engineering.	Geometry: spatial awareness and understanding of positional terms

ICE IN THE WATER TABLE

EARTH SCIENCE

Materials

○ water table

○ ice cubes (colored with red and blue food coloring prior to freezing, if desired)

Activity Description

Children know less about ice than adults may assume (as was revealed in the ice project documented in Project Activity 5.1). Children can learn about ice by periodically having the opportunity to handle it. Therefore, a quick but valuable STEM activity is to occasionally add ice cubes to the water table. As children handle the ice, they can experience the melting process through both sight and touch. Because shadowy images from trapped air are often visible in ice cubes, some children may think that an object is part of the ice. After the ice has melted, children can see that the ice cubes were just frozen water.

Integrating Science

There are three physical states of matter: solid, liquid, and gas. Exploring ice cubes allows children

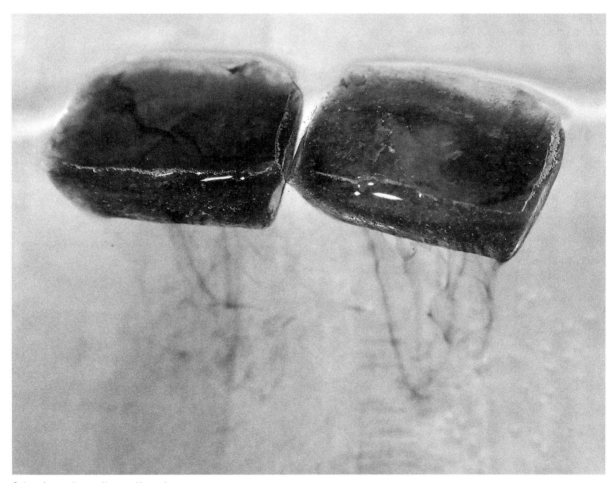

Colored ice cubes melting in the water

to experience a *physical change* in a material. A physical change does not produce a new material. It merely changes the state of that material. This contrasts with a *chemical change*, which results in a new substance. In this activity, the ice cubes were always water, which children can see and feel as they melt. The water simply looked and felt different because it was in a frozen state. Children can reproduce the physical change by refreezing some of the water for exploration on another day. Teachers can also color the water with food coloring before it is frozen. This allows children to see the water from the ice cubes dissipate into the water in the water table.

 Integrating Mathematics

Measurement is a part of this activity because children compare the changing sizes of the ice cubes as they melt. If ice cube trays are available, children can periodically place ice cubes back in the tray and compare the size of the cube to the compartment it previously occupied. It is important to remind children that water from the ice cube has not disappeared. It has now joined the water in the water table.

Table 6.4: STEM Components in the Ice in the Water Table Activity

🔍 SCIENCE	💡 TECHNOLOGY	⚙️ ENGINEERING	➕ MATHEMATICS
Exploring change in the physical state of water	A freezer is the technology connection; without it, children would have to wait for freezing temperatures outside to make their ice cubes.	Knowing the temperature at which various materials experience a change in physical state is important in engineering.	Comparing size changes in ice cubes

INSTANT PARALLEL LINES

MATHEMATICS: GEOMETRY

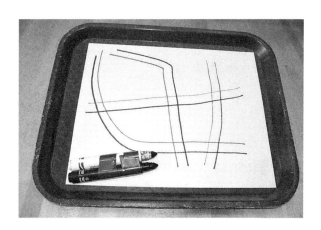

Materials

○ 2 markers, each a different color, taped together

Activity Description

Most of the lines children draw intersect, or cross over, each other at some point. By simply taping two markers together, teachers make it possible for children to instantly draw parallel straight lines. Even if children create loops with the markers, the two colors stay the same distance apart. As children experiment with this phenomenon, teachers can talk about the lines the children are creating and point out parallel lines in the classroom, such as bookcase shelves.

Integrating Science

Parallel lines occur throughout nature. For example, tree trunks and many flowers grow straight upward as they stretch toward the sunlight. This creates parallel lines. Layers of *sedimentary rock*, which can be observed in cuts made for roadways, also create parallel lines. Growth rings in trees, which can be observed in cross sections of tree trunks or branches, form *concentric* parallel lines.

Integrating Mathematics

The concept of parallel versus intersecting lines is important in geometry. There are many parallel lines in the school environment: fence rails, the frames of doors and windows, the borders of the hallway where the walls meet the floor or ceiling, the opposite sides of square floor tiling, steps on a staircase, the opposite edges of a book or puzzle, and so forth. Teachers can point out these lines throughout the day, and children will soon begin drawing attention to them as well.

Table 6.5: STEM Components in the Instant Parallel Lines Activity

⌕ SCIENCE	☼ TECHNOLOGY	⚙ ENGINEERING	+ MATHEMATICS
Exploring parallel lines in nature	Children can observe many examples of parallel lines on a computer keyboard.	Parallel lines are critical in construction. Children can find many parallel lines by looking at buildings.	Geometry: recognizing parallel versus intersecting lines

SAND TIMERS

MATHEMATICS: MEASUREMENT; EARTH SCIENCE

Materials

○ several sizes or types of sand timers

○ standard kitchen timer (optional)

Activity Description

Inexpensive sand timers are readily available. When they are placed around the classroom or at a particular activity, children can visually document the abstract idea of elapsed time. Traditional egg timers have two funnels that are connected at their narrow ends so that sand can flow through. Some versions have three timers mounted in a frame, with different colors of sand for three-, four-, and five-minute intervals. This type may be particularly interesting to children.

The sand timers can be used anywhere in the classroom, but the best opportunities to bring them into a discussion with children might be during special activities or snacktimes. Teachers might comment, "When all of the sand gets to the bottom of the timer, you will have spent three minutes on your project. We can see how much of your drawing is finished after three minutes."

Integrating Science

The sand timer allows children to watch the movement and behavior of fine particles of sand. They

can see how the sand bunches up at the top of the funnel, filters through the small opening, and spreads out again at the bottom. This is the same process that occurs in geology when water and *minerals* filter into the cracks in *rocks*. Teachers can compare the observation of the timer to experiences children have using funnels in the sensory table.

Integrating Mathematics

This quick and spontaneous activity introduces children to the difficult measurement concept of elapsed time. When children measure length with interlocking cubes, they can see both the object they are measuring and the measurement units. Because children cannot see time, the dripping sand visually marks its passage for them.

Table 6.6: STEM Components in the Sand Timers Activity

🔍 SCIENCE	💡 TECHNOLOGY	⚙ ENGINEERING	➕ MATHEMATICS
Movement of fine particles, which illustrates how mineral formations can occur	Use of a classical timing device	The behavior of natural materials is important in engineering, as when a stable foundation material is needed.	Measurement of elapsed time

DRY SPONGE, WET SPONGE

PHYSICS, EARTH SCIENCE

Materials

○ sponges, 3 dry and 3 moist

○ plastic container to hold each type of sponge

Activity Description

Spills are a frequent occurrence in preschool and kindergarten. When they happen, let children try to wipe up a spill with a dry sponge and then a moist sponge. The moist sponge is much more effective in wiping up the spill, and the reason is related to the unique behavior of liquids.

Integrating Science

Liquids have the ability to move against gravity to occupy the small spaces between fibers in certain materials. This process, which is called **capillary action**, allows absorbent materials such as sponges to pick up, or absorb, liquids. Water also has a strong **cohesive property**, which means that it tends to

grab hold of other water molecules. Since the moist sponge already has water in it, this water pulls the new liquid into the sponge.

 Integrating Mathematics

The time lag while children wait for the sponges to absorb the liquid is a good time to model stable order counting. Teachers can have children place a moist sponge on one section of the spill and a dry sponge on the other section. After the teacher and children count to ten, the sponges can be checked to see which one has absorbed the most liquid. Children can use several methods to help them decide: (1) compare which sponge left more of the spill on the table, (2) squeeze both sponges into the sink and see which releases more liquid, and (3) hold both sponges to determine which one feels heavier and is therefore holding more liquid.

Table 6.7: STEM Components in the Dry Sponge, Wet Sponge Activity

🔍 SCIENCE	💡 TECHNOLOGY	⚙ ENGINEERING	➕ MATHEMATICS
Exploring capillary action; water cohesion	Large sponges, called sorbents, are sometimes used to absorb oil when cleaning up oil spills. Disposable diapers usually contain a crystal called sodium polyacrylate, which turns into a super-absorbent gel when exposed to water.	No obvious connections to engineering	Measurement: As the amount of water on the table decreases, the amount of water in the sponge increases, and the sponge feels heavier.

TRANSPARENT, TRANSLUCENT, AND OPAQUE

PHYSICS

Materials

○ variety of materials that are transparent, translucent, and opaque

Activity Description

In a short amount of time, teachers can collect various types of containers, paper, and fabric that are *transparent*, *translucent*, or *opaque*. Children can sort the materials based on whether they can see through them easily (transparent), can see through them somewhat (translucent), or cannot see through them at all (opaque). The objects can be located anywhere in the classroom, but since children especially enjoy looking through the materials at the outside world, placing them in a container near a window may be ideal.

Transparent material

Translucent material

Opaque material

Integrating Science

Transparent materials allow light to pass through them, so objects can be viewed clearly through the material. A transparent material may be clear, or it may have a color. While a translucent material also allows light to pass through it, the light is diffused, and objects cannot be seen clearly through the material. Opaque materials do not let light pass through. Therefore, objects on the other side of an opaque material cannot be seen. Examples of transparent materials are most windows, clear plastic wrap, and pure water. Translucent materials include bubble wrap, wax paper, and velum paper. A canvas bag, a book, and a piece of cardboard are examples of opaque materials.

 Integrating Mathematics

Children can sort the objects into baskets based on whether they are transparent, translucent, or opaque. Sorting and classifying is a component of the algebra standard for young children.

Table 6.8: STEM Components in the Transparent, Translucent, and Opaque Activity

SCIENCE	TECHNOLOGY	ENGINEERING	MATHEMATICS
Exploration of the transparency properties of various materials	Special filters are used in technology to allow particular wavelengths of light to pass through.	Materials used in various parts of buildings are selected based on the need for *transparent*, *translucent*, or *opaque* properties.	Sorting and classifying of materials based on transparency, translucency, and opaqueness

HOLES IN BOTTLES

MATHEMATICS: MEASUREMENT; EARTH SCIENCE; PHYSICS

Materials

○ clear plastic bottles or jars

○ hot glue gun, to melt holes in the bottles

Activity Description

Most young children have had experiences filling plastic bottles with water in the sensory table. A quick variation of this activity is to use the metal tip of a hot glue gun to melt holes in plastic bottles or jars. Children can experiment with water pressure by comparing the height of the water above the hole to the *force* of the water shooting out. Many variations are possible, including positioning the holes at various places on the bottle and adding more than one hole.

the arc of the shooting water changes as the height of the water column, and hence the force it exerts, decreases. Teachers should guide children to observe this relationship.

 ## Integrating Science

This activity allows children to explore the movement of water and the force it exerts. A preliminary response for many children is to start and stop the flow of the water by plugging the hole with a finger. Next, they often notice that water no longer comes out of the hole when the water level is below the height of the hole. Children may not notice how

 ## Integrating Mathematics

The mathematics in this activity is related to measurement. Children will notice that as the water exits the bottle, the height of the water column gets shorter. This measurement is critically related to understanding the force exerted by the water and illustrates how learning in science and mathematics is often closely paired.

Table 6.9: STEM Components in the Holes in Bottles Activity

SCIENCE	TECHNOLOGY	ENGINEERING	MATHEMATICS
Exploring the force exerted by moving water and factors related to water pressure	Water towers, which children often see in their communities, are examples of the use of pressure created by elevated water.	Designers of tall buildings may need to include a water tower in their plans to supply enough water pressure for the building.	Measurement of height

REFLECTION TREASURE HUNT: INDOORS

PHYSICS

Materials

○ no specific materials are needed

○ chart to record findings (optional)

Activity Description

Many objects and materials in the classroom create a reflection. Mirrors, silverware, shiny manipulative materials, faucets, and water are a few examples. Teachers can challenge children to go on a reflection treasure hunt and find as many reflective surfaces as they can throughout the day. Some extra examples can be placed in areas throughout the classroom to make the hunt more exciting. A chart can be hung in the classroom where children can record their findings.

 Integrating Science

The physical laws of reflection are too difficult to try to explain to children; however, children may notice some common properties of materials that are reflective. They tend to be highly polished, shiny, and very smooth. Many of the surfaces are metallic because many metals can be highly polished. *Transparent*

materials, such as windows and water, also create reflections.

 Integrating Mathematics

In this activity, children select items to place in the special category of reflective. Sorting based on a general rule falls into the domain of algebra for young children.

Table 6.10: STEM Components in the Indoor Reflection Treasure Hunt Activity

🔍 SCIENCE	🔆 TECHNOLOGY	⚙️ ENGINEERING	➕ MATHEMATICS
Exploration of the reflective properties of various materials	Children may notice reflective surfaces on technology that they use, such as computer screens.	Materials used in various areas of engineering are selected based on their reflective capabilities.	Sorting and classifying of materials based on their reflective properties

REFLECTION TREASURE HUNT: OUTDOORS

 PHYSICS

Materials

No specific materials are necessary.

Activity Description

This activity is similar to Activity 6.10 but takes place outside. Children can discover reflective surfaces that are made by people or created by nature. Examples of reflective surfaces that children may discover outside are metallic surfaces, such as a drinking fountain or tricycle handlebars, mud puddles, windows, and sunglasses.

Integrating Science

Children are encouraged to look at a specific physical property of materials in this activity—reflectivity. Children will likely notice similarities between the reflective properties of the objects they found outside and those they may have found indoors. Once again, metallic objects, materials made of glass, and water are likely to be materials that children recognize as reflective.

Integrating Mathematics

This activity involves sorting materials into categories based on whether or not they reflect images. Sorting is a component of early algebra for young children.

Reflective materials, including the windowpanes

Table 6.11: STEM Components in the Outdoor Reflection Treasure Hunt Activity

SCIENCE	TECHNOLOGY	ENGINEERING	MATHEMATICS
Exploration of the reflective properties of various materials	Children may notice reflective surfaces on technology that is used outside, such as camera lenses.	Materials used in various areas of engineering are selected based on their reflective capabilities.	Sorting and classifying of materials based on their reflective properties

"RUBBER BAND" BAND

PHYSICS

Materials

○ large rubber bands

Activity Description

Teachers can create a quick but interesting sound activity by passing out rubber bands during group time. Children can make a rhythm instrument by looping a rubber band around their shoe and pulling up on it. The tighter they pull the rubber band, the higher the *pitch* becomes when they pluck it. With teacher guidance, children can produce higher and lower tones together. Then they can strum their rubber bands to create rhythmic patterns, such as "low–low–high–high."

 ## Integrating Science

Pitches that are labeled *low* have fewer vibrations per second than pitches that are labeled *high*. Children can see and feel the rubber bands vibrate, which creates the sound, but they obviously cannot measure the vibrations. Children can learn, however, to apply the cultural labels *low* and *high* to relative tones, particularly if the teacher holds her hand high for the higher pitches and low for the lower tones. Pitch is related to the branch of science known as *acoustics*.

+ Integrating Mathematics

As children learn to classify tones as high or low, they are applying concepts related to algebra. Creating and reproducing patterns are also algebraic concepts. Music is a productive area for teachers to introduce patterning, as many young children seem to repeat auditory patterns more easily than patterns that are visual.

Table 6.12: STEM Components in the "Rubber Band" Band Activity

Q SCIENCE	⚙ TECHNOLOGY	⚙ ENGINEERING	+ MATHEMATICS
Exploring vibrations as producers of sound; relating tautness of a vibrating string to low and high sounds	Understanding of sound production is utilized in recording technology.	Acoustical engineering is specifically related to sound production.	Classifying sounds based on their relative pitch; creating patterns

FENCE PERCUSSION

PHYSICS

Materials

○ spoons

Activity Description

Teachers can bring a few spoons outside for children to use to create rhythmic patterns on the school fence. Tapping the rails or wire creates one type of sound, while strumming across them creates another. By varying their taps and strums, children can create a variety of sound patterns.

 ## Integrating Science

Experimenting with how to create and vary sound is an important part of physical knowledge for young children. The material of the fence affects its **timbre**, or tone quality. A wooden fence produces a different sound from a metal or plastic fence.

 ## Integrating Mathematics

Patterning is an important component of early algebra for young children. Many different patterns can be created with spoons and a fence. Here are a few examples:

- [tap, strum] [tap, strum]
- [tap, tap, strum, strum] [tap, tap, strum, strum]
- [tap, (silence), tap, tap] [tap, (silence), tap, tap]
- [tap, tap, tap, tap, t-a-p, t-a-p]
  (four quick taps followed by two slow taps)

Table 6.13: STEM Components in the Fence Percussion Activity

🔍 SCIENCE	💡 TECHNOLOGY	⚙️ ENGINEERING	➕ MATHEMATICS
Exploring the sounds created by various surfaces	Understanding of sound production is utilized in recording technology.	Acoustical engineering is specifically related to sound production.	Creating sound patterns

THE WONDERFUL WORLD OF COATS

PHYSICS

Materials

none needed

Activity Description

Even arrival and dismissal times offer the opportunity to engage in scientific conversations. Children are often interested in their coats, and discussions can center around the materials used to make them. Some coats are smooth, while others, such as those made of corduroy, are rough. Some coats look metallic and are therefore shiny. Coats may be made of plastic (raincoats), faux fur, cotton, or manufactured fibers. Some children may be interested in what the label indicates their coat is made from. The fasteners on coats are also interesting to discuss. Coats may have zippers, toggles, buckles, or buttons, all of which are interesting technological inventions that children are struggling to master. After repeated discussions, children may be interested in graphing the types of fasteners on their coats during group time.

examine the physical properties of other materials they encounter.

Integrating Mathematics

Exploring and talking about clothing lead naturally to mathematical comments and questions.

- How many buttons are on Eli's coat? Look, two buttons are fastened, and two are still open.

- Eli has four buttons.

- Aren't these toggles interesting? You turn them so that they fit through the hole, and then turn them back to keep the coat fastened. Whoever thought of that had a good idea.

The quantification questions relate to number and operations. Graphing coat fasteners is part of data analysis.

Integrating Science

Investigating and discussing the physical properties of coats help children understand the real-life applications of science. While encouraging children to examine the details of their clothing, also suggest that they

Table 6.14: STEM Components in the Wonderful World of Coats Activity

🔍 SCIENCE	💡 TECHNOLOGY	⚙️ ENGINEERING	➕ MATHEMATICS
Exploring the physical properties of materials	Understanding the technology involved in everyday objects	Physical properties of materials	Quantification and data analysis

TRICYCLES SOUND POPPERS

PHYSICS

Materials

○ several sheets of bubble wrap

Activity Description

One of the great aspects of outside time is that children are free to make noise. A simple addition to the playground that allows children to make noise while exploring the physical properties of materials is a strip of bubble wrap taped to the tricycle path. Children love the popping sound they can create by riding over the bubble wrap. At first there are many loud pops, but gradually the sound decreases as the pops become more intermittent. It is interesting for children to observe the bubble wrap before and after it has been popped.

Integrating Science

Popping bubble wrap allows children to experience the quick release of air that is trapped within the plastic bubbles. They discover that the *force* of the tricycle (or their stamping feet) is enough to split open the plastic and release the air. The rapid release of air produces a loud sound, much like a balloon popping.

Integrating Mathematics

In another part of the playground, children can brush tempera paint over bubble wrap and lay the painted side on top of paper or the pavement. The bubble wrap produces endless rows of circles organized in parallel lines. After the paint dries, children can use markers to connect some of the circles and create shapes.

Table 6.15: STEM Components in the Tricycles Sound Poppers Activity

SCIENCE	TECHNOLOGY	ENGINEERING	MATHEMATICS
Exploring the release of trapped air	Understanding the technology involved in everyday objects	Physical properties of materials	Exploring geometric forms

7

STEM-Based Field Trips

Gina and Pablo carefully examined several cactus plants on the table in front of them. Their class was on a field trip to a garden center, and their group was in charge of finding a cactus to bring back to the classroom.

"I like this one," said Pablo. "It looks like a hot air balloon with spikes."

"No," argued Gina. "Someone might get hurt on those spikes. Feel them."

Pablo carefully touched the end of one of the spines. "You're right," he agreed. "It hurts."

"I like this cactus," said Demetrius. "It has lots of round things like ears. It looks cool."

"Some people call that a bunny ear cactus," said a store employee, who had come over to help the group.

"Let's get that one," said Gina.

"What's this?" asked Katie, the fourth child in the group. "It doesn't have spikes like the other cactus plants."

"That plant is a cactus, too," replied the employee. "We call it a holiday cactus because it gets beautiful flowers right around Thanksgiving. See the buds? It will probably have flowers in about one more week."

"Oh, let's get this plant," said Pablo. "Then we can see the flowers come out."

Gina agreed. "I want that one too," said Gina. "I love flowers. Maybe they'll be pink and purple."

"Me too," said Katie. "I didn't know a cactus would have a flower."

"I still like the bunny ear cactus better," Demetrius said.

"I'll tell you what," said the store worker, "if you buy the holiday cactus for your school, the store will give you the bunny ear cactus for free. That way you'll have two cactus plants for your class."

"Thank you!" the children all exclaimed.

• • •

STEM-BASED FIELD TRIPS

Field trips broaden children's learning by providing concrete experiences with people, places, and things that they may have seen previously only in pictures, in books, or on television. These face-to-face encounters frequently cause children to rethink previous inaccurate assumptions. There are three sources of inaccurate assumptions:

1. Inaccurate portrayals in educational materials or popular culture (for example, talking animals)

2. Information that was incorrectly assimilated

3. Faulty memories

For example, on a trip to a zoo or an aquarium, children will likely observe that, unlike popular movie representations, penguins do not talk, and they appear to have no interest in dancing, although they do swim quite well. At a construction site, children may discover the vast size of the building materials and construction vehicles, as well as the considerable noise they create. Nevertheless, the trucks do not have faces and personalities, as they do in many children's books.

Other places that children visit on field trips may be completely removed from their previous experiences. Many children may never have been inside a car wash, a fabric store, or a garden center. So field trips to places such as these broaden children's views of the world. They also provide a concrete basis for understanding related material that children may later encounter in stories or other school curricula.

Some field trip destinations may already have a strong science component. Visits to an aquarium, an apple orchard, or a pumpkin farm are obvious examples. Even so, teachers must be prepared to enhance and extend the science content or to introduce mathematical components. Otherwise, many STEM learning opportunities may be lost. Technology can be helpful in this regard. Since not all important or interesting topics can be discussed with all children during any outing, digital photographs and videos can preserve the experience for later discussion. In addition, seeing images of places and things that they have recently encountered helps young children better remember the learning experience. They may ask questions that may not have occurred to them before, and they can practice new vocabulary.

PLANNING FOR STEM OUTCOMES

All field trips could arguably be considered STEM-related experiences, because in each case the focus should be on inquiry. What are the physical features of the place we are visiting? What are the materials made from? What are the component parts? How does it work? Why does the animal or object react that way? How is it the same or different from other things we have observed?

These are the types of questions that should be addressed on any field trip, and they are all related to science.

Consider an example that at first glance appears completely unrelated to science or mathematics. Suppose a class has the opportunity to visit an orchestra or band rehearsal at a local high school. This could be an exciting experience for young children, filled with sights and sounds that are new to many of them. But how, one might ask, does music qualify as a STEM activity? The first thing children will likely observe is that instruments that look alike are arranged in groups. Classifying objects based on a particular attribute is a component of algebra. Children may also notice that there are varying numbers of instruments. For example, a band typically has many more clarinets than bassoons, and an orchestra has many more violins than flutes. Quantifying and comparing sets of objects, such as musical instruments, are part of the number and operations standard in mathematics.

As the ensemble rehearses, children can compare the sounds produced by the various instruments. The piccolo has a much higher sound than the tuba, and it is also much smaller. The same is true of the violin versus the string bass. Through these observations, children begin to realize that the size of an instrument affects how high or low it sounds. This is an important science concept. Children will also notice that the instruments are made from different materials: wood for string instruments and some woodwinds; brass for trumpets, trombones, saxophones, and tubas; and a silver-colored metal for flutes and piccolos. These different materials also affect the sound of the instruments. These few examples show that an experience that at first seems unrelated to math or science is actually closely connected to both. This field trip (Field Trip 7.9) is described more fully later in this chapter.

To maximize the learning experiences of children, teachers must plan carefully for science and mathematics outcomes. This may entail a visit to the field trip site, with STEM objectives in mind, prior to the field trip experience. Teachers can note all of the possible science, mathematics, technology, and engineering connections. This information can be passed along to the other adults who will be accompanying the group, with suggestions for topics of conversation. Also, with STEM goals clearly in mind, the teacher can direct preparatory experiences toward these objectives. In reference to the music example in the previous paragraph, teachers might prepare the students by reading aloud a children's book about the orchestra. After hearing the story, the children can discuss questions they would like to answer during the trip, and the teacher can pose some as well. Having some expectations about what they will encounter helps children focus their attention during the field trip.

DOCUMENTING THE EXPERIENCE

Documenting a field trip experience is a critical component of the learning because it preserves information for later discussion and helps children remember the experience. There are several important ways to document learning during field trips. First, if children have generated questions prior to the experience, adults can make sure the children remember to ask them and record the answers. They can also notate the exact comments children make during the field trip.

A second important method for documenting field trips is photography. Modern digital technology makes it possible for teachers or other adults to take numerous photographs during the experience. These can be printed for extension projects or shared with children on a computer. Viewing photographs of their experiences helps children solidify information, ask questions that may not have occurred to them at the time, and put their learning into words.

Videotaping or digital video recording is yet another way to preserve important learning from field trips. Teachers may assign an adult to take videos, or take short clips themselves with a smartphone. Video recording is particularly useful when sound and motion are integral parts of the experience, such as at the zoo or a construction site.

GOING TO THE ZOO

Field Trip Description

Many preschool and kindergarten programs situated in or near large urban areas take an annual field trip to the zoo. By its very nature, a zoo field trip is science oriented. However, zoo field trips often focus mainly on trying to see and identify as many animals as possible. Zoo trips can be transformed into better scientific learning experiences when children have specific questions to answer. When the field trips also incorporate mathematics and engineering, they become true STEM educational activities.

There are so many things to see at a zoo that young children can quickly become overwhelmed and distracted. However, if children are divided into small groups, each with a specific question to answer and an adult to facilitate observations, they can better focus their attention. In the days following the field trip, each group can share its observations and documentation with the entire class.

Preparation

Preparation for the zoo field trip should begin several days prior to the event. At this time, children can become familiar with some of the animals they may see at the zoo. Teachers can begin to draw attention to animal characteristics and habitats. From conversations shared with the children, the teacher can organize their questions into categories and list them on chart paper. Finding answers to these questions

A close encounter with Galápagos tortoises

then becomes the responsibility of specific groups of children. Individuals can sign up for the question they are most interested in, or the teacher can assign children to various groups. Groups should have no more than four or five children. This ensures that the adults designated to chaperone and guide the learning experiences can attend to each child in their group and involve them in the observations and recording of information. Examples of group topics could include animal habitats, how animals move, type and number of feet, relative size of animals, type of body covering, and whether or not the animal has teeth.

To help focus children's observations, each child should have a card with examples of what his or her group will be looking for. Teachers might decide to combine the observation cards with children's name tags, with the child's identification information on one side of the card and the observation clues on the other side. Table 7.1a provides information that could be included on observation cards for various groups. Illustrations as well as labels should be included on the cards.

A series of books by David M. Schwartz, which are part of the Look Once, Look Again Science Series published by Creative Teaching Press, can help both teachers and children identify types of animal body parts through the vivid illustrations. These books include *Animal Noses, Animal Eyes, Animal Tails, Animal Ears, Animal Mouths, Animal Skin & Scales, Animal Feathers & Fur,* and *Animal Feet.*

Implementation

At the zoo, the adults in charge of each group should assemble their respective children to discuss the items on their cards. Naturally, they can also discuss other characteristics of the animals as well. Ensuring that children repeatedly watch for specific traits, however, helps children realize that these are items that scientists use to compare, describe, and classify animals. Adults should ask questions that help children observe particular details of the animals and make comparisons. For example, the adult might say, "What shape is the elephant's foot? Did the monkey's foot look like the elephant's foot? Why not? How was it different? How was it alike?"

Documenting the field trip is an important part of the experience. The adult in charge of each group should attempt to write down the exact words of the children whenever possible. Photography is also an important element of documentation. Ideally, each adult has a digital camera to take photographs of the animals and close-up shots of the characteristics being observed. If this is not possible, one adult can be designated to take photographs. This adult might also make digital recordings of the sounds animals make, or perhaps take digital videos to capture both sound and movement.

Table 7.1a: Zoo Observation Cards

ANIMAL FEET	HOW ANIMALS MOVE	ANIMAL HABITATS	BODY COVERING
claws	walk/run	trees	fur
webbed	hop	rocks	skin
paws (pads and claws)	fly	water	scales
opposable digit	climb	flat ground	feathers
	swim	cave	
		cage	

Extension

Children's reflections about the zoo trip, which are enhanced by the documentation taken during the experience, are an important part of the learning. In the days following the field trip, the teacher can meet with the various groups to discuss their topic and what they discovered at the zoo. The teacher can read the comments written down by the adult leader, look at photographs with the children, and notate observations that the children make as they review these materials. Children can also draw pictures to help them remember and communicate their observations. The teacher can assemble and display the information in a variety of forms: group books, a large class book, or documentation panels mounted in the classroom. The materials can be discussed during group time, and children can return to them again and again to relive their experiences at the zoo.

Door to the elephant house, Cincinnati Zoo

Table 7.1b: Integration of STEM Components in the Zoo Field Trip

🔍 SCIENCE	💡 TECHNOLOGY	⚙ ENGINEERING	➕ MATHEMATICS
Life science: animal characteristics and habitats Scientific observation	Digital photography Audio recording Video recording	Structural design of animal habitats at the zoo	Measurement: size comparisons Geometry: shapes of animal parts, shapes of animal habitats, positions of animals (high, low, above, below, inside, on top of) Quantification: number of animals in particular groups

WHAT LIVES IN OUR NEIGHBORHOOD?

Field Trip Description

Whether urban, suburban, or rural, school neighborhoods are filled with living things, most of which go unnoticed. An interesting topic for a field trip is to discover what lives in the school neighborhood, whether on or under the ground, in the cracks of pavement and walls, in trees, in the air, or high atop buildings. Later, children can discuss their findings and categorize the items as plants or animals—or perhaps *fungi*, which are neither plants nor animals.

Preparation

In preparation for the field trip, teachers may wish to find out what the children already know. During group time, the class can discuss and list what plants and animals they think live near the school. This list can be reviewed just prior to leaving for the neighborhood walk, and the children can be challenged to find even more living things than are on the list. In addition, the teacher may want to read some books with the class about plants and animals.

As with all field trips, the teacher should scope out the territory ahead of time. Sadly, some neighborhoods may have particular areas that need to be avoided. Teachers will want to be vigilant for any dangerous materials, such as broken glass or rusted metal, so that adult helpers can be warned in advance. In addition, the teacher should look carefully for plant and animal habitats and note their locations. For example,

Finding a bird nest in a bush

the teacher may notice an anthill between the cracks of the sidewalk, pigeons that roost on the eaves of a building, or weeds growing between the sidewalk and the curb. These can become stopping points for careful exploration during the class walk.

Wild primroses growing from a crack

Certain tools will help the children in their scientific exploration of the neighborhood. Small spoons or shovels can be used to look for insects under the ground or to dig up samples of plants that are growing wild. Several pairs of children's binoculars enable children to view birds that are high above them. Specimen jars for insects and other small animals (such as worms, snails, and toads) and small bags to collect plants complete the investigation kit.

Implementation

Although the class may stay in a group as they take their neighborhood walk, teachers may wish to assign children to small groups for adult supervision. The adults can serve as mentors, asking appropriate questions (provided ahead of time by the teacher) and answering questions. Since many children do

Using binoculars to look for tree-dwelling animals

not consider insects to be animals, teachers should draw attention to them. Children are also not likely to believe that animals live underneath the ground, so if an appropriate spot is available, a little selective digging may be beneficial. Teachers will also want to direct children's attention upward, since animals may be located on roofs, on telephone wires, or in trees. Areas that are moist and covered in leafy plants may house snails and worms.

As during other important classroom activities, it is helpful if adults can document what children say during their explorations and how they respond to specific questions. Later, hearing these comments read back will help children remember the experience. The notes also document learning. Photographs of specific plants and animals are invaluable for helping children remember the experience.

Extension

Once the children have returned to the classroom, they can examine and discuss what they have discovered. Photographs can be grouped into categories of plant or animal and perhaps be displayed on the bulletin board. As part of this discussion, teachers should help children describe characteristics that determine whether something is a plant or an animal. In some cases, children may have discovered a mushroom or toadstool. These are examples of a third class of living things—*fungi*. (NOTE: As with any material collected on the neighborhood walk, teachers must be careful that children do not taste the objects, as some may be poisonous. Children should wash their hands as soon as they return from the walk.)

If any live animal samples have been brought back to the classroom, children can carefully watch them, write or dictate their observations, and perhaps create drawings of the animals. The animals should then be released into an environment that is similar to where they were found. Plant specimens can be preserved in a variety of ways. One option is to place them overnight under a stack of books so that they lie flat and then seal them between two sheets of self-laminating film. The preserved plants can be viewed on a light table or hung in a window. The plant parts are more visible when light shines through them. As children examine plant and animal specimens, teachers can ask questions to focus their observations:

- Here are pictures of some of the animals we saw: a cat, a bird, and an ant. How many legs does each animal have? Which one has the most legs?

- Of all the animals we saw on our neighborhood walk, which was the largest? Which animals did we find under the ground?

- Here are some of the plant leaves we found. What shapes do you see?

- Here's a plant that we dug up. Let's look at the roots. What do you notice?

- What was the biggest plant we saw?

- Do you think this ant could crawl up the side of the box? What other animals could do that?

Teachers may also wish to create display boards to document the field trip. These boards can include photographs of plants and animals encountered on the walk, the comments of the children, and actual samples of plants.

To further support children's learning, teachers should assemble books related to the plants and animals that the children discovered on their walk. The book *Sparrows* by Hans Post and Kees Heij provides excellent illustrations and information for children about how birds live. *Plants in Different Habitats* by Bobbie Kalman and Rebecca Sjonger illustrates and discusses the parts of plants. Children are also likely to find insects and spiders on their walk. The following books contain vivid illustrations of insects and spiders: *Ants* by Melissa Stewart, *Insects* by Robin Bernard, and *Spiders! Get Caught in the Web of These Eight-Legged Creatures* from Time for Kids.

Table 7.2: Integration of STEM Components in the Neighborhood Walk Field Trip

🔍 SCIENCE	💡 TECHNOLOGY	⚙️ ENGINEERING	➕ MATHEMATICS
Life science: plant and animal characteristics and habitats Scientific observation	Digital photography Binoculars Spoons or shovels (*levers*)	Not a component of this activity	Quantification: animal legs and other body parts Measurement: size comparisons Geometry: shapes of plants, positions of animals (high, low, above, below, inside, on top of)

AT THE CAR WASH

Field Trip Description

A car wash is a fascinating place, full of sights, sounds, machinery, and movement. Although some children may have experienced car washes with their families, others have never had the opportunity. For these children, the sensory experience of being in a vehicle as it moves through the car wash is dramatic. The field trip should therefore include two parts: the actual experience of riding through the car wash, and a background tour of the machinery that operates the car wash. The focus of this field trip is technology and engineering. These areas are less commonly covered in STEM learning activities for young children.

Preparation

Before the day of the field trip, children should participate in washing their play vehicles: tricycles, scooters, wagons, and so forth. This experience highlights the steps necessary to clean a vehicle. It must be wetted down, rubbed with soap suds, rinsed, and then dried. During the ride through the car wash, children will see all four of these steps duplicated by the machinery.

An important part of the trip preparation is to prepare children for the sounds and movements they will hear and see at the car wash. Otherwise, some children may become frightened. Teachers can simulate the experience by waving streamers and twirling large feather dusters. Teachers may also want to share children's books related to the topic, such as *Car Wash* by Sandra and Susan Steen.

Implementation

Teachers must decide ahead of time how best to implement this field trip. If the car wash has a viewing window, children can begin by watching several vehicles proceed through the machinery. They will notice machines that squirt water and soap, pull giant sponges across the vehicles, and blow air to dry them. If their school allows parents to drive children

Children's car wash

on field trips, then children can proceed through the car wash in these vehicles. Some schools have small school buses to transport children. These may be small enough to drive through the car wash, although teachers should check with the business well before the field trip. If the school bus cannot fit through the car wash, then a parent can meet the class at the field trip site, and children can take turns riding through the car wash in this vehicle. Children should not be forced to go through the car wash if they are frightened and prefer just to watch.

Photographs or videos can be taken to help the children remember their experience.

Extension

Once the class has returned to the classroom, children can recount their experience through dictating or writing stories, drawing pictures, or perhaps building a car wash in the block area.

Inside the car wash

Leaving the car wash

Entering the car wash

Table 7.3: Integration of STEM Components in the Car Wash Field Trip

🔍 SCIENCE	💡 TECHNOLOGY	⚙️ ENGINEERING	➕ MATHEMATICS
Physics: use of machinery to perform specific tasks Scientific observation	Digital photography and video Car wash machines	Mechanical: The focus of this trip is the design and use of specific machines to achieve a task.	Sequencing: steps followed by the car wash, use of *ordinal numbers* (first, second, etc.)

VISITING A GARDEN CENTER

Field Trip Description

A visit to a garden center can be highly interesting and educational for young children. And it's free! A well-supplied garden store contains a wide variety of plants—trees, shrubs, flowers, ornamental grasses, and ground covers. There are many varieties of plants:

- plants from tropical climates and desert environments

- plants that grow indoors and outdoors

- large and small plants

- plants with leaves of many shapes and colors

In addition to plants, garden stores sell a wide assortment of tools to assist with gardening. Children can compare clippers that range in size from small (for cutting flowers) to medium (for pruning hedges) to large (that extend up to the branches of trees). Similarly, rakes and shovels vary from short to long and narrow to wide. Other tools include the following:

- wheelbarrows

- wagons

- watering cans

- augers for drilling into the ground

- spreaders to distribute seeds and fertilizer

- mallets for hammering stakes into the ground

Many of these garden tools are **simple machines**. For example, shovels and wheelbarrows are types of **levers**, while an auger is a type of **screw**.

Garden stores also sell many different types of mulch, which are used to slow the growth of weeds, keep the soil moist, and add natural beauty to a garden. Bags of mulch often split open and spill before they can be sold, so the store may be willing to donate several handfuls of various types of mulch for children to explore in the sensory table when they return to school.

Aloe plant

Preparation

Teachers should select a garden center that welcomes classroom visits. Some stores may open early for special visits, and others may have special celebrations for children, such as pumpkin festivals. Be sure to let the store know what types of items you want the children to see. They may be able to provide a guide. Also, teachers should have adequate chaperones to manage small groups of children.

It is helpful for children to have a goal in mind when they go on a field trip. When visiting the garden store, most children would be thrilled to select a plant to bring back to school. Since a plant for each child would likely be a budget breaker for many

Gardening tools

teachers or schools, teachers can compromise by forming the children into four or five groups and allowing each group to choose a plant for the class. Each group might have a specific type of plant to select, such as a cactus, fern, flower, or vegetable plant, or the choices could be left open to the children. Adults will need to help children find a plant within their price range, which should not be difficult since most garden stores sell a range of inexpensive plants. Working in a group to select a plant is a valuable experience for young children, since they must communicate and problem solve with their peers.

As another step in preparation for the field trip, children can list questions they may have about caring for the plants they select. These might include how much water the plants need, whether the plants grow better in sunshine or shade, and how much to fertilize them. Teachers may need to guide this discussion since many children have little experience with caring for plants. As an example, the teacher might say, "At the garden store, we'll see containers of plant food. Plant food contains chemicals that plants need to keep them healthy. Do you think we should ask the store what kind of food to buy for our plants?"

Implementation

When the children arrive at the garden store, they will naturally be excited. It may help to have a schedule in hand for each group. Perhaps they will tour the outside plants first, then look at the mulch, followed by tools. Toward the end of the trip, each group should choose its plant and ask any necessary questions of the store associates. Adults can take photographs of various items that are of interest to the children and lead discussions. The garden store field trip provides many opportunities for adults to increase children's vocabulary. Discussions should focus on descriptions of the various plants and comparisons among them.

Other topics of conversation can focus on mathematical topics, such as the following:

- comparison of the sizes of similar plants and tools

- looking at *symmetry* in plants and leaves (one side is the mirror image of the other)

- describing the shapes of leaves and plants (for example, many fir trees are triangular, or cone shaped)

- counting the flowers on plants

Evergreen shrubs and trees

Extension

On the days following the field trip, children can examine their plants more carefully and perhaps use them as models to inspire creations in many art media, including paint, colored pencils, wire, and clay. Children can also contribute to a class book that documents the field trip. They may recount their favorite part of the trip, tell what they learned, or talk about the plant their group selected. Children's drawings and photographs can illustrate this book.

During group time or when meeting with individual groups, teachers can discuss plans to care for the plants. Perhaps a schedule can be developed for each plant in which children from the group that selected the plant take turns watering and feeding it. All children will be interested in watching as the plant food dissolves in water, in many cases turning the water light blue. Teachers can also introduce books related to plants and plan further planting experiences for the children. Children can measure weekly growth of the plants and track their progress on a chart. The data can be compared during discussion times. Teachers might ask questions or make comments such as the following:

- Which plant grew the most this week?

- This plant isn't very tall, but look how wide it's growing. Let's measure the distance across the plant.

- Do you think the cactus will ever catch up to the sunflower in height?

- What do you notice about the tomato plant that is different this week?

Table 7.4: Integration of STEM Components in the Garden Center Field Trip

🔍 SCIENCE	💡 TECHNOLOGY	⚙️ ENGINEERING	➕ MATHEMATICS
Life science: plant characteristics and habitats Scientific observation	Digital photography and video	Growing frames for certain plants, such as tomatoes	Quantification: flowers, leaves, etc. Measurement: size comparisons Geometry: shapes of plants and leaves Data analysis: comparison of growth rates

EXPLORING A FABRIC STORE

Field Trip Description

Children find a visit to a fabric store to be a fascinating experience. For many, it is their first exposure to a store of this type. Fabric stores are filled with items that interest children:

- fabrics of various colors, designs, and textures

- collections of auxiliary items—buttons, thread, yarn, and trim

- tools to use when sewing—scissors of various sizes, embroidery hoops

- sewing machines

A visit to a fabric store can be transformed into a STEM learning experience by helping children focus on the mathematical, scientific, and technological elements. Fabric stores are filled with mathematical content. Many of the fabrics have distinct patterns that children can discuss and even chant together, such as "teddy bear–star, teddy bear–star," or "red stripe–blue stripe, red stripe–blue stripe." Other items in the store are organized into groups by a distinguishing characteristic. For example, thread is sorted according to color and size, and buttons are often grouped by shape or color.

There are many opportunities for quantifying. As children examine buttons, they may want to count and compare how many are mounted on each card. When they reach the display of scissors, they may want to count how many different types are hanging from the hooks.

Another strong mathematical component of a fabric store is measurement. Children can compare the widths of various bolts of fabrics or observe the way in which embroidery hoops are arranged from smallest to largest. They can watch as store personnel carefully measure fabric before cutting it.

Bolts of fabric with various designs and patterns

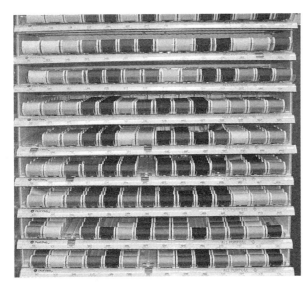

Rows of spools of thread

The physical characteristics of various fabrics present a strong science component for this field trip. Some fabrics are thin and *transparent*, so that children can see through them. Others are thick and *opaque*. Textiles may be ridged, bumpy, soft, scratchy, warm, cool, or smooth to the touch. Fabrics also originate from various sources: cotton and bamboo fibers are plant products, wool is made from sheep or alpaca hair, silk is produced by special worms, and polyester is a man-made material. Children are also likely to find fur, feather, and leather products, although some of these may be manufactured replicas of animal products.

Preparation

For children who are engaged in sewing or art activities that require fabric, a visit to a fabric store is a logical extension. Teachers often include fabric and yarn as collage materials for the art area, but they seldom involve children in the selection process. Before special events such as Valentine's Day, teachers may assemble assorted trims and sequins for children to use when making valentines. Teachers may also purchase fabric to make tablecloths, napkins, or aprons for the dramatic play area, and some teachers engage children in sewing or quilt-making projects. All of these activities provide a logical context for a visit to a fabric store.

Teachers should visit the fabric store and make arrangements for the field trip in advance. As with the garden center field trip (7.4), it is helpful if children have a specific goal when they visit the fabric store. A goal helps focus their attention in a very stimulating environment. Perhaps they will be charged with selecting fabric for a class quilt, trim for the art shelf, or beads for stringing activities. Fabric remnants can be purchased very inexpensively at many fabric stores. Children can be directed to this area to make their purchases. As with other field trips, separating children into small groups is generally a more successful way to tour the store. Adults can engage small numbers of children more effectively in conversations related to STEM components, such as patterns and materials used in various fabrics. Adults can also help groups negotiate as they select a particular material for the school.

As further preparation for the field trip, children can examine fabrics with various textures that they can look for during the field trip. This can become a kind of treasure hunt. The teacher might provide each child with a note card with four types of fabric stapled to it, such as corduroy, velvet, leather, and satin, each of which has a very different appearance and feel. This type of preparation makes the implementation of the field trip more organized and leads to greater learning.

Ribbons and trims

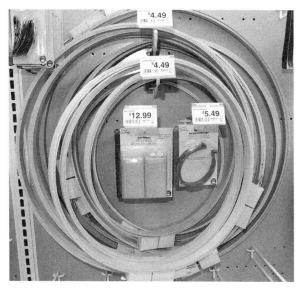

Embroidery hoops

Implementation

Adult chaperones should be given specific objectives as they tour the store with their group of children. If children have "Find It" cards containing particular fabrics or items, helping them locate the items will be one goal. Adults might also be asked to help children find patterns on fabrics, talk about the purpose of various tools sold in the store, and help children describe how collections of items are arranged. Taking photographs so that children can revisit their experiences on the trip may also be a priority. Finally, directing children's attention to the process of measuring the fabric should be a major goal of the trip.

Extension

For children, using the materials from the fabric store will be an important reminder of the store where they purchased them. Teachers may want to photograph children using the products from the field trip in the classroom. These can be displayed along with the pictures from the trip to create a historical timeline. Learning to describe a sequence of events is an important development during the early years.

Teachers can create follow-up activities related to the field trip to deepen and extend children's learning. For example, teachers can present fabrics with patterns during group time and help the children discuss, and perhaps rhythmically chant, these patterns. In addition, the teacher can assemble collections of thread or buttons for children to sort and classify. As children work with the fabrics, discussions about the physical properties of textiles should be encouraged, including whether they are thin or thick, smooth or bumpy, or feel soft to the touch. A wonderful culminating experience is for a staff member, or a member of a child's family, to bring a portable sewing machine to class and demonstrate how this technology is used to sew fabrics together.

Table 7.5: Integration of STEM Components in the Fabric Store Field Trip

🔍 SCIENCE	💡 TECHNOLOGY	⚙ ENGINEERING	➕ MATHEMATICS
Comparison of the physical properties of textiles and other materials Tools used for sewing Origin of various fibers	Digital photography Sewing machine Sewing tools	Machines that aid in design, such as sewing machines, involve mechanical engineering.	Quantification, e.g., buttons Measurement: size comparisons and fabric length Algebra: patterns on fabric and ribbon Sorting and classifying, such as buttons and thread

VISITING A CONSTRUCTION SITE

Field Trip Description

Being able to watch the construction of a building is highly educational for young children, particularly if they can observe the development of the structure over time. Often a fleet of machinery and vehicles is busy digging, hauling away debris, spouting cement, or raising large objects high into the sky. During the building process, children can see the skeleton of the structure, something that is usually not visible. This type of experience makes engineering, use of technology, and applied science highly visible to young children.

Although visitors are typically not allowed on construction sites, there is usually a protective fence erected around the area, and individuals can observe safely from behind this barrier. Teachers should, of course, verify this before visiting a construction zone with children. Major construction takes place over a rather long period. Unless a school is located within walking distance from a construction area, children may not be able to visit the site more than once. In this case, the teacher, another staff member, or a parent can periodically visit the construction area and photograph or videotape the progress. This allows children to observe the stages of construction even if they cannot be present. This is an excellent application of technology to extend the field trip experience.

Excavator

Preparation

Many young children are quite interested in construction vehicles and the building process, so they will likely be eager to participate in this field trip. Prior to the visit, teachers can read books about construction aloud so that the children have a better understanding of what they may observe during the experience. *A Year at a Construction Site* by Nicholas Harris provides colorful, detailed illustrations, which some children may want to pore over for long periods or revisit daily, and the text is easy to understand. *Machines at Work* by Byron Barton consists of clear, graphic illustrations of trucks that are used in construction, along with limited text. *Building a Road* by Henry Pluckrose identifies and describes the trucks used in the construction process.

Implementation

During the visit to the construction site, teachers will want to draw attention to the types of machinery and vehicles that are used, their components, and the type of work they are doing. Teachers can verbalize their own observations and help children to do the same, as in the following examples:

- "I see a bulldozer moving the soil around. Why do you think it is doing that?"

- "Look at that huge excavator digging up the dirt. How many places can the arm on that big shovel bend?" "Which vehicles have wheels, and which have caterpillar tracks? Why do you think they are different?"

- "I see a crane lifting a big beam. It looks like it has a big pulley—kind of like our bird feeder [Activity 4.2], only much bigger."

- "Which truck do you think the cement will come out of? How can you tell?"

- "Why do you think we call that truck over there a *dump* truck?"

Teachers will also want to draw attention to what the workers do; the tools that are used; the components of the building, if they have begun to emerge;

Support columns

and where these components are placed (below or above the ground; on the top, middle, or bottom of the structure; vertically, horizontally, or diagonally). Videos and photographs should be taken of the various components of the construction site so that teachers and children can continue to discuss them in the days ahead. In addition, these photographs provide a historical marker for comparison to additional pictures taken throughout the construction process. Eventually, children can sequence the photographs to create a timeline.

Extension

Teachers can use photographs and videos of the construction site in a variety of ways. Digital photos can be imported into a PowerPoint or slideshow presentation for discussion during group time. Videos can be used in a similar way. If the class has a computer, children can revisit these programs individually or in small groups. Teachers may also want to display enlargements of the photographs in various locations in the classroom. If incorporated into the art and writing areas, they may inspire children to create drawings or write stories that re-create the field trip experience. Photographs displayed in the block area may stimulate children to build similar structures with blocks.

Scaffolding

Teachers who are interested in a project-based curriculum may find that some children are excited about building a structure of their own following the visit to the construction site. This might take the form of a small shed or dollhouse, depending on the interest of the children.

Table 7.6: Integration of STEM Components in the Construction Site Field Trip

🔍 SCIENCE	💡 TECHNOLOGY	⚙️ ENGINEERING	➕ MATHEMATICS
Physical science: properties of materials; use of machines and tools Earth science: materials exposed during excavation Scientific observation	Application of technology to construction work Digital photography Videotaping	This field trip focuses on construction engineering.	Geometry: position, direction, and angle Sequencing: developing a timeline of the construction process

HOW FOOD GROWS IN A VEGETABLE GARDEN

Field Trip Description

Field trips do not need to be limited to public or commercial venues. Many families, whether urban, suburban, or rural, plant small vegetable gardens or container gardens at their homes. In addition, some urban neighborhoods support community gardens. An informal vegetable garden is an excellent destination for a field trip because it conveys to children that people can grow their own food. After children explore and examine how the vegetable plants grow, they can select a small number of assorted vegetables to take back to school. These vegetables can be used to cook vegetable soup (Activity 3.5).

Preparation

Prior to the field trip, the teacher should check with the gardening family about what vegetables grow in their garden, will be ripe at the time of the field trip, and are available for children to pick. It is also important to establish and convey to children the number of each type of vegetable that can be picked. Appropriate tools must be assembled. For example, if potatoes will need to be dug, small shovels should be packed. Garden clippers may be needed for vegetables that grow on thick vines or stems, and children may require small pails or bags to safely carry the vegetables.

Urban community garden

Pumpkin and tomato plants

Children need some preparation for this field trip so that they will be able to locate and identify particular vegetables. Prior to the trip, teachers may want to bring to class examples of the types of vegetables children will encounter so that they can examine them. Books or pictures about vegetable gardens can also provide important background information that children can build upon during the field trip experience.

To further scientific inquiry and sharpen children's observational skills, the teacher may choose a particular vegetable and ask children to predict how this vegetable grows: on a tree, a vine, a stalk or stem, or under the ground. Children's predictions can be assembled on a graph and quantified. Following the trip, children can compare their predictions to what they actually observed.

Implementation

As children prepare to depart for the vegetable garden, they can be separated into small groups, each of which is responsible for selecting and picking a particular vegetable. Children can then be given a photograph, perhaps attached to their name tag, of the vegetable they must find. This will help them in the identification process and encourage them to focus on the characteristics of particular plants. Although all children will want to see, touch, and smell each

type of plant, having only one vegetable that they are designated to pick will help remind children of their responsibility to respect the garden's owner and not take more vegetables than are needed.

During the walk through the garden area, children should be reminded to step carefully so that they do not damage the plants. Adults assigned to small groups can help children describe the plants they see, draw attention to various parts of the plants, and take photographs or videos to document the experience. In particular, children will be searching for the vegetable they have been designated to pick, as well as the plant for which the class made growth predictions. The garden's owner may wish to

Picking tomatoes

take a leadership role and describe the planting and growth process of the various plants. The focus of the children, however, will likely be on what they can see, touch, and smell.

Extension

There are many opportunities for extending the vegetable garden field trip in the days after the trip. The vegetables should be displayed for at least a day so that children can examine them more carefully. Children can group the vegetables by various attributes, such as color, size, or type of vegetable. Sorting and classifying the vegetables is an interesting scientific and mathematical process because each vegetable can fit into more than one grouping. For example, if children picked red, yellow, and green peppers, these vegetables could belong to either a particular color category or to the "pepper" group. Defining groupings for plants aligns this activity to both life science and algebra content standards. Children should also be encouraged to compare the texture and feel of various vegetables; for example, potatoes feel relatively hard when compared to tomatoes or peppers, which have more give when they are lightly pinched.

Another interesting activity for children is to examine the outside coverings of vegetables. Corn cobs are protected by long, thick leaves, while peas are arranged in pods. Children may want to count and compare the number of peas in each pod, and some may attempt to count the number of kernels of corn on a cob. Children may also wish to compare the weights of various vegetables by placing them on a balance scale. All of these activities integrate math and science.

On the day of the cooking experience, children have even more opportunities to observe plants, both from the outside and inside. As children cut open vegetables such as green peppers and tomatoes, they can look for shape and **symmetry** in the inside conformation of the plant. Children may also observe the connection between grooves on the outside of the pepper and growth membranes on the inside, and they can describe how the seeds are connected to the plant. Children can use plastic knives to cut the vegetables into small pieces for the soup. In the process, they can compare the texture and taste of the raw vegetables to the cooked vegetables they will soon eat.

On subsequent days, children can view videos and photographs of their field trip experience. This will help them remember vegetables that they had to dig up (carrots, potatoes, onions) and those that they could pick directly from the plant. An important follow-up activity is for children to write thank-you notes to the garden owners.

Table 7.7: Integration of STEM Components in the Vegetable Garden Field Trip

🔍 SCIENCE	💡 TECHNOLOGY	⚙️ ENGINEERING	➕ MATHEMATICS
Life science: observations of plant growth; comparing parts of vegetables Scientific prediction Physical science: use of tools, including shovels (**levers**) and knives (**wedges**)	Use of tools for cutting and digging up plants Digital photography Videotaping	Mechanical: use of tools designed for a particular purpose	Geometry: shape and symmetry; positional terms (*above, below, on, on top of, inside*) Algebra: sorting and classifying vegetables Number: counting seeds Measurement: weight and size

VISITING A PIZZA PARLOR

Field Trip Description

A visit to a pizza parlor combines aspects of physics, chemistry, life science, geometry, measurement, engineering, and technology. Of course, maximum learning occurs if children have the opportunity to assist in the pizza making. Some local restaurants that open for lunch are willing to let children visit an hour or so before they would normally open. It is a way for restaurants to provide community support, which is good for business. Children may have the opportunity to knead dough and select toppings to put on their pizzas. Children can also observe the large ovens used to bake pizzas; tools used to grate cheese, slide pizzas into the oven, and slice the pizza; and changes in materials that occur during the heating process.

Preparation

Most children in the United States have had many experiences eating pizza, so less preparation is needed for this field trip than for some others. Nevertheless, it is helpful for children to speculate about what they may see at the pizza parlor. They can then compare their predictions to what actually occurs. Teachers might lead children in a discussion of the steps that are needed to make pizza, the ingredients they expect to see, and the equipment that pizza chefs use. This information can be written on chart paper for later comparison to events that occur during the visit.

An excellent way to incorporate mathematics into the preparation phase of this trip is for children to create a representation of how much of each type of

Pomodori Pizza Parlor, Cincinnati, Ohio

topping they want on their slice of pizza. For example, Freddy might decide that he wants three mushrooms, four pieces of pepperoni, and a lot of cheese. To remember this information, Freddy could draw a picture that indicates the type and amount of these toppings, or perhaps glue cutouts of the toppings to his paper. The teacher can then summarize the information in a sentence that models the use of numerals to convey the same information. Children can take these "orders" with them on the field trip.

Implementation

During the field trip, teachers and chaperones should highlight STEM elements as they occur. For example, they can point out the special ovens that are designed specifically to bake pizzas and ask the restaurant manager about them. Children can estimate

Wood-fire pizza oven

Children's thank-you to their hosts

how many pizzas they think would fit into one of the ovens. If children have the opportunity to knead the dough, adults can encourage them to describe how the dough feels. The stretchy nature of pizza dough is particularly interesting to young children. They may wish to measure how long the dough is when they stretch it compared with its length when they let it contract.

Many restaurants will allow the children to place toppings on their pizzas. During this phase, children can refer to their premade order forms that indicate the amount of each ingredient they desire. (Of course, some children may change their minds when they see the actual ingredients.) Teachers should draw attention to how these ingredients look and feel so that children can make comparisons after they are cooked. They can also help children classify the toppings as coming from a plant, an animal, or *fungus*. (Mushrooms belong to the classification *fungus*, which is a distinct category of living thing that is neither plant nor animal.)

While children wait for their pizzas to cool, teachers can lead a discussion about the shape of the whole pizza versus the individual slices. The children can help the teacher count the number of slices on each pizza, and the teacher can introduce language related to fractions. For example, if the pizza is cut into six slices, the teacher can comment and show that each slice is one-sixth of the whole pizza. Children can also consider related math problems, such as how many slices are contained on two or three pizzas. As children begin to eat the pizza, teachers can comment on how many slices there were to begin with, how many have been eaten, and how many are left. This type of mathematical conversation is extremely important for children's understanding of mathematical language.

Teachers should also encourage children to compare the way the pizza ingredients look and feel after they have been cooked. Children may notice that the cheese has melted and individual pieces of cheese no longer exist. Even if the cheese cools and hardens, it does not separate into individual strands. Toppings such as pepperoni may seem essentially the same as before they were cooked, while mushrooms feel more "squishy" and the crust is now stiff rather than bendable.

Extension

Following the field trip, teachers can ask children to recall the steps necessary to make their pizzas. Children can then compare the actual pizza-making process to their predictions of the steps that would be necessary. Teachers can also share books about pizza making with the children, and they can compare their field trip experience to the scenes depicted in the books.

Table 7.8: Integration of STEM Components in the Pizza Parlor Field Trip

🔍 SCIENCE	💡 TECHNOLOGY	⚙️ ENGINEERING	➕ MATHEMATICS
Physical science: effects of heat Scientific observation Life science: categories of living things	Special ovens for cooking pizzas Tools used in the pizza-making process	Design and construction of ovens for baking pizza	Sequencing: *ordinal numbering* of steps (first, second, etc.) Counting and representation Fractional parts Geometry: shapes Problem solving

WATCHING A MUSIC REHEARSAL

Field Trip Description

Watching a music rehearsal is an exciting experience for young children, and it introduces them to a venue that may be completely new for them. Most high schools and many middle schools have some sort of instrumental music ensemble, such as a band or orchestra. Students playing a variety of instruments contribute to a musical performance. With prior planning, young children may be invited to attend a rehearsal, perhaps before an upcoming concert, and experience the amazing sights and sounds of a musical production. They may even be permitted to visit the musicians on stage, perhaps before or after the rehearsal, and ask them questions about their instruments.

Acoustics is a branch of physics that deals with sound. This field trip enables children to experience some of the factors that affect sound. The first thing children are likely to notice is that the instruments are grouped into sections based on type and size. In an orchestra, the string instruments are usually in the front, with the smallest instruments (violins) to the audience's left, and the larger instruments (violas, cellos, and basses) to the right. In a band, clarinets and flutes are likely to be seated in the front, with clarinets to the left and flutes to the right. Behind these front groups are other types of woodwind instruments and brass instruments, and at the very back are percussion instruments.

During a rehearsal, the director often asks particular sections of instruments to play alone. This enables children to compare the sounds produced by various types of instruments. Children may notice that large instruments, such as the string basses and tubas, produce low sounds, while small instruments, such as violins and flutes, create much higher tones. In addition, the sound of instruments depends on the material they are made from and the way they

Playing a bassoon

are constructed. For this reason, instruments made of brass have a characteristic sound, as do string instruments.

Children will also notice that various methods are used to produce musical sounds. In brass and woodwind instruments, the player creates sounds by blowing into the instrument. String players create sounds by drawing a bow across the strings or in some cases by plucking the strings. Percussion players produce sounds by striking the instrument with some type of mallet or stick.

Preparation

Children will be better able to process information from the music rehearsal if they have some prior knowledge about musical instruments. A video that highlights the various instruments in an orchestra or band, both individually and in groups, provides a good foundation for children to build upon when they experience a live rehearsal. Several well-known musical compositions that both tell a story and highlight particular instruments have been recorded on videos for children. These include Saint-Saëns' *Carnival of the Animals*, Prokofiev's *Peter and the Wolf*, and Paul Tripp and George Kleinsinger's *Tubby the Tuba*. (Tubby even has his own website!) Another good example of the instruments of the orchestra is Britten's *Young Person's Guide to the Orchestra*. As children watch instrumental videos, the teacher can draw attention to the sizes and sounds of the instruments, the way they are played, and their names.

Another good way to prepare children for a visit to a music rehearsal is to invite parents or older children who play a musical instrument to perform for the class. Regardless of the level of accomplishment of the performer, young children will enjoy and benefit from watching and listening to the instruments, asking questions, and perhaps having an opportunity to try the instrument themselves. There are also children's books that describe the instruments in a band or orchestra. These can help children begin to recognize and name the instruments they will later see.

Implementation

Before entering the orchestra or band rehearsal, children should be instructed about appropriate behavior. They will need to sit quietly and whisper if they have a question. If it has been arranged previously, the teacher or another adult may be allowed to walk small groups of children around the edges of the ensemble so that they can see the instruments more closely. The children should be instructed not to try to touch the instruments. If possible, children should sit in small groups so that an adult can redirect their attention, whisper comments, and answer whispered questions. If allowed by the school, an adult may be designated to take photographs and video clips for later viewing.

Timing and pacing of the field trip are important, since young children cannot sit still for long periods. For this reason, short walks around the venue are helpful if they have previously been approved by the director. It is especially valuable for children to visit with music students after the rehearsal, if possible. They may be able to gently touch the instruments, ask questions of the performers, and watch and listen to individual instruments.

Extension

Following the music rehearsal field trip, teachers and children should view any videos taken during the experience. So much happens during a field trip that children cannot possibly process everything. By revisiting the experience through videos and photographs, children can review what they learned during the trip and focus on aspects that they may have initially missed. Video recordings of musical instruments introduced prior to the live experience can

Sharing a violin

also be watched again. During these follow-up activities, the teacher can ask children questions related to the following topics:

- measurement: large, medium, and small instruments

- *pitch*: how high or low an instrument sounds (especially as related to its size)

- how a sound is produced on each instrument

- sound quality (*timbre*) of various instruments

Quantification questions can also be posed. Which instrument was played by the most musicians in the orchestra? How many flutes were in the band? Were there more trumpets or tubas? Children may also want to talk about the kind of instrument they would like to play one day, and perhaps graph the class responses for data comparison. An important extension activity is for individual children or the class as a whole to write thank-you letters to the music group. This helps children understand the importance of showing their appreciation for learning experiences and gives them yet another opportunity to think about the field trip.

Table 7.9: Integration of STEM Components in the Music Rehearsal Field Trip

🔍 SCIENCE	💡 TECHNOLOGY	⚙️ ENGINEERING	➕ MATHEMATICS
Physical science: concepts related to *acoustics*, including size and sound relationships Scientific observation	Digital photography Videotaping	Acoustical engineering, which is related to the sound and design of instruments	Measurement: size comparisons among instruments Algebra: sorting and classifying instruments by type and size Quantification and set comparisons Graphing favorite instruments

EXPERIENCING AN ART MUSEUM

Field Trip Description

An art museum is another wonderful site that many young children have never had the opportunity to visit. Many mid- to large-size cities have art museums that may be free to school groups. In addition, colleges and universities often have art exhibits that are open to the public. In some cities, artists from various disciplines rent studios in a particular neighborhood or building, and periodically they may open their studios to the public. All of these venues help connect children to the world of visual art.

At first one may wonder how an art museum is connected to STEM education. Once again, mathematics and science are evident throughout the museum. In terms of mathematics, teachers can draw attention to the types of lines and shapes that artists use, which may be particularly evident in certain styles of painting or sculpture. Children can also make size comparisons, both among the sizes of paintings and sculptures exhibited, which may vary widely, and within an individual work of art. The teacher might ask children to talk about the largest image in a painting and then focus on smaller components that are also important. Children may also discover artworks that invite them to quantify the number of items in a painting. Focusing on mathematical representations in art helps children begin to recognize how mathematics is infused throughout the world.

The following are examples of questions that teachers might use to draw attention to mathematical elements in painting:

- I see horseshoes and lines painted on the horse. Are there more lines, more horseshoes, or the same number of each? (See the painting below.)

- Look at this vase. The design is the same on each side of the star. It's symmetrical. (See the vase on page 217.)

Painted Pony, an oil painting by Carol Kelley. © 2007

Oriental vase by J. B. Owens Pottery Company, Zanesville, Ohio, ca. 1900

- Who is bigger in this painting—the little girl or the dog? Do you think the dog is a puppy or a grown-up dog? (See the painting on page 218.)

- How would you describe the shape of the cello? Do you see any curved lines? Do you see any straight lines? (See the photograph of the cello on page 218.)

- Wow, look at all the sticks the burro is carrying. Can you estimate how many there are? (See the painting on page 219.)

Science is also highly visible in an art museum. Children may notice sculptures created from various rocks and metals, including *granite*, marble, brass, and bronze. Since some children may be particularly interested in color, teachers might help them discover all of the shades of a particular color that are used, or which artists tend to use a particular color as part of their palette. Children will also observe natural science depicted in many works of art. It may be particularly interesting for children to focus on one type of plant or animal and discuss how various artists depict it. The following are among the questions that teachers can pose to help children think about the depiction of scientific elements in art:

- "What did the artist include in the painting so that you can tell it's a burro?"

- "Do you think the artist wanted to paint a horse that looks real, or a pretend horse that she created in her mind?"

- "What did the artist do to make the horse look like it is running?"

- "What kind of land do you see in the back of the picture?"

- "Does the scene in this painting look like a dry place or a rain forest? How can you tell?"

Engineering and technology are also important components of many museums and galleries. There may be sweeping staircases, cathedral ceilings, and balconies that capture children's imaginations. Design elements in the museum itself can also become a topic of conversation. In addition, special types of lighting may be used in various displays to highlight the artwork without damaging it. Children may want to ask a docent (museum guide) why there are so few windows in the building.

Preparation

There are so many galleries and types of artwork in many museums that choices must be made regarding what will be visited. Otherwise, children may become completely overwhelmed and miss out on important learning opportunities. For this reason, it is essential that the teacher visit the museum ahead of time, make note of the various collections, and decide which to focus on during the trip. Children can help in the decision making. The teacher may notice that many animals are depicted throughout the museum and ask the children to decide whether they want to focus on horses, dogs, chickens, or birds during their tour. Perhaps the museum has a large sculpture garden at one end of the facility and a display of colonial furniture at the other end. The teacher may feel that it would be too far for the children to walk to both displays, and ask them to help her decide which one to visit.

Children are better prepared to notice key elements of a new situation if they have some prior indication of what they can expect to see. The teacher can introduce children's books about art museums. In addition, viewing coffee-table books or calendars with color renditions of renowned artwork can generate discussions about art with the children. These prepare them to look at particular elements of art once they reach the museum. The same types of questions that teachers expect to pose at the museum can be topics of conversation as children examine the books and photographs. The children's books from the New York Metropolitan Museum of Art, which include *Museum ABC, Museum 123,* and *Museum Shapes,* are particularly useful.

Museums often sell postcards of some of the most distinguished art in their collection. Teachers can share these postcards with the children prior to their visit so that they can determine special artwork that they definitely want to see. In fact, the teacher might give small groups of children postcards of particular works of art that he knows will be part of their tour. These groups can alert the class when they find the full-scale version of the art.

Some museums have curators or art educators who can help teachers prepare for a field trip. Teachers will need to decide for themselves whether they want to schedule a special tour led by a museum employee or volunteer. Since tour guides are often more accustomed to older students, they may supply more information than young children can digest. Also, if the teacher leads the tour, pacing can be regulated based on the needs of the class.

New Playmate, an oil painting by Carol Kelley, © 2004

Implementation

As children prepare to enter the museum, they should be reminded of museum etiquette. Even though the museum has large, open rooms, they will need to walk. Although they can talk to one another and the teachers, they should use soft voices. Finally, they should not touch any of the artwork. If children have particular works of art that they wish to see, the teacher can remind them to consult their postcards.

Cello, Prague school, ca. 1850

As children may be organized in small groups with an adult to supervise, all adults should have a note card with examples of the types of questions to pose to children, topics of conversation, and particular things to point out to children. This ensures that productive discussions will occur throughout the trip. Museums may not allow photography or videotaping, so teachers should determine this before the field trip. Adults can, however, write notes about what the children say for later reflection.

Extension

Following the trip to the art museum, children may wish to try out some of the art techniques they observed. Examples of prints, cards, and photographs of some of the artwork that was of particular interest to the children can serve as reminders and models of these techniques. Some children may want to experiment with combining shapes to create new images, while others may be more interested in particular designs or colors. Children may want to experiment with creating new colors by combining pigments or adding white or gray. Examples of children's artwork, comments that they made during or after the trip, and photographs taken at the museum (if allowed)

Firewood, an oil painting by Carol Kelley, © 2009

can be assembled into a class scrapbook documenting the experience.

If the children are especially interested in a particular piece of artwork and the artist is still living, they may be able to communicate with her. For example, Santa Fe artist Carol Kelley shared the following information about her painting titled *Painted Pony*

(page 216): "The three painted hoof prints stand for the number of horses captured in raids. The circle around the horse's eye is for alert vision. The three stripes stand for how many battles the horse has been in. Every war pony was decorated with the unique stories of the horse and his rider."

Table 7.10: Integration of STEM Components in the Art Museum Field Trip

🔍 SCIENCE	🔆 TECHNOLOGY	⚙️ ENGINEERING	➕ MATHEMATICS
Earth science: rocks and metals used in sculpture Life science: portrayal of plants and animals by artists	Application of technology to museum lighting	Design and construction of the museum building, such as staircases, floors, and ceilings	Geometry: use of lines and shapes in artwork Measurement: size comparisons both within and between artworks Quantification of selected images in artwork

Glossary

acoustics: A branch of physics that deals with sound production.

adhesion: The ability of water to stick easily to other materials.

agate: A type of *rock* that, when sliced, reveals bands of color formed by quartz deposits.

amber: A hardened resin from ancient trees, which often contains the remains of insects.

amphibian: A member of the Amphibia class of animals that typically undergoes a *metamorphosis* from a larval stage with gills to an adult, air-breathing stage; includes frogs, toads, salamanders, and newts.

angle of incidence: In *optics*, the angle formed between a light ray that strikes a surface and a line perpendicular to that surface at the point of contact.

angle of reflection: In *optics*, the angle formed between a light ray that is reflected from a surface and a line that is perpendicular to that surface at the point of reflection.

apatosaurus: A large, long-necked, plant-eating dinosaur that lived during the late Jurassic period; formerly known as *brontosaurus*.

arachnid: An *invertebrate* animal that has eight jointed legs; includes spiders.

arthropod: An *invertebrate* animal (of the phylum Anthropoda) with an external skeleton, segmented body, and jointed appendages; includes insects, arachnids, and crustaceans.

brachiopod: A marine animal with hard upper and lower shells that are hinged at the back to open and close; the *fossilized* remains of a bivalve sea creature that dominated the ocean floor during the Paleozoic era.

buoyancy: In physics, the upward *force* of a gas or liquid on an immersed object that works counter to the force of gravity; the power to float or rise in a fluid.

capillary action: The ability of a liquid to flow against the *force* of gravity to occupy the narrow spaces between fibers, such as in a sponge.

carapace: In zoology, a bony, protective shell covering the back (or part of the back) of animals such as turtles and crabs.

cardinality: The understanding that when items are counted, the counting word assigned to the last item represents the total.

carnivore: An organism whose diet consists mainly of animal tissue.

chemical change: The formation of a new substance through the combination of other substances.

cohesive property: In chemistry, a property of molecules that makes them mutually attractive or causes them to stick together; water molecules are highly cohesive.

concentric: Describes objects that share the same center with one inside the other, such as concentric circles with the same center but different diameters.

cyan: A color in the blue-green range of the spectrum; when mixing pigments or dyes, cyan (along with *magenta* and yellow) is one of the primary colors that can produce a wide range of other colors.

Doppler effect: A shift in frequency and wavelength created when a wave source is moving with respect to an observer; accounts for the raising and lowering of a siren's *pitch* as it approaches and recedes.

dynamics: In music, the volume of sound.

Fibonacci sequence: A pattern of numbers in which each successive number is the sum of the previous two, as in 0, 1, 1, 2, 3, 5, 8, 13, 21, 34, 55, and so on; a spiral shape created by drawing an arc to connect the opposite corners of square tiles that have sides with lengths that correspond to the Fibonacci sequence; spiral pattern often found in nature that duplicates the Fibonacci sequence.

force: In physics, an influence that causes an object to change movement or direction.

fossil: The preserved, hardened remains or impressions of plants or animals that died long ago.

fulcrum: In physics, the point around which a *lever* (bar) is free to move.

fungus (plural, **fungi**): An organism that is considered to be neither a plant nor an animal; includes yeasts, molds, and mushrooms.

gastropod: A class of animals in the phylum Mollusca, which includes snails and slugs; the *fossilized* remains of a species from the Gastropoda class.

geode: A spherical *rock* containing crystals that formed when groundwater slowly deposited *minerals* inside a cavity in a rock formation; an outer shell, usually *granite*, surrounds the crystals until the rock is cracked open.

glissando: In music, sliding from one *pitch* to another.

granite: A common type of *rock*, composed mainly of the *minerals* quartz, *mica*, and feldspar; granite is widely used in construction because it is hard and durable.

gyroscope: A mechanical device used to maintain orientation and direction; it consists of a spinning wheel with an axis that is free to rotate in any direction.

gyroscopic effect: The tendency for the axle on the spinning wheel of a *gyroscope* to keep pointing in the same direction, allowing the wheel to balance as long as it is spinning.

herbivore: An organism whose diet consists mainly of plant tissue.

humus: In soil science, organic matter that has decomposed to a point of stability (it will not decompose further); it improves the moisture and nutrient retention of soil.

igneous rock: A type of rock formed either underground, when molten rock becomes trapped in small pockets and cools, or aboveground, when volcanoes erupt and lava cools.

inclined plane (or **incline**): A tilted flat surface that can be used to help raise or lower a *load*; one of the six classical *simple machines*.

invertebrate: An animal that does not have a backbone or a bony skeleton.

iridescent: Exhibiting rainbowlike colors that appear to change as the angle of view or the angle of illumination changes.

lever: A rigid bar that can pivot at a single point (*fulcrum*) and move a *load* placed at a second point along the bar by a *force* (effort) at a third point; one of the six classical *simple machines.*
  · **Class 1 lever:** The fulcrum is between the load (resistance) and the effort (force), such as in a crowbar.
  · **Class 2 lever:** The load is between the fulcrum and the effort, such as in a wheelbarrow.
  · **Class 3 lever:** The effort is in between the load and the fulcrum, such as in a pair of tweezers.

load: The object that one is attempting to move when using a *lever*; also called the *resistance*.

magenta: A purple color with a pink hue; when mixing pigments or dyes, magenta (along with cyan and yellow) is one of the primary colors that can produce a wide range of other colors.

mammal: A class of animals whose members are warm-blooded, have a backbone, and produce milk for their young through mammary glands.

metamorphosis: A biological process during which an animal's body structure changes conspicuously between infancy and adulthood; an example is the change of a tadpole to a frog.

metronome: A mechanical device used by musicians that produces pulses, ticks, or flashes of light at regular intervals.

mica: A group of *minerals* that forms in sheets; some forms of mica are *transparent*.

mineral: A naturally occurring substance that has a characteristic chemical composition, is solid at room temperature, and is not of biologic origin.

omnivore: An organism whose diet includes both animal and plant material.

one-to-one correspondence: A relationship in which each item in a group is paired with exactly one item from a corresponding group.

opaque: Describes a material that light cannot pass through; objects on the other side of the material are therefore not visible.

optics: A branch of physics that studies the properties and behavior of light.

ordinal number: A number that indicates position or order in relation to other numbers, such as *first*, *second*, or *third*.

paleontologist: A scientist who studies prehistoric life.

paleontology: The scientific study of prehistoric life.

pendulum: A weight suspended from a fixed point so that it can swing freely.

petiole: In botany, the stalk that attaches a leaf to a stem.

petrified wood: A tree in which all of the organic material has been replaced with *minerals*, thereby turning it to stone.

photosynthesis: The process by which plants convert light energy into chemical energy and store it as sugar.

physical change: A change that affects the form of a substance—such as changing from a gas to a liquid or from a liquid to a solid (or vice versa)—but does not change its chemical composition.

pitch: In music, the perceptual ordering of tones based on their number of vibrations per second.

pulley: A grooved wheel mounted on an axle that can change the direction of a *force* by means of a rope or belt that moves along its circumference; one of the six classical *simple machines*.

pumice: Volcanic *rock* with a pock-marked appearance caused by rapid cooling and the release of gaseous bubbles.

reflection: The change in direction of a wave, such as light or sound, when it encounters a substance that causes it to return to the medium from which it came.

reflective symmetry: The similarity of form on either side of a dividing line (the axis) where each side is the mirror image of the other; also known as *bilateral symmetry*.

reptile: A class of animals that are cold-blooded and have scales.

rock: A substance that is composed of combinations of *minerals* and nonminerals, does not have a specific chemical composition, and is solid at room temperature.

sandstone: A *sedimentary rock* composed of sand-size particles of weathering debris.

screw: A solid cylinder with a spiral groove; one of the six classical *simple machines*.

sedimentary rock: A *rock* formed by a layering of the earth's materials.

sedimentation: The tendency for particles that are suspended in a fluid to settle out of the fluid against some type of barrier.

simple machine: A mechanical device that changes the magnitude or direction of a *force*; the six classical *simple machines* are the *lever*, *incline*, *wedge*, *screw*, *pulley*, and *wheel and axle*.

surface tension: The tendency of the surface of a liquid to resist an outside *force*.

stegosaurus: A genus of armored, plant-eating dinosaurs that lived in the late Jurassic period.

symmetry: The similarity of form, arrangement, or design on either side of a dividing line or around a point.

talc: A soft *mineral* composed of magnesium silicate that is easily scratched and widely used for powder.

timbre: In music, the tone quality of a sound that distinguishes the sound source, such as a voice or musical instrument.

translucent: Describes a material through which light can pass but is diffused; objects on the other side of the material are not clearly visible.

transparent: Describes a material through which light can pass; objects on the other side of the material are clearly visible.

triceratops: A genus of plant-eating dinosaurs that had three horns.

tyrannosaurus: A genus of meat-eating, bipedal dinosaurs; includes *Tyrannosaurus rex*, one of the largest *carnivores* ever to live.

vascular plant: A plant that has woody tissue for conducting water, *minerals*, and *photosynthetic* materials.

vertebrates: Animals that have backbones and spinal columns.

wedge: Mechanical device consisting of two small *inclines* that are joined at one end to create a ridge for cutting or splitting materials; one of the six classical *simple machines*.

wheel and axle: A wheel attached to an axle so that the two parts rotate together and *force* is transferred from one to the other; one of the six classical *simple machines*.

Recommended Children's Books

Chapter 2

Aliki. 1988. *Digging Up Dinosaurs*. New York: HarperCollins.

———. 1990. *Fossils Tell of Long Ago*. New York: HarperCollins.

Barton, Byron. 1990. *Bones, Bones, Dinosaur Bones*. New York: HarperCollins.

———. 1987. *Machines at Work*. New York: HarperCollins.

Bernard, Robin. 2001. *Insects*. Washington, DC: National Geographic Society.

Boruchowitz, David E. 2008. *Aquarium Care of Goldfish*. Neptune City, NJ: T. F. H. Publications.

Branley, Franklyn M. 1996. *What Makes a Magnet?* New York: HarperCollins.

Dickmann, Nancy. 2010. *Farm Machines*. Mankato, MN: Heineman-Raintree.

———. 2010. *Food from Farms*. Mankato, MN: Heineman-Raintree.

———. 2010. *Jobs on a Farm*. Mankato, MN: Heineman-Raintree.

Editors of TIME for Kids. 2005. *Spiders! Get Caught in the Web of These Eight-Legged Creatures*. New York: HarperCollins.

Feldman, Judy. 1991. *Shapes in Nature*. New York: Children's Press.

Fox, Sue. 2006. *Hamsters*. Neptune City, NJ: T. F. H. Publications.

———. 2006. *Rabbits*. Neptune City, NJ: T. F. H. Publications.

Glaser, Linda. 1992. *Wonderful Worms*. Minneapolis, MN: Millbrook Press.

Himmelman, John. 2001. *An Earthworm's Life*. New York: Children's Press.

Hyde, Natalie. 2010. *Life in a Mining Community*. New York: Crabtree Publishing.

Lember, Barbara Hirsch. 1997. *The Shell Book*. Boston: Houghton Mifflin.

Love, Ann, Jane Drake, and Pat Cupples. 1997. *Mining*. Tonawanda, NY: Kids Can Press.

Mancini, Julie. 2006. *Guinea Pigs*. Neptune City, NJ: T.F.H. Publications.

McNamara, Margaret, and G. Brian Karas. 2007. *How Many Seeds in a Pumpkin?* New York: Schwarz & Wade Books.

Merriam, Eve. 1995. *Bam, Bam, Bam*. New York: Henry Holt and Co.

Rau, Dana Meachen. 2006. *Star in My Orange: Looking for Nature's Shapes*. Minneapolis, MN: First Avenue Editions.

Robbins, Ken. 2006. *Pumpkins*. New Milford, CT: Roaring Brook Press.

Chapter 3

Adkins, Jan. 1984. *The Craft of Sail*. New York: Walker and Company.

Aliki. 1988. *Digging Up Dinosaurs*. New York: HarperCollins.

———. 1990. *Fossils Tell of Long Ago*. New York: HarperCollins.

Dickmann, Nancy. 2010. *Farm Animals*. Mankato, MN: Heinemann-Raintree.

———. 2010. *Farm Machines*. Mankato, MN: Heinemann-Raintree.

———. 2010. *Food from Farms*. Mankato, MN: Heinemann-Raintree.

———. 2010. *Jobs on a Farm*. Mankato, MN: Heinemann-Raintree.

———. 2010. *Plants on a Farm*. Mankato, MN: Heinemann-Raintree.

———. 2010. *Seasons on a Farm*. Mankato, MN: Heinemann-Raintree.

Douglas, Lloyd G. 2002. *What Is a Plane?* New York: Scholastic.

———. 2002. *What Is a Pulley?* New York: Scholastic.

Harris, Nicholas. 2009. *A Year at a Construction Site*. Minneapolis, MN: Millbrook Press.

Kalman, Bobbie, and Rebecca Sjonger. 2006. *Plants in Different Habitats*. New York: Crabtree Publishing.

Lember, Barbara Hirsch. 1997. *The Shell Book*. Boston: Houghton Mifflin.

Libbrecht, Kenneth. 2003. *The Snowflake: Winter's Secret Beauty*. Stillwater, MN: Voyageur Press.

Lindeen, Carol K. 2003. *Life in a Pond*. Mankato, MN: Capstone Press.

Macaulay, David. 1976. *Underground*. Boston: Houghton Mifflin.

———. 1988. *The New Way Things Work*. Boston: Houghton Mifflin.

Morris, Ann. 1995. *Houses and Homes*. New York: HarperCollins.

Pfeffer, Wendy. 2004. *From Seed to Pumpkin*. New York: HarperCollins.

Pluckrose, Henry. 1998. *Building a Road*. New York: Franklin Watts.

Reid, George K. 2001. *Pond Life*. New York: St. Martin's Press.

Stewart, David. 2002. *Pond Life*. New York: Franklin Watts.

Chapter 4

Barton, Byron. 1987. *Machines at Work*. New York: HarperCollins.

Dickmann, Nancy. 2010. *Farm Machines*. Chicago: Heineman-Raintree.

———. 2010. *Food from Farms*. Chicago: Heineman-Raintree.

———. 2010. *Jobs on a Farm*. Chicago: Heineman-Raintree.

Harris, Nicholas. 2009. *A Year at a Construction Site*. Minneapolis, MN: First Avenue Editions.

Pluckrose, Henry. 1998. *Building a Road*. New York: Franklin Watts.

Sill, Cathryn. 1997. *About Birds: A Guide for Children*. Atlanta: Peachtree Publishers.

Stewart, Melissa. 2010. *Ants*. Washington, DC: National Geographic Society.

Chapter 5

Castañeda, Omar S. 1993. *Abuela's Weave*. New York: Lee and Low Books.

Cole, Barbara Hancock. 1990. *Texas Star*. New York: Orchard Books.

dePaola, Tomie. 1973. *Charlie Needs a Cloak*. New York: Scholastic,

Flourney, Valerie. 1985. *The Patchwork Quilt*. New York: Dial.

Gilman, Phoebe. 1992. *Something from Nothing*. New York: Scholastic.

Guback, Georgia. 1994. *Luka's Quilt*. New York: Greenwillow.

Hopkinson, Deborah. 1993. *Sweet Clara and the Freedom Quilt*. New York: Knopf.

Johnston, Tony. 1985. *The Quilt Story*. New York: Scholastic.

Jonas, Ann. 1984. *The Quilt*. New York: Greenwillow.

Polacco, Patricia. 1988. *The Keeping Quilt*. New York: Simon and Schuster.

Ziefert, Harriet. 1989. *Before I Was Born*. New York: Knopf.

Chapter 7

Barton, Byron. 1987. *Machines at Work*. New York: HarperCollins.

Bernard, Robin. 2001. *Insects*. Washington, DC: National Geographic Society.

Editors of TIME for Kids. 2005. *Spiders! Get Caught in the Web of These Eight-Legged Creatures*. New York: HarperCollins.

Harris, Nicholas. 2009. *A Year at a Construction Site*. Minneapolis, MN: First Avenue Editions.

Kalman, Bobbie, and Rebecca Sjonger. 2006. *Plants in Different Habitats*. New York: Crabtree Publishing.

New York Metropolitan Museum of Art. 2002. *Museum ABC*. New York: Little, Brown.

———. 2004. *Museum 123*. New York: Little, Brown.

———. 2005. *Museum Shapes*. New York: Little, Brown.

Pluckrose, Henry. 1998. *Building a Road*. New York: Franklin Watts.

Post, Hans, and Kees Heij. 2008. *Sparrows.* Honesdale, PA: Lemniscaat.

Schwartz, David M. 1998. *Animal Ears.* Huntington Beach, CA: Creative Teaching Press.

——. 1998. *Animal Eyes.* Huntington Beach, CA: Creative Teaching Press.

——. 1998. *Animal Feathers & Fur.* Huntington Beach, CA: Creative Teaching Press.

——. 1998. *Animal Feet.* Huntington Beach, CA: Creative Teaching Press.

——. 1998. *Animal Mouths.* Huntington Beach, CA: Creative Teaching Press.

——. 1998. *Animal Noses.* Huntington Beach, CA: Creative Teaching Press.

——. 1998. *Animal Skin & Scales.* Huntington Beach, CA: Creative Teaching Press.

——. 1998. *Animal Tails.* Huntington Beach, CA: Creative Teaching Press.

Steen, Sandra, and Susan Steen. 2001. *Car Wash.* New York: Putnam Juvenile.

Stewart, Melissa. 2010. *Ants.* Washington, DC: National Geographic Society.

References

Abell, Sandra K., and Norman G. Lederman, eds. 2007. *Handbook of Research on Science Education.* Mahwah, NJ: Lawrence Erlbaum Associates.

Carnegie Mellon University. 2008. *STEM Education in Southwestern Pennsylvania: Report of a Project to Identify the Missing Components.* Pittsburgh: Carnegie Mellon University.

Clements, Douglas H., and Julie Sarama. 2007. "Early Mathematics Learning." In *Second Handbook of Research on Mathematics Teaching and Learning,* ed. Frank K. Lester Jr., 461–556. Reston, VA: National Council of Teachers of Mathematics.

Copple, Carol, and Sue Bredekamp, eds. 2009. *Developmentally Appropriate Practice in Early Childhood Programs Serving Children from Birth through Age 8.* 3rd ed. Washington, DC: National Association for the Education of Young Children.

Duncan, Greg J., Chantelle J. Dowsett, Jeanne Brooks-Gunn, Amy Claessens, Kathryn Duckworth, Mimi Engel, Leon Feinstein, Aletha C. Huston, Crista Japel, Pamela Klebanov, Katherine Magnuson, Linda S. Pagani, and Holly Sexton. 2007. "School Readiness and Later Achievement." *Developmental Psychology* 43 (6): 1428–46.

Edwards, Carolyn, Lella Gandini, and George Forman, eds. 1998. *The Hundred Languages of Children: The Reggio Emilia Approach—Advanced Reflections.* 2nd ed. Westport, CT: Ablex Publishing Company.

Gee, Nancy R. 2011. "Animals in the Classroom." In *Animals in Our Lives: Human–Animal Interaction in Family, Community, and Therapeutic Settings,* eds. Peggy McCardle, Sandra McCune, James A. Griffin, Layla Esposito, and Lisa S. Freund, 117–41. Baltimore: Paul H. Brookes Publishing Company.

Gelman, Susan A., and Karen S. Ebeling. 1989. "Children's Use of Non-Egocentric Standards in Judgments of Functional Size." *Child Development* 60 (4): 920–32.

Gersten, Russell, and David J. Chard. 1999. "Number Sense: Rethinking Arithmetic Instruction for Students with Mathematical Disabilities." *Journal of Special Education* 33 (1): 18–28.

Humane Society of the United States. 2012. "Pass on the Classroom Pet." Last modified 2012. www.humanesociety.org/parents_educators /classroom_pet.html.

Kuenzi, Jeffrey J. 2008. "Science, Technology, Engineering, and Mathematics (STEM): Background, Federal Policy, and Legislative Action." Washington, DC: Congressional Research Service.

Moomaw, Sally, and Jaumall Davis. 2010. "STEM Comes to Preschool." *Young Children* 65 (5): 12–18.

Moomaw, Sally, and Brenda Hieronymus. 1997. *More Than Magnets: Discovering the Wonders of Science in Preschool and Kindergarten.* St. Paul, MN: Redleaf Press.

National Center for Education Statistics. 2009. *Highlights from Trends in International Mathematics and Science Studies (TIMSS) 2007: Mathematics and Science Achievement of U.S. Fourth- and Eighth-Grade Students in an International Context.* Washington, DC: U.S. Department of Education.

National Council of Teachers of Mathematics. 2000. *Principles and Standards for School Mathematics.* Reston, VA: National Council of Teachers of Mathematics.

———. 2006. *Curriculum Focal Points for Kindergarten*

through Grade 8 Mathematics: A Quest for Coherence. Reston, VA: National Council of Teachers of Mathematics.

National Research Council. 1996. *National Science Education Standards.* Washington, DC: National Academies Press.

———. 2009. *Mathematics Learning in Early Childhood: Paths toward Excellence and Equity.* Christopher T. Cross, Taniesha A. Woods, and Heidi Schweingruber, eds. Washington, DC: National Academies Press.

———. 2011. *Successful K–12 STEM Education: Identifying Effective Approaches in Science, Technology, Engineering, and Mathematics.* Washington, DC: National Academies Press.

Philipp, Randolph A. 2007. "Mathematics Teachers' Beliefs and Affect." In *Second Handbook of Research on Mathematics Teaching and Learning,* ed. Frank K. Lester Jr., 257–315. Reston, VA: National Council of Teachers of Mathematics.

Piaget, Jean. 1971. *Biology and Knowledge.* Chicago: University of Chicago Press.

Ramani, Geetha B., and Robert S. Siegler. 2008. "Promoting Broad and Stable Improvements in Low-Income Children's Numerical Knowledge through Playing Number Board Games." *Child Development* 79 (2): 375–94.

Reggio Children. 1997. *Shoe and Meter.* Reggio Emilia, Italy: Reggio Children.

Saracho, Olivia N., and Bernard Spodek, eds. 2006. *Handbook of Research on the Education of Young Children.* 2nd ed. Mahwah, NJ: Lawrence Erlbaum Associates.

Starkey, Prentice, Alice Klein, and Ann Wakeley. 2004. "Enhancing Young Children's Mathematical Knowledge through a Pre-Kindergarten Mathematics Intervention." *Early Childhood Research Quarterly* 19:99–129.

Van Hiele, Pierre M. 1999. "Developing Geometric Thinking through Activities That Begin with Play." *Teaching Children Mathematics* 6:310–13.

Whyte, Jemma Catherine, and Rebecca Bull. 2008. "Number Games, Magnitude Representation, and Basic Number Skills in Preschoolers." *Developmental Psychology* 44 (2): 588–96.

Young-Loveridge, Jennifer M. 2004. "Effects on Early Numeracy of a Program Using Number Books and Games." *Early Childhood Research Quarterly* 19:82–98.